# MORAL TALK ACROSS THE LIFESPAN

# LIFESPAN
## COMMUNICATION
*Children, Families, and Aging*

Thomas J. Socha
GENERAL EDITOR

Vol. 7

The Lifespan Communication series
is part of the Peter Lang Media and Communication list.
Every volume is peer reviewed and meets
the highest quality standards for content and production.

PETER LANG
New York • Bern • Frankfurt • Berlin
Brussels • Vienna • Oxford • Warsaw

# MORAL TALK ACROSS THE LIFESPAN

## Creating Good Relationships

EDITED BY **Vince Waldron** AND **Douglas Kelley**

PETER LANG
New York • Bern • Frankfurt • Berlin
Brussels • Vienna • Oxford • Warsaw

**Library of Congress Cataloging-in-Publication Data**

Moral talk across the lifespan: creating good relationships /
edited by Vince Waldron, Douglas Kelley.
pages cm. — (Lifespan communication: children, families, and aging; vol. 7)
Includes bibliographical references and index.
1. Communication in families. 2. Moral development. 3. Families. 4. Interpersonal relations.
I. Waldron, Vincent R. II. Kelley, Douglas L.
HQ519.M67   306.85—dc23   2015003700
ISBN 978-1-4331-2676-5 (hardcover)
ISBN 978-1-4331-2675-8 (paperback)
ISBN 978-1-4539-1551-6 (e-book)
ISSN 2166-6466 (print)
ISSN 2166-6474 (online)


Bibliographic information published by **Die Deutsche Nationalbibliothek**.
**Die Deutsche Nationalbibliothek** lists this publication in the "Deutsche
Nationalbibliografie"; detailed bibliographic data are available
on the Internet at http://dnb.d-nb.de/.

The paper in this book meets the guidelines for permanence and durability
of the Committee on Production Guidelines for Book Longevity
of the Council of Library Resources.

© 2015 Peter Lang Publishing, Inc., New York
29 Broadway, 18th floor, New York, NY 10006
www.peterlang.com

Printed in the United States of America

# Table of Contents

# Series Editor's Preface

## Moral Talk Across the Lifespan: Creating Good Relationships

THOMAS J. SOCHA
Old Dominon University

*Moral Talk Across the Lifespan: Creating Good Relationships*, edited by *the* prominent interpersonal communication scholars, Vincent Waldron & Douglas Kelley represents a significant and long overdue addition about a timeless, yet understudied, topic in lifespan communication research in the ever-evolving communication of contemporary personal and social relationships. Our messages certainly have something to do with defining, creating, and maintaining "good" relationships, and are also something that we learn from early childhood and build on across the human lifespan. This volume takes significant theoretical and methodological steps forward as it fuses communication theories and theories of morality within a lifespan developmental framework.

Like this volume, the book series, Lifespan Communication: Children, Families and Aging invites communication scholars to view communication through a panoramic lens—from first words to final conversations—a comprehensive communication vista that brings all children, adolescents, adults, and those in later life as well as lifespan groups such as the family into focus. By viewing communication panoramically it is my hope that communication scholars and educators will incorporate into their work, the widely-accepted idea that communication develops, that is, it has a starting point and a developmental arc; changing as we change over time. And further, that developmental communication arcs are historically contextualized. As infants we begin our communication education in unique historical and familial contexts that shape our early communication learning as well as the foundations of our communication values. Children born in 2015, for example, will begin their communication learning in a time where humans are seeking to remake themselves to fit a rapidly changing, and increasingly complex landscape that features an ever-widening variety of types of relationships. Of course adults caring for these children—who could have been born anytime between the 1930s to the late 1990s—have experienced vastly different developmental communication arcs, but yet must discursively span the generations, pass along their communication knowledge and values, as well as teach children how to communicate effectively within the current historical context, whether their relationships are grounded in birth or social agreement. Historically-contextualized lifespan thinking raises important new questions such as, what is to be passed along from one generation to the next as "timeless" communication knowledge and practice? In the case of the present volume, how is communication used to create "good" in relationships? In contemporary digital parlance, and analogous to genetic information, what communication is to become memetic, or survive to become the communication inheritance of future generations?

It is my hope that *Moral Talk Across the Lifespan: Creating Good Relationships,* and all of the books published in the Lifespan Communication: Children, Families, and Aging series, will offer the communication field new understandings and deeper appreciation of the complexities of all forms of communication as it develops across the lifespan as well as raise important questions about communication for current and future generations to study.

—Thomas J. Socha

# Preface

DAWN O. BRAITHWAITE
University of Nebraska-Lincoln

I have followed with great interest the development of this book project on *Creating "Good" Relationships*. From the first I heard about it from Doug Kelley and Vince Waldron, the book sounded like a very good idea, even as it made me initially a bit uncomfortable as a researcher for reasons I'll explain below. I am honored that they asked me to write this preface to their book, which I believe makes an important contribution to our understanding of communication in close relationships. As Vince and Doug so cogently describe in their introduction, like most close relationships scholars, once I had some time to think about it, I asked the same question, just what do you mean by "moral dimension of communication?" You would think—given the importance of what people believe is "right" or "wrong"—that this topic would be of central concern to close relationships scholars, but it has not been. This demonstrates a need for this book that brings together essays that get us thinking about, increasing our comfort with, and commitment to, centering the moral dimension of communication into our thinking, teaching, and research.

In the introduction to this volume, Waldron and Kelley take a broad approach to the "moral dimension" as focusing on what persons believe is "right" or "wrong" and they turn our attention toward a communication or discursive focus which means that we look at communication as the primary ways that our relationships, and indeed ourselves, are created and enacted (Baxter, 2004; Craig, 1999). They provide us with several reasons that they believe scholars often ignore the moral dimension of communication. This can help to get all of us—students, teachers, and researchers—thinking about and acting on the moral dimension of communication.

I do agree that, for most academics, there seems to be discomfort and, I believe, an intentional distancing from focusing on the moral dimension of communication in close relationships. Waldron and Kelley point out that the training most of us received as social scientists and the positions we've been hired for in the academy, set us up for taking a cautious and distanced approach to the moral dimension of communication in close relationships. I think this is especially true for those of us working in public colleges and universities. Why is this the case? Well, social scientists are trained to examine those variables related to communication behavior that can be isolated and measured. Thus, we see scholars focusing their research on (a) factors that influence communication choices, such as relational type (e.g., marriage, parent-child, in-law, stepfamily), race and ethnicity, religiosity, or sex differences, (b) communication goals, such as maintaining relationships or communicating competently, or (c) communication processes around which we often theorize, for example, managing privacy boundaries, undertaking facework, or negotiating intergroup differences. To understand and answer questions that spring from these foci, early close relationships researchers started with social science theories and methods and these approaches have accounted for most of the scholarship in interpersonal and family communication since this area of scholarship took off in the 1960s (for more information on this historical development see Braithwaite, Schrodt, & Carr, 2015; Delia, 1987; Miller, 1983).

In fact, to better understand development and current state of research and thinking in interpersonal and family communication, my colleagues and I have been tracking the breakdown of studies of communication in close relationships as to the type of research methods and approaches the researchers take. We have found that most of the research represents social scientific, post-positive (what we often think about as "quantitative") research. Our most recent analysis of all of the studies published in interpersonal communication from 2006–2012 shows that 85% of the studies come out of the post-positivist tradition, up slightly from 1990–2005 (Braithwaite 2015).

The "science" part of social science is, by its nature, focused on how different variables are linked together, and it tends to lead us away from an explicit focus on the moral dimension of communication. Even scholars who undertake research in the interpretive paradigm, where we engage in in-depth interviews, focus groups, or ethnographic research where we focus explicitly on talking with and understanding people's lived experiences (Braithwaite, Moore & Stephenson Abetz, 2014; Tracy, 2013) often shy away from asking people to focus on what they believe is right and wrong. As Waldron and Kelley discuss in the Introduction, if we think about it, the moral dimension is always there and permeates much of our research, but in the cause of science we often put it on the back burner. While this research direction is perhaps understandable, it is also somewhat ironic. The eminent social psychologist Ellen Berscheid, who was one of the founders of the interdisciplinary study of close relationships, reflected on the roots of the discipline, going back to Comte's positivist theory of science of the mid-1800s. Even as the close relationships discipline took off in the mid-1980s and developed squarely in the social science tradition, Berscheid stressed that "the most consistent theme throughout Comte's writings was not his insistence on quantification; instead it was his belief that the aim of the pursuit of knowledge ... [was] to improve society and the human condition" (2000, p. xvi). This tells me that while we of course should always focus on doing sound and credible research we must not ignore a very important part of the human experience.

As most communication researchers are also university professors, we are also mindful, often quite appropriately, about foisting our own values on our students. Out of respect for honoring the diversity of beliefs and perspectives in our classrooms and in the communities in which we teach, we often hesitate to talk about, or even attend to, the moral dimension of communication in close relationships. In fact, I start my own classes in interpersonal communication telling students that my goal is not to prescribe how they should or should not communicate, but rather to help them expand their own repertoire of communication choices. I believe a great number of professors are more likely to center their teaching around knowledge and understanding that will help people ably choose the most appropriate ways to interact in the broad and complex morass of relationships in which they find themselves. However, the authors writing in this present volume lead us to question our instructional approaches and help us see that if we want to teach to the whole of the human experience, we should not be afraid to discuss the moral dimension of communication in our classes. That also means that our students will need to be willing to engage this topic, to think about (and beyond) their own beliefs and values that shape who they are, and to be willing to thoughtfully examine the communicative choices they make.

What might happen if we encourage scholars and teachers to open up their thinking to include more fully the moral dimension of communication? Through this present book, Waldron and Kelley give us the space to do so and that is important. I have seen this play out most fruitfully when scholars are freed from some of the constraints of research methodology and theorizing and are encouraged to cast research findings into narratives or case studies. Julia T. Wood and I have been publishing a collection of case studies of interpersonal communication since 2000 (see Braithwaite & Wood, 2015). We've asked researchers to write case studies that reflect their research findings in narrative form, most often in the story of one or two main characters. In this way, researchers represent how the concepts they study play out in the lives of "real people." For example, Doug Kelley and his co-author Debra-L Sequeira (2015) wrote an excellent case study entitled, "Why Has *Finding God* Changed My Relationships? Managing Change Associated with Religious Conversion." They created the story of John, a football star who has a religious conversion following a serious car accident that resulted in injuries to himself and his sister Katie. In the case study they highlight some of the struggles this young man has when his close friends and his family members are uncomfortable with the changes they see in him. Take a look at this confrontation between John and his sister Katie:

> "John, you know I think you're the best brother ever, even when you're a total dork. And, I know you have just gone through the most traumatic time of your life, but you've changed, and I want my old brother back."

> "Look, I'm still me. The only difference is that God is part of my life, now."

> "It's just that we used to fight and argue all the time, but there was always this real connection between us. I felt like we were so similar, you know? I mean, we could talk about anything."

> "That's exactly what I'm still doing," John replied. "I'm still sharing with you what's most important to me. It just happens that God is a big part of that."

> "I know," said Katie reservedly, "I mean, I guess I'm glad for you and all, but somehow it's just different between you and me now."

> "It doesn't have to be that way," John quickly retorted. "I'm still sharing with you. It seems to me that you're the one who's changed. You're the one who isn't sharing with me!"

> "But ... look, never mind."

> "Never mind what?"

> "It's just that I'm not so sure that you really approve of me and my friends anymore."

> "What do you mean?" John asked in confusion.

> "Well," Katie began hesitatingly, "I mean, you don't really think drinking and getting high is cool anymore and, well, I know what you think about Jennifer and Amy."

In this narrative we can see research findings on communication and relationship development, identity shifts, and uncertainty management infused with a moral dimension as well. We can see the importance of what the characters believe is right and wrong, how they impose these judgments on others in their lives, and perceive others are doing the same, thus giving readers a fuller picture of communication in close relationships. I have experienced this freedom to explore the moral dimension of communication in my own case study writing as well. When we think beyond the borders of research and more in terms of what real people are experiencing and communicating in their everyday lives, the more that we understand the pervasiveness and importance of the moral dimension of communication. This is what Waldron and Kelley are encouraging us to do as we read this volume.

In my own scholarship I certainly can see the moral dimension of interpersonal communication infusing the discourse of stepchildren and their families. For example, in several studies we heard stepchildren talk about being caught in the middle between their parents, as this young woman described in a focus group of other young adult stepchildren:

> I always use the metaphor of the bone between two dogs. I always felt like, because my parents did not talk to one another and if it happened where they were forced to talk to one another it was not pretty at all. Sometimes it was just easier to use me too, so they both wouldn't fight, sometimes I willingly took that role so I didn't have to see my parents fight. But it, I didn't feel much like a person, I felt like a plaything. (Braithwaite, Toller, Daas, Durham, & Jones, 2008, p. 41)

In another example a stepdaughter exclaimed:

> I think that if [my stepmother] would have just said "You kids need to do this: or "You kids need to come home at a decent time" or "We all need to sit down and discuss this curfew thing," I think that if she would have said that to us, we would have had more respect for her in the long run. We would have respected her for coming to us. At the same time we would have been mad because we didn't want to come home early … [Stepparents] need to be involved in [a] child's life. They need to act as if it is their own child but yet give them the space that they need, also. (Baxter, Braithwaite, Bryant, & Wagner, 2004, p. 459)

In both of these studies we used Relational Dialectics Theory to make sense of quotes like these and we analyzed how stepchildren managed the simultaneous need for openness and closure in their stepfamily. I believe these and other studies have made a good contribution to better understanding the challenges of stepfamily communication. However, we can also look at these quotes and see what these stepchildren think is right and wrong, can't we? Stepchildren think it is wrong for their parents to put them in the middle of parental problems and anger, to "trash" the other parent, or for stepparents to overstep stepchild-perceived boundaries and tell them what to do. Similarly it is clear to me from our interviews that stepchildren do think that the right thing for parents and stepparents to do is to be open with them in age appropriate ways—they want to be in the know without being caught uncomfortably between the two people who should be the most important in their lives. It is useful to think about what a more explicit focus on the moral dimension of communication would bring to our studies.

In addition, while it is sometimes easier to turn our attention to all of the communication problems out there, I do believe we also need to focus on what we think is right. In fact, Vince and I, along with a group of co-researchers, are starting a new study of adults who report a positive relationship with a stepparent in their adult years. We will be asking these adults step-"kids" to focus on turning points in the relationship with their stepparent over the years and on communication in these positive relationships. I cannot help but believe that we will hear the moral dimension of communication reflected in their discourse. In the end I believe that a willingness to engage moral aspects of communication will increase our understanding of lived experiences in close relationships. I also believe this may help researchers become more comfortable with, and adept at, translating research findings into practice and, when appropriate, be more prescriptive about what effective communication is. I am hopeful this book will help us to move along that path. In the end, perhaps more recent calls to highlight critical approaches to interpersonal communication and especially calls to understand the central role of power and its misuse will help scholars more fully engage the moral dimension of communication, even if scholars have not talked about it in those terms (for example see Baxter & Asbury, 2015).

As we increase our focus on relational lives as constituted in discourse and highlight the pervasiveness of the moral dimension of communication I would also encourage scholars to apply this lens broadly, for example across relational types and across the lifespan. For example, how does the moral dimension play out in the lives of older LGBT families where partners do not have legal rights of visitation or decision-making when a their partner has become ill and incapacitated? What do we do or say when a longtime friend or family member chooses to play out what we believe should be a private relational conflict on social media like Facebook? What do we do or say when a family member posts political opinions we find offensive or humor we find inappropriately gendered or racist? What do we say to a friend we believe is abusing drugs or alcohol or engaging in sexually risky behavior? All of us will need to confront situations along these lines and the essays in this volume should help us think more fully about the communicative choices we make.

I am grateful to Vince and Doug for their leadership in this area of communication scholarship and thank the authors who have written these thoughtful essays. I do believe this volume can help us better understand communication in close relationships and serve to set the agenda for the future research, teaching, and contributions to the communities in which we live our relational lives.

## REFERENCES

Baxter, L. A. (2004). Relationships as dialogues. *Personal Relationships, 11*, 1–22.
Baxter, L. A., & Asbury, B. (2015). Critical approaches to interpersonal communication: Charting a future. In D. O. Braithwaite & P. Schrodt (Eds.), *Engaging theories in interpersonal communication* (2nd ed., pp. 189–202). Thousand Oaks, CA: Sage.

Baxter, L. A, Braithwaite, D. O., Bryant, L., & Wagner, A. (2004). Stepchildren's perceptions of the contradictions in communication with stepparents. *Journal of Social and Personal Relationships, 21*, 447–467.

Berscheid, E. (2000). Foreword: Back to the future and forward to the past. In C. Hendrick & S. S. Hendrick (Eds.), *Close relationships: A sourcebook* (pp. ix–xxi). Thousand Oaks, CA: Sage.

Braithwaite D. O., Moore, J., & Stephenson Abetz, J. (2014). "I need numbers before I will buy it": Reading and writing qualitative scholarship on close relationships. *Journal of Social and Personal Relationships, 31*, 490–496.

Braithwaite, D. O., Schrodt, P., & Carr, K. (2015). Meta-theory and theory in interpersonal communication. In D. O. Braithwaite & P. Schrodt (Eds.), *Engaging theories in interpersonal communication* (2nd ed., pp. 1–20). Thousand Oaks, CA: Sage.

Braithwaite, D. O., Toller, P., Daas, K., Durham, W., & Jones, A. (2008). Centered, but not caught in the middle: Stepchildren's perceptions of contradictions of communication of co-parents. *Journal of Applied Communication Research, 36*, 33–55.

Braithwaite, D. O., & Wood, J. T. (2015). *Casing interpersonal communication: Case Studies in Personal and Social Relationships* (2nd ed.). Dubuque, IA: Kendall/Hunt.

Craig, R. T. (1999). Communication theory as a field. *Communication Theory, 9*, 119–161.

Delia, J. K. (1987). Communication research: A history. In C. R. Berger & S. H. Chafee (Eds.), *Handbook of communication science* (pp. 20–98). Newbury Park, CA: Sage.

Kelley D. L., & Sequeira, D-L. (2015). In D. O. Braithwaite & J. T. Wood (Eds.), *Casing interpersonal communication: Case Studies in Personal and Social Relationships* (2nd ed., pp. 27–32). Dubuque, IA: Kendall/Hunt.

Miller, G. R. (1983). Taking stock of a discipline. *Journal of Communication, 33*, 31–41.

Tracy, S. J. (2013). *Qualitative research methods: Connecting evidence, crafting analysis, communicating impact.* Malden, MA: Wiley-Blackwell.

# Acknowledgments

Series editor Tom Socha was an early supporter of our efforts to foster scholarly interest in the moral dimensions of family communication. We thank Tom for being such a positive force in the discipline and for his stewardship of this project. Amy Vestal provided the first round of copy editing for each of the chapters. We appreciate her conscientious work. Vince thanks Kathleen Waldron for her 30-year commitment to making (and remaking) a good marriage. Doug is grateful for and to his wife, Ann, for trekking the moral journey together—one that has been profoundly challenging, joyous, and deepening.

# Introduction

## In Search of the Good Relationship

VINCENT WALDRON & DOUGLAS KELLEY

Welcome to a conversation that has been developing for several years among researchers and students of personal relationships—a conversation about the kinds of communication practices that make relationships good, in the moral sense of that word. This emerging dialogue has displaced what we perceive to be an implicit code of silence, a ban self-imposed by many of us in the name of so-cial science. Until recently, to pose a research question about morality along with, say, queries about the appropriate statistical procedures for analyzing parent-child interaction, would seem anecdotal and inconsequential to the "real" purpose of relationship research. However, we strongly believe that "good" questions are essential to research on personal relationships.

Like awkward party guests (no comments from those who know us!), we are steering the conversation toward unfamiliar, even uncomfortable, moral themes. And, like teenagers at their first school dance, we decided not to dance alone. As you will see, the chapters contributed to this volume were penned by top research-ers of family communication, both well-established sages and brilliant new voices. As scholars of family communication, we are self-invited guests stumbling at a late hour into a soirée on the ethics of communication—one convened long ago by colleagues who find their homes elsewhere in our diverse discipline (for exemplary reviews see Arneson, 2007; Arnett, Harden Fritz, & Bell, 2009; Cheney, May, & Munshi, 2011). Indeed, when it comes to examinations of public discourse, the in-fluences of media, or practices of organizations, communication scholars rarely shy away from what we consider to be the central question addressed by this volume: How do relational partners use communication practices to make themselves and their relationships good? It is we, the family communication researchers, who are late to the party.

## MORAL DEVELOPMENT: IT'S NOT JUST FOR KIDS ANYMORE

Although it is true that we are behind the curve when it comes to moral matters, family communication scholars are leading the pack when it comes to another of our guiding questions: *How do moral communication practices change as people and their relationships move through the life course?* This book is one in a groundbreaking series on communication across the lifespan. Published by Peter Lang and edited by Tom Socha, one of our leading scholars of lifespan communication, the series provides the perfect opportunity for our band of contributors to explore this question. Of course, a stupendous amount of good work has been conducted on moral development in children, much of it by developmental psychologists. Tom and his coauthor Angela Eller provide a nice synthesis in their chapter. And they argue quite convincingly that much more research is needed on the kinds of parent-child communication that cultivate moral development in families. We hope readers will heed their call.

This volume conceptualizes moral development as a *lifelong* process, one shaped by crucial conversations with those we care about. These are often spurred by life events that challenge or disrupt our moral sensibilities: starting college, entering the workforce, marrying (or divorcing), birthing children and launching them into adulthood, dealing with serious illness, caring for parents, growing old, facing death. As we make sense of these experiences familiar moral commitments may feel outdated, too simple or, maybe, just *wrong*. What do we do? Well, we *talk* about it. But, who do we talk with? About what? How? The authors of these chapters can address those questions because they make it their business to observe, carefully, the talk that shapes personal relationships.

For example, the emerging adults (18–25 years old) Vince studied with his colleagues are talking about the nature of good relationships. Who are they talking with? Well, it appears that their parents remain important sources of "memorable moral messages" even as these young persons reach for independence and adulthood. The moral impact of intergenerational relationships is confirmed in the chapter authored by Soliz and Rittenour. They show that moral guidance is an important element of generativity, the legacy grandparents hope to leave their grandchildren. A diagnosis of breast cancer is the kind of disruptive event that spurs family members to talk about, and sometimes redefine, what it means to be a "good" daughter, son, or spouse. Carla Fisher and Bianca Wolf provide compelling insights regarding family conversations about the moral responsibilities of care-givers. In his study of justice talk, Doug listens closely to the conversations of long-term (30 years or more) romantic partners, searching for the kinds of moral commitments that remain important late in the lifespan of good relationships. You might be surprised at the types of words couples use to express their joint commitment to the relational justice that appears to makes these relationships good.

## IN SEARCH OF THE GOOD RELATIONSHIP

Doug's decision to analyze the talk of successful long-term partners, people who presumably have developed some degree of relational expertise over the years, be-lies a belief that we share. In our view, our personal relationships can be potent sites of moral learning, development, and relationship definition. Indeed, it is often our parents, siblings, friends, and lovers who model virtuous behavior, challenge us to refine our moral commitments, and inspire us to be our best selves. They are also uniquely positioned to do us wrong, to be the objects of our grudges and bitterness, to be the casualties of our moral transgressions. Family researchers have been quite successful in mining this darker side of our personal relationships, unearthing practices that make relationships hurtful, unsatisfying, and even dangerous (e.g., Cupach & Spitzberg, 2011; Olson, Wilson-Kratzer, & Symonds, 2012). Recent volumes have, also, set out to chronicle the brighter side, the factors that make relationships positive, satisfying, and healthy (Socha & Pitts, 2012). Yet, as we surveyed the literature and talked to respected colleagues, we came to suspect that few of us had really considered that central, nagging question, How does communication make us, and our relationships, good?

A challenge to look again. So we invited (*challenged* might be the better word) a group of prominent relationship researchers to explore new ground. We asked them to reflect on their personal programs of research with a new set of eyes. Would they temporarily put aside the theoretical lenses they typically employed as social scientists to reflect on the moral dimensions of family communication practices?

The initial responses to our invitation were enthusiastic. Yes, relational morality is a thorny topic, but we are game. Bring it on! But as the conference date drew near, anxious questions began to trickle in. "Can you tell me what you mean by morality, exactly?" "Wait. Are you asking me to pass judgment on the people I study?" and, "I wasn't really trained to do this. Shouldn't we be asking the rhetoricians and philosophers these questions?" Our responses to these questions were "no," "no," and "definitely, but we, too, have an important perspective to bring."

We had no single definition of morality in mind and we certainly weren't asking our colleagues to serve as the moral arbiters of family life. Instead, we wanted them to focus on the *communication* part of morality. We goosed the conversation a bit by offering a few guiding questions: How are personal values and community standards expressed when we talk to our family members, partners, and friends? What kinds of communication (re)define, impose, resist, negotiate, and evaluate what we consider to be right and wrong behavior in close relationships?

## ELECTRIFIED (BUT TONGUE-TIED)

As things turned out, the preconference conversation created quite a stir. Indeed, we all left the conference thinking a little differently about what we do. Certainly it became clear that *family members*, ours included, often view their essential communication issues from a moral perspective. When someone we love violates our trust, we do not simply describe it as dissatisfying, inappropriate, inconvenient, or unhealthy. We say it is *wrong*. When a parent chastises a child for an act actually committed by her brothers or sisters, the accused cries out, "*Unfair!*" When an adolescent embarrasses his family by performing a reckless act, the family may feel dishonored. Wronged. Shamed. These words suggest a moral vocabulary of family life, one that most of us haven't really been listening for.

The limitations of our academic vocabulary left some of our conference presenters struggling to think about relationships in moral terms. Indeed, some of us seemed confounded, practically tongue-tied, as we mined our data and theories for moral meanings. Why? Well, first, most of us who study personal relationships were not socialized to consider the moral dimensions of communication, unless we happened to stumble into an elective course on communication ethics, rhetoric, or critical theory as we pursued our Ph.D.s.

Second, we find that the role of communication in negotiating relational morality is rarely the focal concern of theorizing on personal relationships. Even comprehensive reviews of theory (e.g., Braithwaite and Baxter's comprehensive *Engaging Theories of Family Communication*) have offered little on the subject. Our part of the discipline lacks the language that theories of morality provide to our colleagues in other spheres of communication scholarship. Third, it turns out that, while many of us *do* study communication practices with moral implications, we just tend to "lump" the moral part in with the dimensions we have been trained to see. For example, studies of "memorable messages" reveal how various communications shape our understanding of mothers (Heisler & Butler Ellis, 2008) and older people (Holladay, 2002). Although, these kinds of communication express family and societal values, reflect moral judgments about the kinds of mothers who are most worthy and the types of elders who most deserve our respect (and those who don't), and provide guidance on the qualities of good people ("always be honest") and relationships ("treat your step-siblings with the respect they deserve"), this morality-shaping function is rarely the focus of research questions or hypotheses (for a shining exception to this norm, see early work by Smith, Ellis, & Yoo, 2001).

This last observation hints at a fourth reason many of us ignore the obvious moral significance of family communication: professional incentives. Grant-makers and hiring committees are interested in researchers who can demonstrate how family communication practices lead to better health, longer marriages, success in school, or economic productivity. We see few employment advertisements seeking relationship researchers who study the family communication practices that foster good citizens, honest business executives, or students who choose not to cheat, although there are a few philanthropic organizations that reward such work (see fetzer.org, templeton.org, goodventures.org).

All that said, this book evolved from that messy, but exciting, meeting of minds during the preconference at the annual meeting of the National Communication Association. As difficult and frustrating as the process was at times, and as formidable the obstacles just listed, most presenters were ready to give it another go when asked to write for this tome.

## WITH A LITTLE HELP FROM OUR FRIENDS: FINDING A MORAL VOCABULARY

So, what do we mean by relational morality? The short answer is this. We are seeking to understand how relationship partners co-construct that which is right and wrong, good and bad, worthy and unworthy. In relationships, morality seems to be enacted as that which is best for you, and best for me. At the same time the morality of our conduct is measured against standards that transcend a given relationship; those enshrined in religious principles, basic human rights, and systems of human governance. Practically speaking, morality is expressed in the "should"s and "ought"s of our relationships.

Of course, the nature of moral communication has been the focus of much theorizing by our humanities-oriented colleagues. For rhetoricians, ethicists, critical scholars, philosophers of communication—this is familiar terrain. So, at the risk of oversimplifying things, we offer our own synthesis of prevailing frameworks. (By the way, we find particularly valuable a volume edited by Pat Arneson, *Exploring Communication Ethics: Interviews with Influential Scholars in the Field* [2007].) The concluding chapter by Ron Arnett, Arneson, and Leeanne Bell provides a thorough historical review and documents a "dialogic turn" in the study communication ethics. We see several vantage points from which to view moral communication. One associates morality with certain good individual qualities. This "bag of virtues" approach, popularized by Plato and Aristotle among others, yields a list of inherently (a priori) admirable characteristics, such as trustworthiness, honesty, courage, and compassion. Socha and Eller (in this volume) highlight modern positive psychology work by Peterson and Seligman (2004) that similarly highlights *character strengths* such as wisdom, courage, humanity, temperance, and transcendence. From this point of view, good relationships arise from bonds formed by people with good character and relational communication is the means by which individuals express these qualities and endorse them or encourage them in others. This virtues/character strengths orientation is evident in this volume. Chapters contributed by Socha and Eller, Soliz and Rittenour and Waldron and his colleagues reveal that parents and grandparent messages often convey moral virtues across generations.

A different line of thinking imagines morality as a matter of respect for the individual. Good behavior is that which supports the basic humanity, dignity, and autonomy of people. From this viewpoint, good relationships involve mutual respect, equality, fairness. They preserve the capacity of partners to make informed and free choices. Relational communication is the process by which these commitments are enacted. Among the contributions of the chapter by Carla Fisher and Bianca Wolf is their exploration of how family communication practices may support or threaten the dignity of breast cancer patients. Doug's chapter examines the words romantic couples use to enact fairness, equality, and respect. And our reading of Valerie Manusov's chapter is that to be mindfully present in conversations with others is, by its very nature, to acknowledge their humanity and dignity.

A third approach concerns obligation to behave in ways that advantage the larger culture, community, or family to which one belongs—good relationships are those conducted within generally-accepted community standards. From this vantage point, relational communication is the means by which members enact these obligations and, when necessary, are reminded of them. The chapter written by Anita Vangelisti and Erin Nelson explores standards of secrecy and the circumstances under which breaching them might be justified. Laura Guerrero and Megan Cole show that powerful emotions accompany violations of moral standards. Emotions may be part of the "moral glue" that keeps relationships good. As Leslie Baxter, Sarah Pederson, and Kristen Norwood reveal, poetic justice is one communication tactic used to restore moral order after a violation.

Fourth, understandings of right and wrong are also grounded in the wisdom of moral authorities, including religious leaders and judges. Such sources as the Christian Bible (see Waldron's chapter) and Buddhist texts (see the Manusov chapter) influence what people have to say about the conduct of their relationships. Explicitly or implicitly these sources often influence our expectations, aspirations, and evaluations of ourselves, and those with whom we share the bonds of love, friendship, or family. Indeed, one theme emerging across these chapters is the ubiquity of The Golden Rule as a moral standard in the evaluation of relational conduct. Based on our own analyses of forgiveness in personal relationships

(Waldron & Kelley, 2008) it would be hard for us to overestimate the power of religion as a source that stimulates moral discussion and obligation.

A fifth approach to understanding morality, and the one that most informs our own work, is the dialogic tradition (Arnett et al., 2007; Haste & Abrahams, 2008). This tradition views morality as emerging from an ongoing cultural *conversation* about right and wrong, rather than a particular set of virtues, standards, or moral authorities. We participate in this conversation when we offer our moral understandings to our partners or family members and listen to their own. From this point of view, relational communication is a means of expressing the virtues, standards, and practices we have come to think of as "good." Our relationships and life experiences expose us to alternate moral views and compel us to negotiate moral commitments that apply in a given relational context. Drawing from Arnett and colleagues, we argue that a good relationship is one that respects the moral positions formed by the individual parties while simultaneously creating opportunities for relationship partners to create and explore joint commitments.

## A CASE IN POINT: NEGOTIATED MORALITY THEORY

Our interest in moral dimensions of personal relationships stems from our work on forgiveness in long-term romantic relationships (and other relationship contexts), synthesized in the book *Communicating Forgiveness* (Waldron & Kelley, 2008, Sage). This work convinced us that a central function of forgiving communication, that distinguishes it from other conflict management techniques, is to renegotiate the moral commitments that define a threatened relationship. Although forgiving communication can be conceptualized in a number of ways previously addressed by family scholars (e.g., it can be viewed as an effort to redress face threats, to manage uncertainty, and to exchange resources to compensate for loss), there is no theory of family communication that adequately addresses the "moral part" of what forgiveness-seekers and -granters are up to. Negotiated morality theory (NMT) seeks to fill this theoretical gap from the dialogic morality tradition.

Of course forgiveness is just one of the many moral dialogues that take place in personal relationships. The chapters of this book identify a handful of other moral negotiations. Here we update the NMT framework as a way to frame the chapters in this current volume and, we hope, as a means of promoting additional research that takes into account the moral dimensions of our relationships. You can find more details in our book, *Communicating Forgiveness* (Waldron & Kelley, 2008).

**Assumptions.** NMT views personal relationships as sites where people negotiate their moral values. These values are obtained from various sources, including culture, religion, family, and the previous commitments worked out by relationship parties. The desire to preserve moral codes motivates certain kinds of communication behavior (such as seeking forgiveness) particularly when those codes have a long history and are presumed to be shared. NMT claims further that partner behavior that violates our most internalized, shared, and valued moral codes elicits emotional responses. Relational communication is the means by which partners express, negotiate, and attempt to restore the moral agreements that define their relationship as trustworthy, intimate, and just.

Several chapters in this book unpack these assumptions, revealing how they might be enacted in various kinds of personal relationships. Several chapters address how parties in personal relationships might be influenced by the moral messages conveyed by family members, religious sources, and ongoing cultural conversations about such matters as the obligations of "good" sons or daughters (Soliz & Rittenour; Socha & Eller; Waldron & colleagues). And, Guerrero and Cole help us understand the role of emotion as a response to serious transgressions and, presumably, a stimulus for efforts to restore moral order to a disrupted relationship.

**Functions.** According NMT, relational communication performs a variety of moral functions in relationships. Among these are (1) (re)defining moral standards, (2) holding ourselves and our partners accountable, (3) engaging the tensions created by differences in the moral values of the parties, (4) restoring relational justice, (5) honoring the dignity of the self, and (5) increasing the safety and respect experienced by the partners. What kinds of communication perform these functions? We asked the authors of these chapters to help us answer these questions, and what they provide is both interesting and provocative.

For example, Anita Vangelisti and Erin Nelson explore moral standards concerning the revealing of secrets. While it is culturally normative in the U.S. to consider the telling of secrets among friends to be wrong, it turns out that standard is subject to considerable negotiation. Other moral obligations (e.g., keeping friends safe) may be deemed more important. Poetic justice, a kind of socially acceptable "sweet revenge," is one way people perform the second function mentioned above—holding others accountable. As Baxter and her colleagues demonstrate, the act itself is the subject of moral communication, as members of a social network try to determine if an act of poetic justice is justified or too damaging.

Fisher and Wolf illustrate family discourses that emerge around differences in moral obligations to a mother under treatment for breast cancer. Family caregivers often honestly disagree over a host of obligations. Is it right for us to hire a caregiver for mom or should we do all of the caregiving ourselves? Should we encourage mom to "stay positive" or is it best for us to help her prepare for death? In helping us listen to families working out these differences, Fisher and Wolf prepare us for crucial end-of-life conversations.

Most of us know intuitively that fairness is important in our relationships, but in his chapter on *just marriage* Doug looks beyond the intuitive to explore the justice-restoring function of marital communication, including what he terms "processual" justice. Through analysis of transcripts from long-term couples we hear how marriage partners talk their way into just relationships. When it comes to communication that supports the dignity of self and partners, Valerie Manusov writes with care about the practice of mindfulness. As she argues quite convincingly, people have evolved a set of cognitive shortcuts that are *efficient* but, perhaps, not *good* as we are defining it here. These shortcuts make it too easy to evaluate situations and people with simplistic snap judgments. The result? The denial of the humanness of others (and ourselves) when we fail to be fully present, open to the possibilities of conversation and human potential.

## DO WE HAVE A MORAL AGENDA? WELL, YES. SORT OF.

Dialogical approaches to morality, including our own, are more about the process than the content of moral communication. Our interest is in how communication practices shape moral commitments, not in the positions themselves, and how communication practices can create a moral presence, rather than simply engaging "moral" strategies. But, we do bring certain moral commitments to our project (as do our chapter authors). We do believe that some communication practices are better than others. For example, we believe that coercion is typically wrong when practiced in families, as it is in other contexts, because it violates what we consider to be a bedrock moral principle. The right to choose one's course of action is at the core of our humanness and should be honored whenever possible. As another example, we believe that forgiveness is typically a better response to wrongdoing than is revenge, in part because it disrupts cycles of retribution and reduces the likelihood of undue harm. Causing unnecessary harm to other human beings is wrong.

As educators we think these kinds of moral commitments should be the subject of conversation and principled argument. In fact, for many of us, they already are. It is just that we have had few ways to ground these discussions in our own research traditions, so we have discounted the importance of these conversations and given credence to the things we can more easily measure. But consideration of moral matters shouldn't (always) be displaced by discussions of research methodology or the variables that make relationships effective, satisfying, or healthy. Of course these are also great topics for discussion. But in the chapters that follow, communication researchers help us learn how to give voice to the moral experience of our personal relationships. We think that is a good thing. And yes, we just made a moral judgment.

## WHAT YOU WILL FIND IN THESE CHAPTERS
## (AND WHAT YOU WON'T)

This book was intended to be accessible for students but also interesting to family communication researchers. So here is what you will find as you peruse the chapters. We asked the authors of each chapter to do some original thinking. Often this meant *rethinking* the work they are known for, reimagining it from a moral perspective. As we mentioned above, that is a tall task for those trained as traditional social scientists. But we are pleased that each chapter adds fresh perspective, sometimes in the form of informed speculation, about the moral dimensions of communication in personal relationships. We think readers will find their own research imaginations stimulated by the creative stretching offered by our authors.

With the exception of the conceptual contribution from Socha and Eller, each chapter shares empirical observations of communication. We want you, the reader, to see and hear moral discourse as expressed in words, messages, excerpts from conversation, and interview data. We asked our authors to study moral communication in a specific relational context. Although in some cases that proved difficult, you will find that most chapters are deeply situated in real relationships—marriage, parent-child, grandparent-grandchild, friendship, and so on. The lifespan approach of the book is also reflected in individual chapters that focus on developmental periods ranging from childhood to old age. You will also notice that the first section of the book is devoted to life stages (e.g., emerging adulthood) and events (e.g. illness) while the second focuses on communication practices that could spur moral development at any point in the lifespan (e.g., poetic justice; recollection of memorable messages). In the end, each chapter views moral development though a distinctly communicative lens.

What we hope you *won't* find in this book is excessive jargon, dense passages of methodological detail, or boring prose. The chapters are relatively brief and the prose is intended to be interesting and accessible to students as well as researchers. Each chapter is designed to creatively move our thinking about personal relationships into new moral arenas. Sections addressing methodological and statistical procedure are abbreviated; details are available from the first authors.

We are grateful to the authors who agreed to join this project. Not only are they accomplished scholars, but we found them to be collaborative colleagues, conscientious, and committed to exploring the moral implications of their research. They are good in every sense of that word.

# REFERENCES

Arneson, P. (Ed.). (2007). *Exploring communication ethics: Interviews with influential scholars in the field.* New York: Peter Lang.

Arnett, R. C., Harden Fritz, J. M., & Bell, L. M. (2009). *Communication ethics literacy: Dialogue and difference.* Los Angeles: Sage Publications.

Cheney, G., May, S., & Munshi, D. (Eds.). (2011). *The handbook of communication ethics.* New York: Routledge.

Cupach, W. R., & Spitzberg, B. H. (Eds.). (2011). *The dark side of close relationships II.* New York: Routledge.

Haste, H., & Abrahams, S. (2008). Morality, culture and the dialogic self: Taking cultural pluralism seriously. *Journal of Moral Education, 37*(3), 377–394.

Heisler, J. M., & Butler Ellis, J. (2008). Motherhood and the construction of "Mommy Identity": Messages about motherhood and face negotiation. *Communication Quarterly, 56*(4), 445–467.

Holladay, S. J. (2002). "Have Fun While You Can," "You're Only as Old as You Feel," and "Don't Ever Get Old": An examination of memorable messages about aging. *Journal of Communication, 52,* 681–697.

Olson, L. N., Wilson-Kratzer, J. M., & Symonds, S. E. (2012). *The dark side of family communication.* Cambridge: Polity.

Smith, S. W., Ellis, J. B., & Yoo, H. (2001). Memorable messages as guides to self-assessment of behavior: The role of instrumental values. *Communication Monographs, 68*(4), 325–339.

Socha, T., & Pitts, M. (Eds.). (2012). *The positive side of interpersonal communication.* New York: Peter Lang.

Waldron, V., & Kelley, D. L. (2008). *Communicating forgiveness.* Thousand Oaks, CA: Sage Publications.

# PART ONE

# Key Relationships AND Life Events

# CHAPTER ONE

# Parent/Caregiver-Child Communication AND Moral Development

## Toward a Conceptual Foundation of an Ecological Model of Lifespan Communication and Good Relationships

THOMAS J. SOCHA & ANGELA ELLER

Play nicely! "Stop fighting!" "Eat your vegetables!" "Do your homework!" "Clean your room!" "How would you feel, if she/he took your toy?" "Make good choices." These are a just a few examples of the thousands of messages served up daily by parents and caregivers to children. At a foundational level, most of these kinds of messages are intended to halt children's and adolescents' undesired behaviors and redirect them toward more positive ones. But, simultaneously, whether direct ("What would Jesus do?") or indirect ("What would be a nice thing to do here?"), these kinds of parental/caregiver messages also serve up lessons in morality—with sides of parental/caregiver power—intended to nourish children's moral sensibilities, develop their consciences, raise their social consciousness, create moral selves, and more (for a review, see Thompson, 2012). Further, although these kinds of parental/caregiver messages may tend to figure prominently in episodes where parents/caregivers seek to "discipline" their offspring (Socha, 2006), they are actually a mainstay of the everyday discourse of parents and caregivers seeking to raise "good" children (Laible & Thompson, 2000).

Parental/caregiver communication with children is multi-purposed and multi-leveled, containing many kinds of lessons that can include furthering children's communication education (Socha & Yingling, 2010), facilitating their moral development (Kochanska, Koenig, Barry, Kim, & Yoon, 2010), and much more. And, although far less studied, children's messages to parents/caregivers too can potentially serve up similar lessons in both positive communication as well as morality: "Mom! Daddy said a bad word!" Simply introducing a child into the presence of others can, for example, increase mindfulness of standards of politeness and decorum (Socha & Pitts, 2012a) and remind communicators to be on their best communication behavior. To this point, most recently, for example, five elementary schools in Washington, D.C., have adopted a program imported from Canada—Roots of Empathy (2014)—where infants are brought to schools during the day to interact with the children. "The idea is that recognizing and caring about a baby's emotions can open a gateway for children to learn bigger lessons about taking care of one another, considering others' feelings, having patience" (Andrusko, 2014). According to the Roots of Empathy (2014) website,

> Roots of Empathy began in 1996 as a pilot program reaching 150 children in the Toronto District School Board. As of 2011, every Canadian province is taking part in Roots of Empathy. To date, Roots of Empathy has reached almost 480,000 students in Canada.

Further,

> Roots of Empathy has been recognized by His Holiness, the Dalai Lama, Emotional Intelligence author Daniel Goleman, and the World Health Organization, among others. The organization works in partnership with Indigenous people globally, and has been endorsed in Canada by National Chief Shawn A-in-Chut Atleo (and former Chief Phil Fontaine) of the Assembly of First Nations. Mary Gordon has won numerous awards, and the program has also won an international Changemakers award from the Ashoka organization.

Recent empirical research about the Roots of Empathy program also shows that interacting with infants is a promising avenue to reduce children's aggression, foster prosocial behavior, and improve children's comforting skills (Schonert-Reichl, Smith, Zaidman-Zait, & Hertzman, 2012).

Although the field of communication is late to the table when it comes to studying children (see Miller-Day, Pezalla, & Chestnut, 2013; and for a recent review, Socha & Yingling, 2010, chapter 1), this chapter seeks to join the fields of early childhood education and developmental psychology by outlining how and what the field of communication can add to the discussion of children's moral development and positive character development (e.g., Peterson & Seligman, 2004).

First, we offer our conceptualization of morality and review theories of children's moral development with an eye toward the role that communication processes may play. Second, using Bronfenbrenner's (1979) ecological model as a general framework of lifespan development, we begin to gather and organize elements for future use in building an ecological model of positive lifespan communication and good relationships. A lifespan ecological approach is essential here, as social recipes for raising children to become "good adults," who contribute positively to "good relationships," are complex, culturally varied, and operate simultaneously in multiple social systems (e.g., families, schools, churches, governments, etc.). Such a model would need to consider, for example, ingredients from classic theories of children's moral development, as well as, updated understandings about children's character development from positive psychology (e.g., Lyubomirsky, King, & Diener, 2005; Peterson, 2006; Seligman, 2002, 2011; Seligman & Csikszentmihalyi, 2000; Snyder & Lopez, 2011) along with findings from positive interpersonal communication (e.g., Socha & Pitts, 2012b). For example, "good relationships" would seem to include a desire for communication excellence (Mirivel, 2012) and feature positive communication qualities such as relational synchrony (Y. Y. Kim, 2012), deep listening (Bodie, 2012), and considering morality, positive communicative virtues (Miczo, 2012), pro-social forms of communication (Kinney & Porhola, 2009), as well as positive affective communication (Floyd & Deiss, 2012), heightened senses of spirituality (Baesler, Derlega, & Lolley, 2012) and more.

## THEORIES OF MORAL DEVELOPMENT AND CHILDREN

### Conceptualizing Morality

Before we review theories of children's moral development including Piaget (1965), Kohlberg (Kohlberg & Turiel, 1971), Gilligan (1982), and Turiel (1983), we first offer our perspective on defining "morality." Here, we draw on the recent and evocative work of Bloom (2010) who has been studying the moral life of infants:

> Morality, then, is a synthesis of the biological and the cultural, of the unlearned, the discovered and the invented. Babies possess certain moral foundations—the capacity and willingness to judge the actions of others, some sense of justice, gut responses to altruism and nastiness. Regardless of how smart we are, if we didn't start with this basic apparatus, we would be nothing more than amoral agents, ruthlessly driven to pursue our self-interest. But our capacities as babies are sharply limited. It is the insights of rational individuals that make a truly universal and unselfish morality something that our species can aspire to. (Bloom, 2010)

We agree with Bloom and a growing number of developmental psychologists and evolutionary anthropologists (e.g., see Warneken & Tomasello, 2009), who argue collectively that the foundations of processes of morality such as human empathy and altruism are present in infancy and are molded throughout an infant's interactions with people in the world. Hamlin, Wynn, and Bloom (2007), for example, found that children as young as 6 months of age can differentiate "helping" others from "hindering" others. In a study of 6- and 10-month-olds, infants were presented with a puppet show in which a character tried, but repeatedly failed on its own, to reach the top of a steep hill. On alternating attempts, the climber was helped up the hill by a second puppet, and hindered—pushed down the hill—by a third puppet. Infants were shown these events repeatedly until they lost interest in the displays (indicated by decreased looking at the events). Each infant was then offered a choice of the helping character or the hindering character. The large majority of both 6- and 10-month-old infants chose the helper puppet—presumably because it had "helped" the climber achieve its goal, and infants resonated with "helping." In a similar study, Warneken and Tomasello (2007), examined 14-month-old children's orientations toward helping and cooperation using multiple and varied experimental situations such as dropping a clothes pin or a marker and then recording children's unsolicited responses. Warneken and Tomasello (2007) concluded, "The study establishes that children at 14 months of age understand another person's unfulfilled goal, and altruistically help him or her to achieve it" (p. 291).

Thus, in this chapter we think of morality and its development, interactionally. That is, like language development, morality may start with some form of prewired, genetic/biological roots but its development is affected by and through interaction with the world. Like communication itself, a person's moral competencies may display themselves in primitive forms in childhood, but may (or may not) increase in complexity across the lifespan, dependent in part on the kinds of contexts and kinds of interactions a person encounters.

## Theories of Moral Development

Most discussions of children's moral development begin with Piaget's (1932) famous theory of cognitive development that he connected to understanding the moral behaviors and lives of children. To decipher children's views on "right" and "wrong" behaviors Piaget observed how they interacted during game play. Piaget believed that children made moral judgments based on their own direct observations of the world while at play with other children. For Piaget, it was peers, and not necessarily parents, who were key sources of moral concepts such as equality, reciprocity, and justice. Piaget's views on development were that it ultimately occurs from actions of the individual; she/he learned about the world from interacting with their environment. These ongoing interactions are constantly restructuring the knowledge that individuals possess. Through Piaget's observations of children's game play, and following his theory of cognitive development, he concluded that like cognition, morality was a developmental process.

Piaget's (1932) research included interviewing children about their views on lying and stealing. He found that while younger children acknowledged that lying was "bad," they had a difficult time explaining why it was discouraged. Somewhat older children were able to explain that "it wasn't right"—indicating a higher level of moral reasoning. But, the oldest group of children also showed an understanding of being aware of one's intentions in relation to a lie; that is, the difference between knowingly telling a lie versus making an honest mistake.

Piaget (1932) proposed that children begin in a "heteronomous" stage of moral reasoning that is characterized by strict adherence to rules and duties, as well as obedience to authority (see Nucci, 2006, for an overview). Two factors come into play with this heteronomy: the child's cognitive structure and their general social relationship with adults. According to Piaget, egocentrism is a central theme among children's cognitive structure, as they have a difficult time processing their views and the views of others simultaneously. This can lead to children projecting their views and thoughts onto others (Nucci, 2006).

However, as children age and play together they find that a rigid heteronomous adherence to the rules is not always the best way to approach situations. At this point children are reaching the "autonomous" stage, where they approach the rules with a mutual respect for others in hopes of reciprocity. This marks a shift from egocentrism to perspective taking (Nucci, 2006).

Kohlberg (1973; and see Nucci, 2006, for an overview) followed a similar path to Piaget in some ways. He also suggested that children form their morality through life experiences, however, he proposed that moral maturity took longer to achieve than did Piaget. Kohlberg identified six stages of moral reasoning, which he sectioned into three levels. The first level is considered preconventional, as the person makes decisions based around a strict and individualistic point of view. At Stage 1 of this level, heteronomous orientation focuses on avoiding breaking rules that are backed by punishment, obedience for its own sake and avoiding the physical consequences of an action to persons and property. This stage is similar to Piaget's theory as those within it are unable to see the perspectives of others and experience egocentrism. Stage 2 is where individuals begin to comprehend moral reasoning, they learn that "what is right is what's fair in the sense of an equal exchange, a deal, an agreement" (Nucci, 2006, p. 659). The understanding that everyone has their own sets of wants and needs that they pursue comes into light. At the conventional level, Stage 3 involves a deeper understanding of what is considered "right" to those close to them in their lives, and there is more comprehension of what it means to be "good" in terms of stereotypical roles. Stage 3 includes understanding views of family and community on a local level, but not yet considering the generalized social system, which shows through Stage 4. This stage is characterized from shifting the individual's views from the local level to the larger societal level; i.e., obeying laws. The post conventional level is highlighted by reasoning centered on principles. Stages 5 and 6 are demonstrated typically when an individual will reason using principles that are central to various societal rules, but they will not accept the rule being used uniformly. This final level is where the application of laws can be found.

Kohlberg (1973) advanced understanding of morality beyond that which was previously rooted in behavioral traditions where "virtues" were taught through direct communication, then given opportunities to practice, followed by positive (or negative) reinforcement. However, Kohlberg assumes, problematically, a uniformity of agreement among entire communities on what a specific moral virtue is, or should represent. Also, following Kohlberg, teachers are given curricula written by administrators that are predisposed to certain cultural values that may not be consistent with all of the children in a given classroom, and therefore they may present a biased view toward beliefs that are not preferred by a given community (e.g., the debate concerning the inclusion of evolution and creationism in school texts).

Kohlberg (1973) believed that the goal of moral education is to encourage individuals to develop to the next stage of moral reasoning. Development in this model is not only based on cognitive development and gaining more information, but how an individual thinks and acts with their environment within each stage. When the individual is faced with new information that clashes with prior knowledge, it forces him/her to adjust views on the subject, which is known as equilibration.

In response to Kohlberg's work, *Domain Theory* was created by Elliot Turiel (1983, 2002). According to Turiel, morality and social norms are derived from the child's attempts to understand differing kinds of social experiences focusing on intrinsic effects. Specifically, morality is framed by concepts of fairness, harm, and welfare as they are experienced in live interaction. For children, social conventions, at a conceptual level, have little intrinsic meaning and interest beyond that which is needed and experienced as consequences of their interpersonal interactions. Basically, morality consists of the more or less agreed upon rules for how a given interpersonal exchange should function. How this system varies from Kohlberg's model is that although morality and convention are considered distinct frameworks, they are framed within the same conceptual experiential system. In the ebb and flow of these two elements, children at various developmental levels have the opportunity to learn, for example, about how social norms such as turn-taking are also a form of justice. They therefore gain a deeper understanding of morality and what is to be expected from them and others, at their given level of development.

In reaction to Kohlberg, Carol Gilligan (1982, 1988) founded her views, specifically on the morality of care, by listening to women's experiences. She proposed that the morality of care can serve in place of the morality of justice that was suggested by Kohlberg. Gilligan believed that justice and care are distinct, yet possibly connected. With respect to the moral development of children, in a study of children's (grades K–8) patterns of choices in attempting humorous communication, Socha and Kelly (1994) found that boys' and girls' message choices paralleled that of the ethic of care (girls) and ethic of justice (boys). That is, children in early grades tended to not make fun of others, but rather played with words, sounds, and faces. However, starting in grade 3, many boys began to make fun of others (e.g., telling jokes about "dumb blondes," unintelligent people, minorities, etc.), whereas girls added making fun of themselves in relational situations (but not others). These patterns of humor choices continued for most of the children through grade 8. Socha and Kelly concluded that the ethic of care (no one is to be hurt) might have prevented girls from making fun of others, whereas the ethic of justice (everyone is to be treated the same) may have shaped boys' choices of targets of humor as they attempted to "equalize by diminishment" (e.g., We are all the same, no one is really any "better" than anyone else). Assuming the results are replicated, from a lifespan perspective, they have potential implications for adolescents' and adults' humor message production and humor appreciation as connected to morality. That is, especially today, telling racist, sexist, or ageist jokes, for example, will reflect negatively on the image of the teller (and intended audiences), and will raise questions concerning his/her morality.

However, when discussing the development of morality one might overlook many of the achievements that an individual may accumulate incrementally over the early years of their lives and instead focus on what comes later. Thompson (2012) proposes that children start out with "a non-egocentric awareness of the goals, feelings, and desires of people and of how those mental states are affected by others' actions" (p. 426). And, through the early years of development children begin to understand themselves as part of a whole in relation to social groups, the moral obligations implied as a member of these groups, and begin viewing the world more outwardly sooner than originally anticipated. Warneken and Tomasello (2007, 2009) (mentioned earlier) found that 14-month-old children could aid an unfamiliar adult if the need was apparent but also if they knew how to help. Important to note here is that as long as children understood how to help, that the toddlers would aid the unfamiliar adult regardless of maternal support or any kind of reward they would receive. Further, and also important is that the children were **not** verbally requested to help—they did so of their own accord. This indicates that even at such a young age, children are able to perceive intentions and goals through others' behavior and understand how to alter events to aid in the achievement of those goals. However, as Socha and Kelly's (1994) study suggests, children will display a level of learning similar to the adults that surround them (which for the boys in the study included examples of dark humor undoubtedly learned from those around them. Although the study does not report data to support this, the first author suspects the individuals to include older brothers and uncles).

To summarize, thus far our understanding of children's moral development has progressed to what is now a fairly comprehensive framework that considers the role of cognitive development and social development, specifically perspective taking, but less so the development of communication abilities. It is clear, however, that with increasing age, experience, and instruction children's moral abilities do improve. However, such development is not necessarily a straightforward process, nor an easy one.

Conry-Murray (2013) conducted a study that examined whether children under 5 years of age would have a difficult time understanding beliefs that varied from their own, particularly where the social contexts imply how to behave. By using theory-of-mind research (Wellman & Liu, 2004) as her foundation Conry-Murray (2013, p. 493) theorized that "beliefs endorsing moral violations may be more difficult to understand than beliefs endorsing conventional rule violations." In her study she found that children were much less flexible accepting another's idea of what counted as a moral violation (such as hitting someone) versus the violation of a social norm (like wearing pajamas to school—unless it's pajama day). Conry-Murray (2013) used an interview process with the children where the protagonist character within the survey was either a teacher or another child. It was reported that the violation of social rules was generally not OK and that 89% of participants agreed on this regardless whether the character committing these violations was a teacher or another child. When asked about what were generally considered to be unusual, or atypical beliefs (e.g., it is OK to hit others), the majority of children noted that they were indeed unusual or atypical beliefs, but they were also more flexible with accepting what might be considered a "plausible mistake" with said beliefs (e.g., it is OK to hit bullies). With older children, "using norms to predict beliefs may be more common for moral than conventional beliefs perhaps because moral norms are based on inherent consequences" (Conry-Murray, 2012, p. 508).

## POSITIVE PSYCHOLOGY AND CHARACTER DEVELOPMENT

In the past decade academic discussion of moral development (of children and adults) has widened considerably by adding human character development and recently communication (Socha & Pitts, 2012b). Of course, learning to make choices that reflect moral standards of "right" and "wrong" is a significant part of positive human development, however, "good people" not only make moral choices, but also display a wide range of positive human character strengths, such as honesty, fairness, forgiveness, hope and more. In this section we review the work of Peterson and Seligman's (2004) VIA Character Strengths and the VIA Institute on Character (see https://www.viacharacter.org).

Peterson and Seligman (2004), in response to a history of looking for human deficits in the field of psychology, developed a highly significant and ground-breaking volume that examined human strengths. They organized the volume into six core virtues and twenty-four character strengths: **wisdom** (creativity, curiosity, open-mindedness, love of learning, perspective), **courage** (bravery, persistence, integrity, vitality), **humanity** (love, kindness, social intelligence), **justice** (citizenship, fairness, leadership), **temperance** (forgiveness, humility, prudence, self-regulation), and **transcendence** (appreciation of beauty, gratitude, hope, humor, and spirituality).

Peterson and Seligman's (2004) highly significant volume outlines what we envision as a potentially useful template for future theorizing and research about communication and good relationships. Specifically, communication is the means through which individuals display, and invite others to display positive character strengths, that is, to be at our best, as we endeavor to co-create good relationships. Extending this work in positive psychology to communicating with children, Socha and Yingling (2010) argued that positive communication plays a significant role in parenting and caregiving insofar as it focuses attention on using communication in ways that seek to bring out the best in children, as a means of inviting and facilitating them to display desirable qualities such as a love of learning, curiosity, and more.

Imagine, for instance, if parents' and caregivers' communication with children was oriented toward enhancing the particular character strength of children's core virtue of "wisdom" by creating contexts where children wanted to display virtues of creativity, curiosity, open-mindedness, love of learning, and a respect for multiple viewpoints. Of course, some of this is already taking place in parents'/caregivers' efforts in raising children, but, much like in psychology, the emphasis in communication has been on noticing when children have "not" been doing these things, and then using communication punitively as a means of course correction, rather than positively as a call to kids to hop aboard the exciting positive communication train heading to wisdom world!

## CONTEXTS

As we have seen thus far, children learn about morality from many sources and in varied circumstances. However, sometimes the meanings of morality can be misinterpreted or skewed toward a particular standpoint. "Moral values are a group of psychological arrangements acquired by the individual in living in a social sphere. In sum, morality is developed according to learned customs, traditions and ideals in relation to a certain community and its values" (Al-Hooli & Al-Shammari, 2009, p. 389). In this section we review literature about the contexts of communication and children's moral development. What the reader should notice in this section is that although the goals of developing "good" children may be somewhat similar across contexts, the communication strategies and tactics used in service of children's moral development vary.

## HOME

To date, the literature focusing on teaching children morality in the home features mostly applications of educational and psychological literature, along with religious-based instructions and tips. Berkowitz and Grych (1998), for example, focused on five psychological foundations they argued are related to morality. These are: social orientation, self-control, compliance, self-esteem, and endeavor. Berkowitz and Grych then seek to connect parents' behaviors to these outcomes. Importantly, they conclude:

> … perhaps the single most powerful parental influence on children's moral development is induction. Explaining parental behavior and its implications for the child and others is linked to greater empathy, more highly developed moral conscience, higher levels of moral reasoning and altruism. (p. 389)

Specifically, parents who "talk aloud" their thinking when making decisions, that is, letting children peer behind the scenes, especially in those decisions concerning moral choices, are likely to be successful in teaching children to make similar choices.

It is important that parents be mindful of the sources of values connected to their choices including their personal and family's values, as well as those of connected systems such as neighborhoods, religious institutions and more. And, also, that sources and values change over time. For example, today, parents searching the internet for tips and advice about teaching children morality will find that the LIVESTRONG Foundation (LIVESTRONG.com) features an article "How to Teach Morals to Children" in four steps (Ireland, 2013). Of course, the highly publicized ethical and moral controversies surrounding the choices made by its founder (Lance Armstrong), will require that today's parents also give this particular source (as well as all internet sources) a very close and critical reading (i.e., its credibility as a source of moral advice has become suspect).

A good example of a study of parent-child communication and moral development at home is Laible's (2004) study that "examine[d] the relations between both the content and style of mother-child discourse (about the child's past behavior) at age 30 months and their relation to a child's socioemotional and sociomoral development 6 months later" (Laible, 2004, p. 174). Mothers were instructed to discuss two behavioral events with their child—one where the child behaved appropriately and one where the child did not. It was found that one of the largest predictors for children's more complex sociomoral understanding of their actions was when the mother discussed these two events in a rich, narrative fashion. By reflecting on how the behavior positively or negatively affected others, children were able to better understand moral norms. Six months after the initial assessment, the participants were asked if these conversations had affected their children, and children were again tested for their understanding of sociomoral behavioral expectations. Those children whose mothers had previously given rich narratives scored substantially higher than those who did not. This suggests that when children have opportunities to reflect on moral consequences, as facilitated by conversations with guardians or caregivers, they have a better chance of more clearly understanding the implications than peers that do not experience similar kinds of parental/caregiver coversations.

Investments of time and effort in communicating with their children about morality at home, such as shown in Laible's (2004) study, is typically regarded to be among the most significant investments parents can make in their children's moral development. Although most of this kind of research tends to focus on a Judeo-Christian moral code, it is important to consider that children are exposed to many systems of moral thought in the world. B. Kim and Sung (2011), for example, discuss the teachings of the Buddhist Sutra, which is revered in many East Asian nations and is considered to be a valuable tool for teaching children the kindnesses their parents passed along to them and how to repay them. It is socially expected in this cultural system for a child to respect and care for their parents as they age. Mothers are held in particularly high regard. According to Kim and Sung, "the teacher is ten times more venerable than the assistant teacher, the father is a hundred times more than the teacher, and the mother is a thousand times more than the father" (Kim & Sung, 2011, p. 901). Many Buddhists not only aim for the salvation of their parents, but for every living thing. Learning to appreciate the kindnesses one's parents passed along opens individuals up to extend their kindness, love, and gratitude to others. And, to also act in concert with the Buddhist belief of karma: an ideology that an individual has been in relationship with all living entities and therefore owes a great debt of gratitude to all (Kim & Sung, 2011).

## Educational Institutions

When children leave the home, many questions can be asked regarding teaching children morality in educational institutions. What should be taught? Who should teach them? How are they qualified to teach them? What if the morals being taught are different than values represented in some of the families?

Al-Hooli and Al-Shammari (2009), for example, argued that one of the most important characteristics of a teacher is that they love teaching and that they are able to convey their love and appreciation for the art of teaching itself to their students. Since teachers are responsible for creating and maintaining safe and respect-filled environments for students, teachers should be able to approach new ideas and new people with open minds. By conveying they are open, loving, and happy to teach, teachers can more effectively pass along socially normative morals throughout the day in their structured domain. When students arrive home, however, they will be confronted with social norms within a familial structure that may be different from and possibly at odds with the classroom. Both contexts afford children structured places to discover and practice social scripts, as well as to work out what might be conflicting moral lessons between contexts.

According to Al-Hooli and Al-Shammari (2009) moral values are a group of psychological arrangements acquired by the individual as she/he lives in social spheres. Within the context of US public schools, Al-Hooli and Al-Shammari (2009) reported that unfortunately there are limited avenues for teachers to teach specific moral values in their classes, but rather teachers can more broadly focus on moral values that pertain loosely to secular humanism, or "being a good person" (The Golden Rule, play fair, etc.). Although careful to not advocate one particular moral vantage point as to what to teach children, in another study Zeece (2009) suggested that teachers employ an expanded selection of prosocial literature aimed at young children to expand their understanding of morals and socially positive behaviors. By providing children published picture books, for example, that display and focus on morally relevant issues, children have the opportunity to express their thoughts as well as express them in ways they may not have had words for previously. By having a teacher read these stories with their students they are also opening a discussion that lets children have a glimpse into an adult's view as well as hear the views of their peers. To reinforce the lessons and sentiments conveyed through school-based literature, the teacher can use characters from the books to promote morally positive behaviors that were emphasized throughout the story. This both reiterates the point (sometimes repetition is the key to retention), and offers a different context for the child to look at the underlying moral point.

## Media

Beside books, children are exposed to various forms of media throughout the day and may encounter prosocial and positive entertainment, especially if they are consuming age-appropriate materials (rather than "adult"). While there are some television shows that clearly promote prosocial values (e.g., *Sesame Street*), children's moral interpretations of shows have been researched sparingly. In general, Mares and Acosta (2008) argued that the mainstream broadcast television messages received by children are often not what the writer intended, and also that pro-tolerance messages, for example, have a very short shelf life in television form. Specifically, Mares and Acosta's (2008) study sought to understand how kindergarteners comprehended a pro-tolerance television show. Their data supported their assumptions—the children were not comprehending the material as intended. They usually took the stories at face value and could not separate what the moral theme was. Their results showed that "for young children, the relationship between story comprehension and moral lesson comprehension depends on specific features of the plot, such as whether there are potentially confusing negative elements" (e.g., such as a character having a change of conscience) (Mares & Acosta, 2008, p. 393). Having a parent or caregiver co-view the material and discuss it with the child during and after can make such programming more productive as moral lessons (Van Evra, 2004).

Lemal and Van den Bulck (2009) studied how children in fourth to sixth grade understood moral reasoning within the domains of violent and non-violent television viewing. Many of the "perpetrators in violent TV programs are portrayed as attractive characters who commit justified violence and are frequently rewarded for such actions. In addition, victims often appear to experience little to no harm" (Lemal & Van den Bulck, 2009, p. 305). Thus, violence is often portrayed as an appropriate way to approach moral discrepancies and dole out justice. Lemal and Van den Bulck's (2009) results indicated that the younger children in their study preferred authority-based reasoning about violence while older children utilized rights-oriented reasoning in such dilemmas.

In summary, children are learning about morality as they communicate in multiple contexts and with multiple sources who are all attempting to teach children varying kinds of moral lessons. What is needed in order to move forward in our understanding of children and moral development is an organizing framework within which to conduct future research.

## TOWARD AN ECOLOGICAL MODEL

Using Bronfenbrenner (1979) and work appearing in Socha and Pitts (2012a), Pitts and Socha (2013), and Socha (2009), in this section, we begin to identify some of the elements that an ecological model of lifespan communication development in support of good relationships might contain. We focus specifically on childhood as the foundation of lifespan moral development and present a general framework to help organize past work and provide a clearer focus for future research. Further, it is our belief that as moral processes begin in infancy and extend throughout the entire human lifespan, and operate between and among various contexts, that a lifespan-ecological approach is warranted. According to Stoyneva (2014) "Ecological models aim to employ various levels of influences in a particular process (such as attitude formation and behavioral change), while striving to make their description more comprehensive and closer to the real-life occurrence. Such models typically visualize a particular human process (behavioral, cognitive, developmental, etc.) as being influenced by multiple layers of the human experience: close family and friends' influences, socio-economic influences, media, as well as cultural and political influences" (pp. 9–10). Among the most famous and widely used is the ecological model of Urie Bronfenbrenner (1979).

Bronfenbrenner (1979) offers a model of human development that "… involves the scientific study of the progressive, mutual accommodation between an active growing human being and the changing properties of the immediate setting in which the developing person lives" (p. 21). Such a model is situated particularly well to study the nested levels of systems in which developing humans reside, and especially when attempting to comprehensively study a topic as complex as moral development.

Four levels of systems are included in Bronfenbrenner's model: "A microsystem is a pattern of activities, roles, and interpersonal relations experienced by the developing person" (p. 22). "A mesosystem comprises the interactions among two or more settings in which the developing person participates (such as, for a child, the relations among home, school, and neighborhood peer group ...)" (p. 25); "An exosystem refers to one or more settings that do not involve the developing person as an active participant, but in which events occur that affect, or are affected by, what happens in the setting containing the developing person" (p. 25), and last "The macrosystem refers to consistencies, in the form and content of lower order systems ... that could exist at the level of the subculture, or the culture as a whole, along with any belief systems or ideology underlying such consistencies" (p. 26).

Following Bronfenbrenner's ecological model and given this chapter's focus on children, Table 1 illustrates some of the communication contexts as well as organizing questions (arranged using his levels) that a study of "politeness," for example, would consider.

Table 1. Elements of a Preliminary Conceptual Ecological Model of Children, Communication and Moral Development as Applied to Children Learning Politeness.

| Level | Foci of Communication | Potential Organizing Questions |
| --- | --- | --- |
| Microsystems | Parent-child communication<br>Sibling communication<br>Friendship communication<br>Caregiver—child communication | How is politeness understood, valued, and communicated within children's microsystems? |
| Mesosystems | Home and School<br>Home and Neighbors<br>Home and Sports Fields | How does communicating politeness differ as children move between systems? |
| Exosystems | Societal discourse | How do adults understand, value, and talk about politeness in society? |
| Macrosystems | Children's television shows<br>Family comedies | How is politeness portrayed in media that children view? |

As Table 1 illustrates, if the focus is on teaching children to communicate politely, communication researchers following a social-ecological approach would study: (a) politeness in children's microsystems (e.g., interaction in children's immediate environments about their politeness); (b) how children manage politeness in their mesosystems (e.g., children's interactions between multiple social systems as in parent-teacher-child triangles talking about their politeness, and for an extended treatment of family triangles, see Socha & Stamp, 2009); (c) discourse about politeness in societal exosystems (e.g., interactions among adults about politeness of their children and other parents' children), and (d) communication about politeness in macrosystems (e.g., television shows displaying politeness that children are likely to view). Comprehensive ecological analyses would consider that "… the properties of the person, and of the environment, the structure of the environmental settings, and the processes taking place within and between them must be viewed as interdependent and analyzed in systems terms" (Bronfenbrenner, 1979, p. 41). Thus, an individual's levels of moral competencies, for example, are "reflected in the substantive variety and structural complexity of the moral activities which she initiates and maintains in the absence of instigation or direction by others" (p. 55). That is, children's moral competencies will rise to the levels of that which is displayed in their microsystems, learned well enough to be able to execute on their own, as well as their ability to transfer these skills as they move between systems. Further, their understandings or morality are situated in adults' discourse about politeness as well as societal portrayals of politeness in media.

## Outcomes

What kinds of outcomes should be considered to be at the center of an ecological model of lifespan communication and moral development in support of good relationships? This raises questions about the outcomes that family communication scholars have been considering. Socha and Stoyneva (2015) have argued that family communication scholars have been shy about reaching for new heights of relating by studying "satisfaction" rather than "elation." When it comes to the development of an ecological model of morality focused on parent/caregiver discourse with children, and based on the previous review, we argue that there are at least three primary, inter-related outcomes to consider for development: (a) character strengths, (b) moral reasoning competency, and (c) positive interpersonal communication competencies.

First, if the goal is to raise "good" children into "good" adults, then the Peterson and Seligman's (2004) positive character strengths would seem to be critically important as goals or outcomes of interaction. That is, parents should communicate with their children so as to increase their children's **wisdom** (creativity, curiosity, open-mindedness, love of learning, perspective), **courage** (bravery, persistence, integrity, vitality), **humanity** (love, kindness, social intelligence), **justice** (citizenship, fairness, leadership), **temperance** (forgiveness, humility, prudence, self-regulation), and **transcendence** (appreciation of beauty, gratitude, hope, humor, and spirituality). Imagined as a whole the list does appear utopian, however, as Socha and Stoyneva (2015) argue the field of communication does not yet know much about the upper bounds of most of its outcomes, in part because it has yet to ask.

Second, moral reasoning competency would seem also to be critically important. Children need to be taught the many ways humans go about making moral judgments, so that they can learn to make their own. Thus, parent/caregiver communication about how they go about making moral judgments would seem to be of particular importance as an input.

And, third, in general, positive communication competencies would seem to also be necessary in order for children to display, and invite others to display the variety of desired outcomes. That is, sometimes individuals may know what the "right" thing to do in a situation might be, but may also lack the abilities to reach their goals. For example, deep and empathic listening would seem to be fundamental positive communication skills that are essential to making "good" moral decisions.

## Inputs

This review has included numerous sources of moral communication education that can affect children's development. These include a heavy emphasis on the people and discourses in children's micro-, and mesosystems:

- Informal modeling by parents, caregivers, teachers, coaches, religious leaders, friends, and media personalities
- Parent/caregiver-child communication
- Friend-child communication
- Teacher-child communication
- Coach-child communication
- Religious leader-child communication
- Media-child communication

There are indeed so many sources of potential input that future studies will have to sort out relative influences of each of these. And, as children are spending increased amounts of time consuming digital media, the ecological model would predict that its influence on moral development would also increase proportionately. Thus, it follows, for example, that children "raised by TV" would to some extent reflect the moral values presented by that system. There are already concerns that children's spending too much time using mobile media may be having detrimental effects on their social skills (Hwang, 2011).

## CONCLUSION

We conclude the chapter by arguing that human's moral development and positive communication development are inextricably linked and are connected to health, happiness (especially eudemonic), and harmony (e.g., see Lam et al., 2012; Leaming, 2004). Further, an ecological, lifespan communication framing opens many new and unexplored questions concerning how parents and offspring, as well as flourishing married couples (De La Lama, De La Lama, & Wittgenstein, 2012), talk about moral issues across the entire human lifespan, and not just during the formative childhood communication years. Questions such as: How are children raised during particular historical periods of time affected by societal discourse about morality? How are cross-generational differences in standards of morality communicated and addressed? And more. Indeed, although positive interpersonal communication may be, tongue-in-cheek, considered "child's play" (Socha & Pitts, 2012b), it is those habits learned through parent-caregiver-child communication in childhood that create a foundation upon which all future human development occurs. And, upon which future "good" relationships rest.

## REFERENCES

Al-Hooli, A., & Al-Shammari, Z. (2009). Teaching and learning moral values through kindergarten curriculum. *Education, 129*(3), 382–399.

Andrusko, D. (2014, June 2). School uses babies to show inner city children how to be kind. *LifeNews* .com. Retrieved from http://www.lifenews.com/2014/06/02/school-uses-babies-to-show-inner-city-children-how-to-be-kind/

Baesler, E. J., Derlega V. J., & Lolley, J. (2012). Positive spiritual/religious coping among African-American men living with HIV in jails and/or prisons. In T. J. Socha & M. J. Pitts (Eds.), *The positive side of interpersonal communication* (pp. 259–277). New York: Peter Lang.

Berkowitz, M. W., & Grych, J. H. (1998). Fostering goodness: Teaching parents to facilitate children's moral development. *Journal of Moral Education, 27*(3), 371–381.

Bloom, P. (2010, May 5). The moral life of babies. *The New York Times Magazine* Retrieved from http://www.nytimes.com/2010/05/09/magazine/09babies-t.html?pagewanted=all&_r=0

Bodie, G. D. (2012). Listening as positive communication. In T. J. Socha & M. J. Pitts (Eds.), *The positive side of interpersonal communication* (pp. 109–126). New York: Peter Lang.

Bronfenbrenner, U. (1979). *Ecology of human development: Experiments by nature and design.* Cambridge, MA: Harvard University Press.

Conry-Murray, C. (2013). Young children's understanding of beliefs about moral and conventional rule violations. *Merrill-Palmer Quarterly, 59*(4), 489–510.

De La Lama, L., De La Lama, L., & Wittgenstein, A. (2012). The soul mates model: A seven-stage model for couple's long-term relationship development and flourishing. *Family Journal, 20*(3), 283–291. doi:10.1177/1066480712449797

Floyd, K., & Deiss, D. M. (2012). Better health, better lives: The bright side of affection. In T. J. Socha & M. J. Pitts (Eds.), *The positive side of interpersonal communication* (pp. 127–142). New York: Peter Lang.

Gilligan, C. (1982). *In a different voice: Psychological theory and women's development.* Cambridge, MA: Harvard University Press.

Gilligan, C. (1988). *Mapping the moral domain: A contribution of women's thinking to psychological theory and education.* Cambridge, MA: Harvard University Press.

Hamlin, J. K., Wynn, K., & Bloom, P. (2007). Social evaluation by preverbal infants. *Nature, 450*, 557–560. doi:10.1038/nature06288

Hwang, Y. (2011). Is communication competence still good for interpersonal media?: Mobile phone and instant messenger. *Computers in Human Behavior, 27*, 924–934.

Ireland, K. (2013, October 15). How to teach morals to children. LIVESTRONG.com. Retrieved from http://www.livestrong.com/article/176293-how-to-teach-morals-to-children/

Kim, B., & Sung, K. (2011). Teaching repayment of parents' kindness. *Educational Gerontology, 37*(10), 899–909. doi:10.1080/03601277.2010.487750

Kim, Y. Y. (2012). Being in concert: An explication of synchrony in positive intercultural communication. In T. J. Socha & M. J. Pitts (Eds.), *The positive side of interpersonal communication* (pp. 73–90). New York: Peter Lang.

Kinney, T. A., & Porhola, M. (Eds.). (2009). *Anti- and pro-social communication: Theories, methods, and applications.* New York: Peter Lang

Kochanska, G., Koenig, J. L., Barry, R. A., Kim, S., & Yoon, J. E. (2010). Children's conscience during toddler and preschool years, moral self, and a competent developmental trajectory. *Developmental Psychology, 46*, 1320–1332.

Kohlberg, L. (1973). The claim to moral adequacy of a highest stage of moral judgment. *Journal of Philosophy, 70*(18), 630–646. doi:10.2307/2025030

Kohlberg, L., & Turiel, E., (1971). Moral development and moral education. In L. Kohlberg (Ed.), *Collected papers on moral development and moral education* (pp. 410–465). Cambridge, MA: Harvard.

Laible, D. J. (2004). Mother-child discourse surrounding a child's past behavior at 30 months: Links to emotional understanding and early conscience development at 36 months. *Merrill-Palmer Quarterly, 50*(2), 159–180.

Laible, D. J., & Thompson, R. A. (2000). Mother-child discourse, attachment security, shared positive affect, and early conscience development. *Child Development, 71*, 1424–1440.

Lam, W. W. T., Fielding, R., McDowell, I., Johnston, J., Chan, S., Leung, G. M., & Lam, T. H. (2012). Perspectives on family health, happiness and harmony (3H) among Hong Kong Chinese people: A qualitative study. *Health Education Research, 27*(5), 767–779.

Leaming, L. (2004). One big happy family? Gross national happiness and the concept of family in Bhutan. Gross national happiness and development—Proceedings of the first international conference on operationalization of gross national happiness, Thimphu, Bhutan. Retrieved from http://archiv.ub.uni-heidelberg.de/savifadok/volltexte/2010/1361

Lemal, M., & Van Den Bulck, J. (2009). Television and children's moral reasoning: Toward a closed-end moral lessons. *Media Psychology, 11*(3), 305–321. doi:10.1080/15213260802204355

Lyubomirsky, S., King, L., & Diener, E. (2005). The benefits of frequent positive affect: Does happiness lead to success? *Psychological Bulletin, 131*(6), 803–855.

Mares, M., & Acosta, E. (2008). Be kind to three-legged dogs: Children's literal interpretations of TV's measure of moral reasoning on interpersonal violence. *Communications: The European Journal of Communication Research, 34*(3), 377–399. doi:10.1515/COMM.2009.019

Miczo, N. (2012). Reflective conversation as a foundation for communication virtue. In T. J. Socha & M. J. Pitts (Eds.), *The positive side of interpersonal communication* (pp. 73–91). New York: Peter Lang.

Miller-Day, M., Pezalla, A., & Chestnut, R. (2013). Children are in families too! The presence of children in communication research. *Journal of Family Communication, 13*, 150–165.

Mirivel, J. C. (2012). Communication excellence: Embodying virtues in interpersonal communication. In T. J. Socha & M. J. Pitts (Eds.), *The positive side of interpersonal communication* (pp. 57–72). New York: Peter Lang.

Nucci, L. (2006). Education for moral development. In M. Killen & J. G. Smetana (Eds.), *Handbook of moral development* (pp. 657–681). Mahwah, NJ: Lawrence Erlbaum.

Peterson, C. (2006). *A primer in positive psychology.* New York: Oxford University Press.

Peterson, C., & Seligman, M. E. P. (2004). *Character strengths and virtues: A handbook and classification.* New York: Oxford University Press.

Piaget, J. (1932). The moral judgment of the child (M. Gabain, Trans.). Loudon: Routledge & Kegan Paul.

Piaget, J. (1965). The moral judgment of the child. New York: The Free Press.

Pitts, M. J., & Socha, T. J. (Eds.). (2013). *Positive communication in health and wellness.* New York: Peter Lang.

Roots of Empathy. (2014). *Roots of Empathy* [website]. Retrieved from www.rootsofempathy.org

Schonert-Reichl, K., Smith, V., Zaidman-Zait, A., & Hertzman, C. (2012). Promoting children's prosocial behaviors in school: Impact of the "Roots of Empathy" program on the social and emotional competence of school-aged children. *School Mental Health, 4*, 1–21.

Seligman, M. E. P. (2002). *Authentic happiness.* New York: Free Press.

Seligman, M. E. P. (2011). *Flourish: A visionary new understanding of happiness and wellbeing.* New York: Free Press.

Seligman, M. E. P., & Csikszentmihalyi, M. (2000). Positive psychology: An introduction. *American Psychologist, 55*, 5–14

Snyder, C. R., & Lopez, S. L. (Eds.). (2011). *The Oxford handbook of positive psychology.* New York: Oxford University Press.

Socha, T. J. (2006). Orchestrating and directing domestic potential through communication: Towards a positive reframing of "discipline." In L. Turner & R. West (Eds.), *Family communication sourcebook: A reference for theory and research* (pp. 219–236). Thousand Oaks, CA: Sage.

Socha, T. J. (2009). Family as agency of potential: Towards a positive ontology of family communication theory and research. In L. R. Frey & K. Cissna (Eds.), *The Routledge handbook of applied communication* (pp. 309–330). New York: Routledge.

Socha, T. J., & Kelly, B. (1994). Children making fun: Humorous communication, impression management, and moral development. *Child Study Journal, 24*, 237–252.

Socha, T. J., & Pitts, M. J. (2012a). Positive interpersonal communication as child's play. In T. J. Socha & M. J. Pitts (Eds.), *The positive side of interpersonal communication* (pp. 523–524). New York: Peter Lang.

Socha, T. J., & Pitts, M. J. (Eds.). (2012b). *The positive side of interpersonal communication.* New York: Peter Lang.

Socha, T. J., & Stoyneva, I. (2015). Positive family communication: Towards a new normal. In L. Turner & R. West (Eds.), *The Sage handbook of family communication* (2nd ed). (pp. 386–400). Thousand Oaks, CA: Sage.

Socha, T. J., & Stamp, G. H. (Eds.). (2009). *Parents and children communicating with society: Managing relationships outside of home.* New York: Routledge.

Socha, T. J., & Yingling, J. A. (2010). *Families communicating with children.* Cambridge, UK: Polity Press.

Stoyneva, I. (2014). *An exploratory study of generational differences in health information seeking and smoking behaviours in Bulgaria* (Unpublished master's thesis). Old Dominion University, Norfolk, Virgina.

Thompson, R. A. (2012). Whither the preconventional child? Toward a lifespan moral development theory. *Child Development Perspectives, 6*(4), 423–429. doi:10.1111/j.1750-8606.2012.00245.x

Turiel, E. (1983). *The development of social knowledge: Morality and convention.* New York: Cambridge University Press.

Turiel, E. (2002). *The culture of morality: Social development, context, and conflict.* New York: Cambridge University Press.

Van Evra, J. V. (2004). *Television and child development.* New York: Taylor & Francis.

Warneken, F., & Tomasello, M. (2007). Helping and cooperation at 14 months of age. *Infancy, 11,* 271–294.

Warneken, F., & Tomasello, M. (2009). Varieties of altruism in children and chimpanzees. *Trends in Cognitive Science, 13*(9), 397–402.

Wellman, H. M., & Liu, D. (2004). Scaling of theory-of-mind tasks. *Child Development, 75,* 523–541.

Zeece, P. (2009). Using current literature selections to nurture the development of kindness in young children. *Early Childhood Education Journal, 36*(5), 447–452.

# CHAPTER TWO

# Which Parental Messages ABOUT Morality Are Accepted BY Emerging Adults?

VINCENT WALDRON, JOSHUA DANAHER, CARMEN GOMAN,
NICOLE PIEMONTE & DAYNA KLOEBER

Which kinds of moral guidance offered by parents during childhood and adolescence are accepted later in life, when young adults solidify their own moral commitments? This chapter addresses that question by examining acceptability ratings of 470 "memorable moral messages" reported previously in a survey of 303 emerging adults (Waldron et al., 2014). On average, the messages had been received when the participants were 16 years old. The analysis revealed that young adults reported being more accepting of some kinds of parental messages. Those that helped the offspring develop empathy, prioritize moral virtues, and deal with "real world" situations were rated more positively than those which focused on family/cultural obligations, issued commands, or invoked external moral authorities. The results reveal the wide variety of messages that parents use to convey moral content. Parents and moral educators may find the results helpful as they evaluate their current communicative approaches and consider alternatives that might prove useful as children and adolescents transition to young adulthood.

## WHICH PARENTAL MESSAGES ABOUT MORALITY
## ARE ACCEPTED BY EMERGING ADULTS?

The period of emerging adulthood, which ranges from the end of adolescence through the mid-to-late twenties, is a time when most people re-evaluate their moral commitments (J. J. Arnett, 2004). Prior to this, during childhood and into early adolescence, young persons' ideas about right and wrong are highly influenced by parents and other authority figures, such as faith community leaders, sports coaches, or older relatives. As young people gain independence, these traditional sources of moral learning are supplemented by others (Jensen, Arnett, Feldman, & Cauffman, 2004). Peer group norms may increasingly compete with family norms (Grusec & Davidov, 2008). As exposure to media and popular culture expands, children are exposed to new role models of good and bad behavior. Previously taken-for-granted assumptions may be challenged as young adults seek advanced education or encounter new codes of conduct in the workforce (Waldron et al., 2014). Young adulthood may bring exposure to unfamiliar spiritual and religious traditions, some of them intent on conversion of new adherents. All of this suggests that emerging adults negotiate a complex moral landscape, one that requires them to forge their own moral positions from those offered by a chorus of multiple and often contradicting voices (Haste & Abrahms, 2008).

Having "absorbed" certain moral commitments in the process of socialization, emerging adults must now decide whether to reject, accept, or modify them as adulthood beckons. This choice-making is often prompted by moral tensions that emerge in personal relationships. For example, one of our students explained that he was struggling over whether it was right to forgive (a commitment emphasized in his faith tradition) a former friend who had badly hurt him by spreading rumors. Or would doing so just excuse bad behavior? Young adulthood also offers experiences that help young adults forge and articulate their own virtuous qualities. Asked to describe her own virtues, a survey respondent described the "courage" it took to admit that she was responsible for mistakes made at her new job. For this student, courage was a moral virtue that helped her communicate in the "right" way.

This time of life challenges young adults to find the moral positions to which they will be most and least committed as they move into adulthood (Coles, 1986). Moral *commitments* are enduring obligations, the important principles that guide a person's behavior and define the core of their moral identity. In discussing his willingness to marry, one of our students described his commitment to the value of fidelity. He wouldn't marry, he said, until he was sure he and his partner could be sexually exclusive. For him, sexual fidelity was a key part of a good marriage and a "lifelong commitment."

As these examples suggest, young adulthood is a time of moral sense making. What kinds of moral questions are being mulled over at this point in the life course?

In our previous research, 18–25 year olds described a number of pressing concerns (Waldron et al., 2014). Some of them involve honesty and cheating: "Is it ok to ask my college roommate for help on a 'take home' test?" Others involve romantic relationships: "Do I tell my long-distance boyfriend that I went to the movies with one of my guy friends last weekend?" Religion is sometimes involved: "I don't really buy into the beliefs of the church I grew up in. Is it ok to stop going?" Sexual behavior is another prominent concern: "Is it wrong to watch pornography?" Some questions relate to matters of privacy and disclosure: "Should I tell my parents that I think smoking pot is ok?" Responsibilities to others frequently emerge. "Should I be spending more time with my old high school friends, even though we have little in common these days?" Emerging adults also struggle with personal virtues: "I feel like I am so focused on myself. How do I become less self-centered?" The answers to these and many other moral questions help emerging adults decide what their values "should" be as they become independent persons, start new careers, and seek fulfilling relationships. In this chapter we focus on determining the kinds of communication that influences emerging adults in their moral decision making.

## A Communicative Perspective on Morality

For our purposes, morality is a person's sense of what is right or wrong, bad or good. It includes virtuous characteristics of individuals, such as honesty or unselfishness (Aristotle, 1954). Social practices can also be viewed through a moral lens, such as condemning cruelty or offering assistance to less fortunate persons. Although the definitions of certain immoral or moral behaviors (e.g., harming children) are the subject of widespread consensus, morality is often a subject of debate. At the time of this writing, a local newspaper has been publishing a stream of letters to the editor concerning members of the local homeless population who often station themselves at busy intersections seeking donations of spare change. Are better-off citizens fulfilling a moral obligation when they respond favorably to these requests? Or, as several writers argue, are they wrongly cultivating a sense of dependence that will ultimately be harmful to the homeless person and society at large? Moral dialogues of this type are important because they express, and sometimes prompt change in, the moral positions of individuals and communities. Participation in such discussions is shaped by a number of forces. One of these is developmental. Some kinds of moral reasoning require a facility for understanding the perspectives of others and the capacity to apply abstract principles. Children and young adolescents may lack the cognitive capacity to transcend egocentrism or think in a nuanced way about such matters as justice (Kohlberg, 1981, 1984).

However, *emotion* is another force that shapes moral dialogue. It appears that certain "moral emotions," such as guilt or shame, have evolved to help members of complex social groups recognize and enforce moral obligations. The experience of these feelings may be a precursor for moral dialogue, as when a feeling of guilt is the catalyst for an apology. See Darwin (1872/2009), and more recently Keltner (2009), for detailed discussion of the evolutionary value of these kinds of emotional experience.

However, developmental readiness and emotional prompting go only so far in helping us understand how moral commitments get "worked out" in personal relationships. To learn more, we must look to the kinds of communication that help people express their values and negotiate those values that appear to be in tension. This emphasis on communication places our work loosely within the dialogical tradition of moral theorizing (R. C. Arnett, Fritz, & Bell, 2009; Haste & Abrahams, 2008; Levinas, 1981), which examines the role of the ongoing moral dialogues orchestrated by families, communities, cultures, and theological traditions. As Bakhtin (1986) suggested, these influences create a "polyphony"—a chorus of simultaneous and sometimes contradictory voices. For us a key question is this: How do moral decision-makers, especially young adults, forge moral positions from these ongoing and sometimes competing influences? For example, how do persons in a dating relationship decide which level of sexual involvement is "right," given the competing positions offered by peers, partners, parents, and faith community leaders?

Our research begins to answer this question by closely examining moral conversations conducted in the context of influential personal relationships. Waldron and Kelley (2008) propose negotiated morality theory (NMT) as a framework for exploring the "moral functions" of relational communication. The theory suggests that—in addition to communicating information about such relational dimensions as intimacy, trust, or control—our interactions with family members, peers, and intimates often convey our understandings of what is right and wrong. This can be done explicitly ("I'm sorry, but that is just *wrong*") or more implicitly by, for example, refusing to laugh when a friend cruelly mocks another person. Focusing on explicit messages, Waldron and colleagues (2014) established that young adults report clear recollections, even years after they were originally received. Survey data further established that parents were often the source of these memorable moral messages. In an effort to further develop NMT, the purpose of the current study is to understand which of these memorable messages are actually accepted as emerging adults form their own moral positions.

## Memorable Messages about Morality

Memorable messages are concise, influential communications received early in life and recollected years later (Knapp, Stohl, & Reardon, 1981). They are often conceptualized as tools of socialization—aids to navigating new, complicated, or confusing situations. Indeed, early studies established them as important sources of wisdom for newcomers to the workplace (Stohl, 1986). Examples might include cautions ("Mind your own business"), axioms ("The early bird gets the worm"), and affirmations ("Believe in yourself"!) among many others. But people recall such messages when facing other challenges, such as balancing work and personal commitments (Medved, Brogan, McClanahan, Morris, & Shepherd, 2006), defining gender roles (Heisler, 2002), aging successfully (Holladay, 2002), being a good mother (Heisler & Butler Ellis, 2008), adjusting to college life (Kranstuber, Carr, & Hosek, 2012; Nazione et al., 2011), and assessing romantic partners (Kellas, 2010).

Working within the framework provided by NMT (Waldron & Kelley, 2008) we find good reason to view memorable messages as forms of communication that serve important moral functions within families. Although memorable messages do not always concern moral matters, they often help recipients assess how their behavior, or that of others, might be considered good or right, bad or wrong. Faced with decisions about how to be a good employee, parent, or friend, individuals appear to search for guidance in the archive of messages received from respected elders and other sources of moral influence. The studies reviewed above reveal that the sources of such messages are often parents and other older family members. For example, Holladay (2002) reported that mothers were often the source of memorable messages about aging well, and it appears that new mothers often recall messages from their own mothers. Heisler and Butler Ellis (2008), for example, found that new mothers more often recalled helpful messages from their own mothers than from other sources of advice. College students have been shown to recall parental messages when reassessing their values, especially when their behavior seems to vary from family expectations (Butler Ellis & Smith, 2004; Smith & Ellis, 2001; Smith, Ellis, & Yoo, 2001). This theme of parental influence also emerged when Kellas (2010) studied the messages that daughters remembered receiving from their mothers. "Characteristics of good relationships" was among the most commonly cited topics. Keeley (2004) found that messages exchanged as the end of life approached sometimes recommended moral principles grounded in spiritual commitments.

Guided by this previous work, we previously surveyed emerging adults about the moral messages they recalled receiving from their parents (Waldron et al., 2014). In that earlier report, we addressed the *content* of these messages. What aspects of morality were addressed by parents? And we wanted to know about the *form*—how were they delivered? Indeed, a wide range of communicative approaches might be used to convey a moral lesson: cautionary tales, commands, proverbs, rhetorical questions, and so on. Which kinds were most likely to be recalled?

With regard to content, the results suggested that memorable messages often concerned relational ethics. By far the most common theme (cited by 35% of messages), included moral qualities of personal relationships (How should a good friend behave?), sexual mores (Is it ok to watch pornography?), and guidelines for behaving toward people in general ("Err on the side of compassion"). Second in frequency was the theme of honoring the self, as manifested in messages about self-development ("Do your best at all times") and self-respect ("Believe in yourself"). Themes of honesty and deception were cited in about 15% of the messages. Qualities of virtuous people (e.g., courage, fortitude) were cited in 9.5% of the messages and references to external sources of moral authority, such as laws, scripture or God, were relatively rare (6.8%). The finding that young adults recall messages about relational morality is consistent with theorizing about the unique concerns of emerging adulthood, a stage of life in which negotiating romantic and friendship ties is of paramount concern (J. J. Arnett, 2004, 2007). Most relevant to NMT, parental guidance about relationships clearly emerged as one kind of communication that may have been useful in helping young adults negotiate the moral landscape of personal relationships.

The form of a communication, in addition to its content, may determine whether a message is memorable late in life. Which forms are most memorable? The literature provides a partial answer to this question. From previous studies we know that memorable messages tend to be brief, that some take the form of injunctions ("Don't ever get old"; Knapp et al., 1981; Stohl, 1986). Stories are often memorable, so we can speculate that some messages are delivered in the form of narratives (Glonek & King, 2014). In our earlier study we examined more deeply the message forms used by parents, classifying them by the way they redirected or transformed the offspring's moral frame of reference (Waldron et al., 2014). Eleven major categories emerged from this analysis along with several prominent subtypes.

*Identity-shaping* messages were most common, accounting for about 21% of the 470 messages reported in the study. Parents used two major approaches. Affirming messages attempted to transform moral self-doubt to self-confidence: "When you are feeling down about yourself, just remember you are a good person at heart." In contrast, obligating messages directed the offspring to focus less on individual identity and more on their responsibilities to the cultural groups to which they belonged. These messages reminded the recipients of their responsibilities as a member of an ethnic or religious community, extended family, or gender ("A member of our family would not even consider getting drunk and carrying on in public").

*Reality-defining* messages (14% of messages) helped youth adapt moral principles to real-life circumstances ("Divorce is not a good thing, but sometimes it is necessary to avoid something worse …"). These messages seem to redefine morality from a set of idealized principles to a matter of practical choice-making, often by balancing competing moral commitments. From this standpoint, good behavior is that which adapts to new and changing circumstances while remaining in conversation with key moral commitments.

Several other message forms were reported by more than 10% of the 303 emerging adults surveyed for the study. *Future-casting* messages (13.1%) directed attention to the consequences of what the parent considered to be immoral conduct ("Think

about how that [a marijuana arrest] will look when you apply for a job someday.").
*Virtue-prioritizing* messages (12.3%) called attention to what parents considered to
be the best qualities of good people ("More than anything else, you have to be seen
as an honest person"). *Commands* (11.4%) attempted to restrict the youth's moral
decision-making autonomy by imposing the parent's authority. These were typically injunctions, such as "Do not ever use drugs of any kind." The messages were
offered without explanation or context. *Perspective-taking* (11.2%) communications
encouraged offspring to consider others rather than the self in the process of moral
decision-making. The most common of these (empathy-enhancing messages) emphasized the feelings and circumstances of other people ("How do you think she
felt when you called her that name?" "How do you think his life might have been
different than yours?").

In addition, several message forms were less commonly used, including *in-
voking external authority* (6.3%) an approach that referenced scripture, the law, or
non-parental authority figures (e.g. judges, pastors, coaches). The sharing of maxims or proverbs, a type of memorable message prominent in earlier studies (Knapp
et al., 1981), was rarely reported by our sample of emerging adults (4.2%). Other
less common forms were the use of emotions (*emotion emphasizing messages*), such
as guilt or fear, to convey the moral message (2.8%); *inviting moral dialogue* (1.9 %),
and *coercion* through actual or threatened force (1.5%).

## What Kinds of Messages Do Emerging Adults Accept?

Our previous work yields an improved understanding of the content of moral
messages recalled by emerging adults. And it yields a taxonomy of the approaches
parents apparently use when communicating them. What remains, however, is an
important question: Which of these moral messages are actually *accepted* by young
adults? It is one thing to recall a message, another to accept it—that is to incorporate
the moral position into one's own worldview. After all, parental messages might be
memorable because they are simply disagreeable, impractical, or forceful. Yet emerging adults might reject these messages out of hand. Communication researchers
increasingly want to know how communication occurring among family members
affects decisions and behaviors later in life (Bylund, Baxter, Imes, & Wolf, 2010;
Kellas, 2010; Socha & Yingling, 2010). This work suggests that important adult decisions about such matters as health practices and relational roles could be shaped by
the qualities of parent-child communication on these topics. It certainly seems likely
that parent-child conversations about morality should be similarly consequential.

Previous research yields some guidance regarding the kinds of moral communication that emerging adults might find most acceptable. In previous analyses of
the moral orientations expressed by young adults, researchers categorized them
using three overarching "moral ethics" (Jensen, 1995; Shweder, Much, Mahapatra,

& Park, 1997). The researchers found considerable concern among young adults for an ethic of autonomy (i.e., the right to pursue a fulfilling life and form one's own identity) and community (i.e., commitments to family friends, and others), but less concern for the ethic of divinity (commitments to God or scriptural teaching; J. J. Arnett, Ramos, & Jensen, 2001). Indeed, reluctance to conform to traditional expectations, including religious ones, is not uncommon at this time of life (J. J. Arnett, 2004; Jensen, Arnett, Feldman, & Cauffman, 2004). This literature suggests that parental messages will be most accepted when they help offspring answer questions about moral identity and relationship obligations. How can I best develop my potential as a good person? What commitments should I make—and which should I expect—in friendships, romantic relationships, and with coworkers? The specific kinds of parental messages that prove most helpful to emerging adults are not yet clear. For that reason we posed Research Question 1. Fortunately, unanalyzed data collected in our earlier study (Waldron et al., 2014) created an opportunity for us to identify the kinds of moral messages that emerging adults find most and least acceptable.

RQ1: What kinds of memorable moral messages communicated by parents are most accepted by emerging adults?

## METHOD

The current report analyzes data originally collected, but not analyzed, by Waldron and colleagues (2014). In that study a survey with both open-ended questions and standardized measures was administered to 303 emerging adults who could clearly recall a moral message communicated by their parents. The form of those messages and their content were analyzed previously. The current report focuses on unanalyzed measures of message acceptance. Only a synopsis of the original data collection procedure is provided here, as details are available in the original publication and from the first author.

### Participants

A total of 303 emerging adults (ages 18–25) completed the online survey. The mean age of respondents was 21.3 years at the time of survey completion. On average, they were 15.8 years of age when they received the memorable message. A substantial majority (71.9%) of the respondents were female. Most described their ethnicity as Caucasian/European (71%), but Hispanic (14%), Native American (5%), Asian/Pacific Islander (5%), and African American (3%) participants were also represented. Most respondents had completed some college (80.5%) or were college graduates (13.9%). When asked to rate their agreement on a 7-point scale with the statement, "Religious beliefs were an important part of my upbringing," 53.8% of respondents moderately or strongly agreed.

## Data Collection Procedures

Participants were recruited from a large metropolitan area in the southwestern United States using social media, solicitations at meetings of community and religious groups, and announcements in university courses. To participate, volunteers needed to be 18–25 years old and they had to be able to recall a memorable message, one about "right and wrong," from a parent or guardian. As an incentive, participants were entered in a lottery to win a $50.00 gift certificate to a local cinema. Additional survey opportunities were available to those who did not meet screening criteria. Volunteers were provided a link to an anonymous survey and informed consent was obtained.

**Measures.** Participants were asked to recall a specific and concrete instance when a moral message was delivered by one or more parents. Survey items encouraged them to describe in detail the setting and participants. Consistent with previous studies (e.g., Holladay, 2002), open-ended survey questions were used to collect descriptions of memorable moral messages. These included: "Describe the behavior or practice that your parent(s) thought was right or wrong. In other words, what did the message identify as the right or wrong thing to do?" Two items asked about communication practices: (1) "… write the message that was communicated to you. If you remember the message exactly, place the words in quotation marks" and (2) "How did your parents communicate the moral message? Provide a detailed description of the verbal and nonverbal behaviors they used…." Additional questions asked participants to describe their reactions to the message, why the message was memorable, why they agreed or disagreed with it, and to evaluate the communicative approach used by parents ("Do you think they did a good job in communicating the message?").

To measure the acceptance of these messages, we adapted a process used to analyze compliance with parental rules about risky behavior (Bylund et al., 2010). Respondents considered their reaction to the message at the time it was delivered and currently (the concern of this study). We operationalized acceptance as (1) agreement ("At the present time I agree with the moral message"), (2) influence on beliefs ("At the present time the message influences my beliefs"), and (3) influence on behavior ("At the present time the message influences my behavior"). Ratings were completed on a 7-point scale ranging from strongly agree (7) to strongly disagree (1). At both points in time, Cronbach's alpha for the three items was high (.88 and .90). Results of the three items pertaining to the present time were summed to form a single acceptance measure. The mean acceptance rating was 17.9 with a range of 5 to 21.

The current analysis also used an interpretative approach (see Miles & Huberman, 1994) to better understand the messages and how respondents' interpreted them. Working in pairs, members of the research team read and reread the survey data, generated interpretative notes, and developing initial themes, and culled illustrative examples. These were presented to the whole team, discussed, and revised. Additional data were analyzed until no new themes emerged. For the current analysis, data and interpretative notes to several open-ended questions were most useful. These asked respondents to describe why they remember the message, why they agree with the message (or not) and why they think the parent did "a good job of delivering" this message (or not)? Data and interpretative notes relevant to these questions were reviewed and interpreted primarily by the first author who presented themes to the larger research team and solicited their feedback. Ultimately, this process yielded insights about why emerging adults appeared to accept or reject the moral messages communicated by their parents.

## RESULTS

Our research question asked about the types of parental messages that were most accepted by emerging adults. To answer that question, we report the results of statistical procedures (analysis of variance) used to examine differences in mean acceptance ratings of those who reported receiving a given message type as compared to the rest of the sample. We also report the themes that emerged from qualitative analysis of the open-ended responses, as they reveal why young adults may have accepted certain messages and rejected others.

### Quantitative Ratings: Which Messages Were Rated Highest in Acceptability?

For each message type, the mean acceptance rating for emerging adults who received the message was compared with the mean acceptance rating of the rest of the sample (those who had received another type of message). Statistical details are footnoted.[1] Only message types used by a sufficient portion (at least four percent) of the sample were subjected to statistical analysis. Table 1 presents those message types with significant differences in the acceptance ratings of our sample of emerging adults. For example, respondents who reported receiving a moral maxim from parents (as indicated by the "yes" column) averaged an acceptance rating of 20.4. This was significantly higher than the 17.9 average rating provided by the remainder of the sample. Message types which showed no significant difference (future-casting, affirmation) are excluded. Table 1 also indicates the percentage of the sample that reported receiving each message type. Only 4.2% of all reported messages were moral maxims. So this type of message is rarely reported, but it is rated highest in acceptance.

Table 1. Differences in Message Acceptance as a Function of Parental Message Type.

| Message type | Did parent reportedly use this message? | | % of all messages[1] |
| --- | --- | --- | --- |
| | Yes | No | |
| Maxim sharing | 20.4[2] | 17.9** | 4.2 |
| Virtue prioritizing | 19.9 | 17.6*** | 12.3 |
| Empathy-enhancing | 19.8 | 18.0* | 5.1 |
| Reality-defining | 19.3 | 17.7** | 14.2 |
| Commanding | 16.6 | 18.4** | 11.4 |
| Obligating | 16.0 | 18.4*** | 8.3 |
| Invoking authority | 15.4 | 18.4* | 6.3 |

[1]4.2% of the 303 respondents reported receiving a maxim-sharing message.

[2]20.4 is the average acceptance rating (maximum score is 21) reported by respondents who reported receiving a maxim-sharing message from parents (versus a 17.7 for the remainder of the sample).

$* p < .05, ** p < .01, *** p < 001.$

As further noted in Table 1, acceptance ratings were significantly higher for those respondents that reported receiving messages that prioritized virtues, cultivated empathy, or adapted moral positions to real life situations ("reality defining" messages). Some types of memorable messages seemed to engender the opposite response; emerging adults who recalled them reported significantly *lower* levels of acceptance when compared to those of the remainder of the sample. This was true of obligating, authority-invoking, and commanding messages.

The quantitative results are qualified by the observation that all message types were positively rated on the three-item acceptance measure. Even the least accepted authority-invoking messages averaged a rating of 5 (moderately agree) on the 7-point scale items. One implication is that *many* types of parental messages can have lasting moral influence on the lives of emerging adults. As a group, our respondents made only modest distinctions between those message types that were most and least accepted. Nonetheless, the results are statistically significant, and they do suggest that some parental messages are particularly significant at this phase of life.

## Qualitative Analysis: Why Are Messages Accepted?

For the most and least accepted messages, we examined respondent assessments of their parents' communicative approach, looking for answers to this question:

Why were these messages considered acceptable or not? One theme that emerged was *simplification*. Axioms and proverbs pack an important moral message into relatively few words. Sometimes linked to a narrative ("they left their feelings out of it and told me a story"), these conveyed concisely *the moral of the story*. "It really stuck with me," was a theme noted by several recipients of these messages. Axioms serve the function of making moral decision-making less complicated. In the face of a moral dilemma, these messages may have made it easy to remember the advice offered by mom or dad, even if it was years later.

Yet messages rated lowest in acceptance, such as commands and injunctions, were also simple and brief. They were described as "clear," "repeated a lot," or "hard to forget." So it appears that the more accepted axiomatic messages must have offered more than mere clarity; perhaps they helped the recipient see that parents and offspring were part of an ongoing cultural discussion about moral values, the joint beneficiaries of collective wisdom that had been encapsulated in a memorable phrase or telling proverb. By drawing on these larger social discourses, by supplementing their own perspectives and feelings, parents may have increased the acceptability of the message.

Another theme was *humanizing*. Rather than enforce particular moral positions, accepted communications recognized or revealed the role of human characteristics in moral decision making. Some of the most accepted messages seemed to be those in which the parent revealed something previously unknown about themselves or their own moral journey. "[Mother] gave her own personal story, which connected us." In some cases, the parent's vulnerability came through. One young man reported: "My father has a strong character. That strong character was fragile that day." Another reported seeing "the fear in her eyes" as his mother expressed concern about his moral recklessness. Recognition of the young person's unique feelings and circumstances was important: "It meant a lot to me to know that my parents understood what I was going through ..." In contrast, less accepted messages depersonalized the parties ("She did not have enough reasons to judge one of my best friends without trying to get to know her."). In general, parents who delivered messages appeared to use what has been previously identified as a person-centered approach, which reflects "an awareness of and adaptation to the subjective, affective, and relational aspects of communicative contexts" (Burleson, 1987, p. 305).

A third theme was *relational navigation*. Accepted messages may have helped emerging adults adjust moral principles to the real-life relationships they participate in now. This theme was perhaps most associated with reality-defining messages, but it was expressed by numerous respondents: "I always took to heart the things she said about bonding with a partner you plan to be with and committed to"; "I ended up marrying my [boyfriend] and I always keep in mind what my dad told me ..."; "It helped me develop better relationships with people." These relationship-navigating messages translate the abstract into the concrete and practical. As discussed previously, the themes of narrative and identity are important in the landscape of moral dialogue. Stories about heroes and heroines overcoming trials or facing adversaries provide a rich, contextual backdrop for translating beliefs and values into actions. Messages focused on relational navigation have the ability to guide emerging adults in shaping a story in which they are an important moral agent.

*Confidence building* was a fourth theme. Accepted messages imbued offspring with the desire, and often the confidence, to be good. The message "made me realize I was not being the best version of myself," noted one young woman. "I want to be seen as someone who is easy to talk to and gives others good advice." Others noted, "It helps reassure me that I am doing the right thing" and "I know I can overcome the worst things that come my way." Memorable messages in the final conversations reported by Keeley (2004) had a similar effect in many cases. End-of-life conversations served an affirming function—for survivors, for persons facing end of life, and for the community to which they belonged. They encouraged surviving individuals to express and "live out" these beliefs. We find a similar role for influential moral messages between parents and children, building confidence of the child as a moral agent in the world or reinforcing the child's moral nature (as opposed to amoral, not immoral). In contrast, less accepted messages expressed disappointment or elicited guilt. "I felt accused," said one respondent. "I still feel guilty over it," said another who remembered the message clearly but rated it low on the acceptance measure.

Finally messages appeared to be accepted because they helped emerging adults *refine moral reasoning*. One young man indicated that his parents helped him see both the positive and negative consequences of parties and alcohol. Others appreciated the opportunity to engage in reasoned dialogue with the parent(s): "It was a conversation; not him nagging me." These parents seemed bent on preparing their children to be moral decision makers later in life: "They presented me with both options allowing me to make my own choice." A son noted that his father took the time to "explain why it was wrong" rather than just admonishing him for misbehavior. In contrast, less accepted messages imposed a moral solution by force of emotion ("He could have communicated the same message without the angry tones"), ridicule ("She had no rational reasoning and her tone was condescending"), or the exercise of raw authority ("It was a bit brutal").

## IMPLICATIONS

The most significant contribution of this work may be its identification of the kinds of moral messages that are more or less accepted as emerging adults negotiate a developmental landscape complicated by multiple and competing moral voices. More broadly, these results answer recent calls for a richer understanding of the communication practices that make moral development a dialogical process (Haste & Abrahams, 2008; Waldron & Kelley, 2008; Waldron et al., 2014). As has been argued previously, communication patterns established in the family should shape the skills and orientations children develop as they enter adulthood (Socha & Yingling, 2010). This study supports that claim by suggesting that parental communication about moral matters during adolescence remains influential years later.

The memorable messages construct has proven useful in previous studies of communication about values and spiritual commitments (e.g., Keeley, 2004; Smith & Ellis, 2001). Our study extends that work, confirming that such messages perform functions anticipated by negotiated morality theory, including prioritizing values in relationships and honoring the moral identity of the individual. Our results also contribute to ongoing discussion about the nature of emerging adulthood (J. J. Arnett, 2007; Jensen et al., 2004). In particular, it appears that memorable messages help emerging adults with the developmentally salient task of defining relationships that are good in the moral sense of that word. Importantly, the *way* in which parents communicate about "good relationships" may influence whether or not their children adopt similar perspectives.

## IMPLICATION FOR PARENTS

All messages reported in this study were memorable by definition and most met with high levels of acceptance. But it does appear that some approaches were more effective, at least as perceived by emerging adults. What can parents do to increase the moral force of parenting messages? Ironically, one suggestion is to be less forceful. Messages from parents who issued commands or demanded conformity with external authorities certainly were remembered, but recipients were less likely to incorporate them into their own beliefs and behavior. What explains this reluctance? Most messages were received during adolescence, a time when children are becoming aware of alternative sources of moral guidance, a time when children are experiencing increased autonomy (Kohlberg, 1981). Compared to other approaches, highly directive messages may be less well-calibrated to the needs of the child. Of course, the very concept of authority is changing at this time in life as the child is exposed to education and alternative forms of thinking. Given that the development of reasoning is one focus of education—a move away from autocratic, personal, or blind authority toward that based on insight—messages from authority figures that offer guidance *without reasoning* may be less well-received.

Emerging adulthood may be a period when moral dialogue is both a valued and necessary communication competency (Jensen et al., 2004). It is partly through discussion with friends and coworkers that young adults articulate and refine their moral outlook. And even as maturing offspring value their autonomy, many continue to welcome open conversation with parents (J. J. Arnett, 2007). Parental messages that invite such dialogue may be perceived as more helpful during this period. Presumably, young adults with parents who established this dialogue during adolescence may be more inclined to welcome it later.

Person-centered approaches may be more successful than position-centered ones. Person-centered communication values the subjective experiences of the parties (Burleson, 1987). It acknowledges that moral decisions are filtered through life experiences and emotional reactions and seeks a rich subjective understanding of the parties involved. It can be contrasted with position-centered communication, which seeks to articulate a convention or generally applicable argument. "The church is against it" or "the cost of your relationship should not outweigh its rewards" are position-centered parental responses. They preclude discussion of the degree to which parent and offspring value the church over other sources of guidance and the exploration of the kinds of rewards the offspring finds in the relationship. Our results do not suggest that position-centered communication is ineffective; it just appears to be less so, as it tends to ignore the contextual details or nuance of the situation at hand. This follows from our findings on the strong acceptance of reality-defining messages, which seem to be focused on bridging the gap between abstract principles or axioms and lived experience or particular trials.

One theme in our data is that emerging adults may view relationship questions through a moral lens. Many of the most influential messages concerned relationship themes. What are the most important virtues to look for in self and partner? When is it right to give up on a relationship commitment? What degree of emotional and physical intimacy is acceptable in which kinds of relationships? How do I fulfill my potential as an individual yet still meet my commitments to a spouse, family, and friends? Parental messages that addressed these issues in a practical way, often by sharing personal experiences, tend to be appreciated. This general finding is consistent with previous work establishing that the primary moral concerns of emerging adults are the nature of good relationships and the quest to fulfill their potential as human beings (J. J. Arnett et al., 2001).

It appears that messages that build confidence during adolescence seem to have lasting effects. When faced with difficulties later in life—a relationship break-up or a bad decision at work—respondents sometimes found reassurance from their parents' earlier messages—that the young adult was essentially a "good person" or that they generally tried to "do the right thing." Rarely were the parents offering their offspring a free pass for bad behavior. Rather than overlooking immoral behavior, these messages conveyed a sense that all people made mistakes, no one was perfect. But the parents did convey a belief in their offspring's core commitments and their capacity to "make things right" after a moral transgression.

These messages appeared to foster self-confidence as emerging adults tested moral boundaries and encountered challenging relationships or circumstances.

Finally it appears, not surprisingly, that parental communication can be instrumental in helping adult offspring continue to develop moral reasoning. Parents who offered concrete reasons or examples to support their positions were often viewed positively, as were those who explored "both sides" of a moral question. Some of these parents promoted mutual moral learning, by inviting their children to explore the possible consequences of behavior they thought was morally wrong, such as illegal drug use. A similar stance was taken by a parent who invited his child to read a religious text as the pair collaboratively sought guidance. Emerging adults rarely appreciated a parent's abdication of moral authority. In fact, several criticized parents who failed to provide moral direction; as emerging adults, they seemed to appreciate their parents as moral teachers who provided the decision-making tools that were now proving useful.

## LIMITATIONS AND CONCLUSIONS

These results are subject to some obvious limitations. Males were underrepresented in our sample as were certain ethnic minorities. Nonetheless, nearly a third of the sample self-identified with a minority cultural or ethnic group. Parental messages about moral matters might vary across subcultures. For example, the message type we labeled group-obligating may be more common or acceptable in families belonging to collectivist cultures or those who seek to resist assimilation into a majority culture. This possibility deserves further investigation.

Despite our efforts to recruit beyond the student population, most of our sample reported having completed at least some college education. College students live in a somewhat unique ethical context. They are less likely to be married, for instance, and more likely to be working part-time. The exploration of relational ethics so clearly expressed in our data may reflect the unsettled and developing nature of their relational networks. Other ethical concerns, those related to parenting or sustaining a career, may be underrepresented in our data. More research is needed on moral communication as it occurs in families with different education profiles. These concerns are closely related to concerns raised by the "emerging adulthood" framework. Emerging adulthood serves as an interpretive lens through which we can view some 18–25-year-olds, but not all. The concept is influenced by socio-economic status, culture, and it is subject to revision in light of generational differences as well. Is an "emerging adult" who is also a Millennial facing the same challenges and bringing the same presuppositions as someone in generation X or Y?

Self-report biases may have influenced our data. We took steps to make self-reported messages accurate, asking respondents to describe single, concrete, and memorable communication encounters. As with previous memorable messages studies, respondents seemed to have little difficulty in doing so. Nonetheless, a memorable messages framework, by definition, overlooks communicative practices that shape current thinking but are no longer available for recall. In future work, we hope to study parents and offspring together, to assess how their memories of moral messages converge or diverge. Finally, we are aware that moral discourse is interactive, messy, and ongoing; these qualities can never be fully captured by a study of discrete messages. However, from previous work on memorable messages it seems clear that young adults often interpret past family interactions as discrete communications. We recognize that process may involve the consolidation of a variety of recalled feelings, thoughts, and behaviors into a coherent "message."

Taken together, these findings illustrate the communicative "scaffolding" that parents provide to help offspring climb to higher levels of moral development (Reese, Bird, & Tripp, 2007; Vygotsky, 1978). As moral mentors, parents take quite different approaches. However, we noted previously that most emerging adults in this study viewed their parents as supportive (Waldron et al., 2014). This could be a unique feature of our sample but more likely reflects the general tendency of emerging adults to maintain amiable relationships with their parents (Jensen et al., 2004). Average message acceptance ratings were also quite high. It could be that children with supportive parents may be reluctant to describe messages that they reject. But a more parsimonious explanation is that this generation of emerging adults is receptive to moral advice offered by parents.

Given previous observations that conversations about morality are relatively rare in some contemporary families (Coles, 1986), one conclusion is obvious. Parents should recognize that they can have a significant impact on the moral reasoning of their children. While some observers have worried that the current generation of parents may be guilty of anxiously meddling into the affairs of their adult offspring (cf. Nelson, 2010) a more encouraging thought is that parental communication is a potent force in developing responsible young adults (Socha & Yingling, 2010). We see this as ample reason for providing parents with the encouragement and, in some cases, the communication training that will help them talk about morality with their kids.

# REFERENCES

Aristotle. (1954). *The Nicomachean ethics* (David Ross, Trans.). New York: Oxford University Press.

Arnett, J. J. (2004). *Emerging adulthood: The winding road from the late teens through the twenties.* New York: Oxford University Press.

Arnett, J. J. (2007). *Socialization in emerging adulthood: From the family to the wider world, from socialization to self-socialization.* New York: Guilford Press.

Arnett, J. J., Ramos, K. D., & Jensen L. A. (2001). Ideological views in emerging adulthood: Balancing autonomy and community. *Journal of Adult Development 8*(2), 69–79.

Arnett, R. C., Fritz, J. M., & Bell, L. M. (2009). *Communication ethics literacy: Dialogue and difference.* Los Angeles: Sage.

Bakhtin, M. M. (1986). *Speech genres and other late essays.* (C. Emerson & M. Holquist, Eds.; V. McGee, Trans.). Austin, University of Texas Press.

Braithwaite, D. O., & Baxter, L. A. (2006). Engaging theories in family communication: Multiple perspectives. Thousand Oaks, CA: Sage.

Burleson, B. (1987). Cognitive complexity. In J. C. McCroskey & J. A. Daley (Eds.), *Personality and interpersonal communication* (pp. 305–349). Newbury Park, CA: Sage.

Butler Ellis, J. B., & Smith, S. W. (2004). Memorable messages as guides to self-assessment of behavior: A replication and extension diary study. *Communication Monographs, 71*(1), 97–119.

Bylund, C. L., Baxter, L. A., Imes, R. S., & Wolf, B. (2010). Parental rule socialization for preventive health and adolescent rule compliance. *Family Relations, 59*(1), 1–13.

Coles, R. (1986). Our moral lives. *Society, 23*(4), 38–41.

Darwin, C. (2009). *The expression of emotions in man and animals.* New York: Philosophical Library. (Original work published 1872).

Glonek, K. L., & King, P. E. (2014). Listening to narratives: An experimental examination of storytelling in the classroom. *International Journal of Listening, 28*(1), 32–46.

Grusec, J. E., & Davidov, M. (2008). Socialization in the family: The roles of parents. In J. Grusec & P. D. Hastings (Eds.), *Handbook of socialization: Theory and research* (pp. 284–308). New York: Guilford Press.

Haste, H., & Abrahams, S. (2008). Morality, culture and the dialogic self: Taking cultural pluralism seriously. *Journal of Moral Education, 37*(3), 377–394.

Heisler, J. M. (2002). Parental memorable messages to their children: Adolescent recall of parents' communication about gender/Unpublished doctoral dissertation. Michigan State University Lansing, MI.

Heisler, J. M., & Butler Ellis, J. (2008). Motherhood and the construction of "Mommy Identity": Messages about motherhood and face negotiation. *Communication Quarterly, 56*(4), 445–467.

Holladay, S. J. (2002). "Have Fun While You Can," "You're Only as Old as You Feel," and "Don't Ever Get Old": An examination of memorable messages about aging. *Journal of Communication, 52*, 681–697.

Jensen, L. A. (1995). Habits of the heart revisited: Autonomy, community and divinity in adults' moral language. *Qualitative Sociology, 18*, 71–86.

Jensen, L. A., Arnett, J. J., Feldman, S. S., & Cauffman, E. (2004). The right to do wrong: Lying to parents among adolescents and emerging adults. *Journal of Youth and Adolescence, 33*, 101–112.

Keeley, M. P. (2004). Final conversations: Survivors' memorable messages concerning religious faith and spirituality. *Health Communication, 16*(1), 87–104.

Kellas, J. (2010). Transmitting relational worldviews: The relationship between mother-daughter memorable messages and adult daughters' romantic relational schemata. *Communication Quarterly, 58*(4), 458–479.

Keltner, D. (2009). *Born to be good: The science of a meaningful life.* W. W. Norton & Company.

Knapp, M. L., Stohl, C., & Reardon, K. K. (1981). "Memorable" messages. *Journal of Communication, 31*(40), 27–41.

Kohlberg, L. (1981). *The psychology of moral development: The nature and validity of moral stages.* San Francisco: Harper & Row.

Kohlberg, L. (1984). *Essays on moral development (Volume 2). The psychology of moral development: The nature and validity of moral stages.* San Francisco: Harper & Row.

Kranstuber, H., Carr, K., & Hosek, A. M. (2012). "If you can dream it, you can achieve it." Parental messages as indicators of college success. *Communication Education, 61,* 41–66.

Levinas, E. (1981). *Otherwise than being: Or, beyond essence* (Alphonso Lingis, Trans.). Hague, Boston: M. Nijhoff.

Medved, C. E., Brogan, S. M., McClanahan, A. M., Morris, J. F., & Shepherd, G. J. (2006). Family and work socializing communication: Messages, gender, and ideological implications. *Journal of Family Communication, 6*(3), 161–180.

Miles, M. B., & Huberman, A. M. (1994). *Qualitative data analysis: An expanded sourcebook.* Thousand Oaks, CA: Sage.

Nazione, S., LaPlante, C., Smith, S. W., Cornacchione, J., Russell, J., & Stohl, C. (2011). Memorable messages for navigating college life. *Journal of Applied Communication Research, 39,* 123–143.

Nelson, M. (2010). *Parenting out of control: Anxious parents in uncertain times.* New York: New York University Press.

Reese, E., Bird, A., & Tripp, G. (2007). Children's self-esteem and moral self: Links to parent-child conversations regarding emotion. *Social Development, 16*(3), 460–478.

Shweder, R. A., Much, N. C., Mahapatra, M., & Park, L. (1997). The "big three" of morality (autonomy, community, divinity), and the "big three" explanations of suffering. In A. Brandt & D. Rozin (Eds.), *Morality and Health.* New York: Routledge.

Smith, S. W., & Ellis, J. B. (2001). Memorable messages as guides to self-assessment of behavior: An initial investigation. *Communication Monographs, 68*(2), 154–168.

Smith, S. W., Ellis, J. B., & Yoo, H. (2001). Memorable messages as guides to self-assessment of behavior: The role of instrumental values. *Communication Monographs, 68*(4), 325–339.

Socha, T. J., & Yingling, J. (2010). *Families communicating with children.* Cambridge, UK: Polity.

Stohl, C. (1986). The role of memorable messages in the process of organizational socialization. *Communication Quarterly, 34*(3), 231–249.

Vygotsky, L. S. (1978). *Mind in society: The development of higher psychological processes.* M. Cole, (Ed.). Cambridge, MA: Harvard University Press.

Waldron, V., & Kelley, D. (2008). *Communicating forgiveness.* Thousand Oaks, CA: Sage.

Waldron, V. R., Kloeber, D. K., Goman, C., Piemonte, N., & Danaher, J. (2014). How parents communicate right and wrong: A study of memorable moral messages recalled by emerging adults. *Journal of Family Communication, 14,* 274–397.

# NOTE

1. Higher acceptance ratings were provided when parents used empathy-enhancing messages, $F(1,299) = 3.6, p = .025, \eta^2 = .01$; virtue-prioritizing, $F(1,299) = 12.3, p = .001, \eta^2 = .04$; maxim-sharing, $F(1,299) = 5.8, p = .01, \eta^2 = .02$; and reality-defining $F(1,299) = 6.3, p = .005, \eta^2 = .02$, messages. Significantly lower acceptance ratings were reported when parents used obligating, $F(1,299) = 9.6, p = .001, \eta^2 = .03$; authority-invoking, $F(1,299) = 12.0, p = .001, \eta^2 = .04$; and commanding messages, $F(1,299) = 5.4, p = .02, \eta^2 = .02$.

# CHAPTER THREE

# Generativity IN THE Family

## Grandparent-Grandchild Relationships and the Intergenerational Transmission of Values and Worldviews

JORDAN SOLIZ & CHRISTINE E. RITTENOUR

"Maybe it was a grandparent, or a teacher, or a colleague. Someone older, patient and wise, who understood you when you were young and searching, helped you see the world as a more profound place, gave you sound advice to help you make your way through it" (www.mitchalbom.com). This introduction to *Tuesdays with Morrie* (Albom, 1997), a memoir chronicling life lessons communicated by an older man in his final days, encapsulates the popular notion that with aging comes wisdom and that life is best (and perhaps only) understood as you actually experience life. Similarly, a quotation attributed to actor William Holden states "Aging is an inevitable process. I surely wouldn't want to grow younger. The older you become, the more you know; your bank account of knowledge is much richer." Whereas quotations, books, and poems about a life well-lived commonly romanticize the morals and wisdom that comes with growing older, very little attention is afforded to interactions in which these life messages and wisdom are actually passed down across generations.

One of the reasons—if not, the most significant reason—for this lack of attention is that, unfortunately, we live in an age-segregated society (Hagestad & Uhlenberg, 2005) in which intergenerational contact between younger and older adults is fairly minimal compared to other relationships. For young adults, *intra*generational (i.e., peer) relationships are the most common and, often, most socially acceptable relationship. The potential consequence of this intergenerational divide is amplified by research consistently showing that younger adults hold negative attitudes toward older adults and aging (Kite, Stockdale, Whitley, &

Johnson, 2005). Thus, we seem to experience a paradox wherein we "wax poetic" about the wisdom that comes with aging (e.g., "older and wiser") and the moral values and wisdom passed down from older generations. Yet, we do not live in accordance with that mindset. Instead our negative intergenerational attitudes often serve as a barrier to younger adults receiving insights from another's long-lived life. However, it is the grandparent-grandchild relationship that may bridge this divide, benefitting young *and* old alike.

For younger adults, grandparents provide the most common and, typically, the most long-lasting relationship with an older adult; thus, the grandparent-grandchild bond has the greatest potential for in-depth and meaningful intergenerational interactions (Williams & Giles, 1996). Whereas popular culture (e.g., commercials, magazine pictures) tends to depict grandparents with very young grandchildren, this relationship lasts well into adolescence and adulthood (Geurts, Van Tilburg, & Poortman, 2012), which are formative times for younger adults (Arnett, 2004). Early work on grandparenting showed many grandparents playing a significant role in their grandchildren's lives (Cherlin & Furstenberg, 1986), arguably second only to that of parents (Kornhaber, 1985) in terms of socialization of identity and transmission of values. Although increasing, empirical inquiries into the grandparent-grandchild relationship are still relatively limited, especially compared to other family relationships (Soliz & Lin, 2013). We believe this partially stems from views that older adulthood relationships are not that dynamic and often maligned with some of the same negative attitudes toward older adults mentioned above (i.e., "Older people are not that interesting to study!"). In line with the premise of this volume and recognizing the significance of this intergenerational family tie, we draw from grandparent-grandchild literature to paint a conceptual landscape of the various ways morality is explicitly and/or implicitly communicated within intergenerational relationships. We take a broad view of morality by including value-laden perspectives of what is "right and wrong" and also general worldviews about *what is to be valued* in other people and *what is to be valued* in life. Further, we articulate a perspective in that worldviews also encapsulate *values* of *aging* (i.e., what does it mean to age well?) as this is clearly tied to our perceptions of what is important across the lifespan and successful aging, in general (Giles, Davis, Gasiorek, & Giles, 2013).

Drawing from disciplines of communication studies, gerontology, family studies, psychology, and sociology, we highlight research findings that demonstrate grandparents' "concern in establishing and guiding of the next generation" (Erikson, 1963, p. 267). This prosocial focus on the morality and growth of future generations is often conceptualized as "generativity." Though not explicitly labeled as such by all researchers whose work we will now begin to highlight, "generativity" captures the overarching trend of grandparents teaching their children what it means to age and to live, and what to value along the way. We classify this generativity into three categories: socialization of values and beliefs, intergroup contact, and memorable messages. We recognized that transmission of values and morals can be both explicit (e.g., specific messages passed down from generation to generation) and more indirect or implicit (e.g., modeling behavior, relationships shaping worldviews). In fact, the final section on memorable messages includes our own inquiry and findings on memorable life messages that are infused with moral prescriptions about how one *should* view life and treatment of others. This inquiry, combined with the reviewed works, inform our concluding thoughts on grandparents' transmission of values and worldviews.

## SOCIALIZATION OF VALUES AND BELIEFS

Grandsons and granddaughters have reported on grandparents' transmission of family rituals and values (Brussoni & Boon, 1998), culture (Wiscott & Kopera-Frye, 2000), and religion (King, Elder, & Conger, 2000). By citing their grandparents' impact on the ways they see and approach the world, grandchildren consistently reinforce Kornhaber's (1985) assertion that grandparents play a significant role in socializing younger generations; especially in the family. Quite often, the grand*mothers* are the ones who bestow these life lessons. This is unsurprising given that there is a strong, positive association between grandparent-grandchild closeness and perceived similarity in life views (Roberto & Stroes, 1992), and that the grandmother (especially the maternal grandmother) is frequently deemed the grandparent with whom grandchildren form the closest bond (Chan & Elder, 2000). "Life views" is a broad concept and scholars have identified several specific avenues of life views that grandchildren learn about and adopt from their grandparents. As such, the family is an excellent context for generativity (McAdams & de St. Aubin, 1992) given that many older adults enact generativity through their bonds with grandchildren (Thiele & Whelan, 2008).

The outcomes of generativity are profound. Generative grandparents transmit prosocial values through storytelling, modeling, and shared time and skillsets, and as a result their grandchildren have strong prosocial concerns (Pratt, Norris, Hebblethwaite, & Arnold, 2008). In short, young adults who have been *taught* to think and do for others are more likely to think and do for others (McAdams, de St. Aubin, & Logan, 1993). For instance, younger adults enact more interpersonal helping behaviors and community volunteer efforts (Frensch, Pratt, & Norris, 2007), and tend to be active in their places of worship and in government affairs (e.g., voting, being informed; Hart, McAdams, Hirsch, & Bauer, 2001) when raised in familial contexts—including grandparents—who focus on more prosocial and other-centered behavior.

While these findings demonstrate the power of generative grandparents upon the thoughts and actions of their grandchildren, there is some evidence to suggest that generativity of those younger family members might influence their treatment of the older generation—a kind of "reversed generativity" if you will (given generativity's conceptual focus from "older" *to* "younger"). There is some evidence that young people's generativity can positively influence their attitudes about caring for an older family member (Peterson, 2002). It may be that generative grandparents communicate that a life well-lived is one in which others are put ahead of oneself, and that there is great pride in both being cared for *and* caring for others. This leads to adult children's ideals of reciprocity, joys of caring for those who cared for them, and—perhaps, given these demonstrated links with positive attitudes, improved comfort with the changing roles of older adulthood (i.e., upward or reciprocal care). Generative behaviors flourish in the presence of social support from family and friends, enabling parents to act as role models to their children and grandchildren (Hart et al., 2001). Finally, people who feel and enact generativity also tend to experience enhanced life satisfaction (McAdams et al., 1993) and relationship (e.g., grandparent/grandchild) satisfaction (Thiele & Whelan, 2008)—all the more reason for its promotion among all age groups.

In addition to grandparents' bestowed broader messages of "doing for others," researchers evidence transmission of values about other aspects of life including education, family, and politics. In addition to—or perhaps *because* of—grandparents' (re)inforcement of family history and family identity, grandparents' communication affects these to varying degrees (Franks, Hughes, Phelps, & Williams, 1993). Grandchildren reported that their own beliefs were *most* affected by their closest grandparent in the following realms: family ideals, moral beliefs, and work ethic (Brussoni & Boon, 1998). This is also evident in Thompson and colleagues (2009) work on family legacies. Family legacies are defined as "strands of meaning that run through the family in ways that give it identity ..." (p. 108). Embedded in legacies are messages about what it means to be a member of this particular family, especially the values associated with this collective identity (e.g., our family is "hard-working" and "doesn't make excuses"). Some family legacies were clearly linked to the aforementioned prosocial concern and behavior (e.g., "we are a family that helps others"). Grandparents' storytelling helps them to pass on family legacies, whether directly from the grandparents themselves or indirectly through *parents'* retelling of these stories. In this way, grandparents create and perpetuate a sense of family identity for young generations. Given that identity and values are linked, the transmission of family legacies is in and of itself a transmission of values and morals.

We should note, however, that there is not always congruence between values of the older and younger generations; especially when grandchildren disagree with the values and beliefs espoused by the grandparents. In fact, Brussoni and Boon (1998) found that values and beliefs revolving around sex and politics were the least frequently bestowed values in grandparent-grandchild relationships. Unfortunately, this is reflected in grandparents' and grandchildren's avoidance of these topics during conversations. Of course, avoidance of sex and politics is not new, nor is it reserved for grandparent-grandchild relationships as these are also among the most taboo topics between parents and children (Guerrero & Afifi, 1995). We believe this is an ironic and sad trend given that informative, deep conversations about these topics (sex, in particular) are so meaningful for physical, emotional, and relational wellbeing (e.g., Fisher, 1986). Further, because they have experienced more years of relationships and affection, grandparents' life-learned wisdom on the topic may be more meaningful than lessons taught in formal education settings, or even those taught by parents.

With years of wisdom about relationships, and a slightly more removed status compared to that of parents, grandparents may be the *most* optimal teachers about sex and psychosexual topics like romance, jealousy, and verbal affection. Conversations about sex, though incredibly uncomfortable for families, are also often met with satisfaction from the younger generation (e.g., "we think it's 'icky' while we are talking, but we are also glad after we have talked about it"; Heisler & Ellis, 2008). Though not empirically confirmed, we can not help but think that our avoidance of sex-related topics among older adults is associated with our negative stereotypes of older adults as not being sexy and as less sexual than younger adults (Hummert, Garstka, Ryan, & Bonnesen, 2004). Similarly, the notions that we avoid topics like politics may coincide with the prominent myth that older adults are (more) "set in their ways" and unable to change. Because our values are so central to how we see ourselves and how we communicate (e.g., Hitlin, 2011), and given the power of grandparents to transmit morals in other realms, we see it as disadvantageous that we would censor our conversations *about* values within the context of one of our important relationships—our relationship with our grandparent.

Because many grandchildren turn to grandparents for moral consult, even when they know or perceive that they disagree on morally "taboo topics" (Franks et al., 1993), we think that they *might* be able to overcome their insecurities about discussing these topics. Given that grandparents have some emotional distance (unlike parents), they might even be in a *more* comfortable, and thus more beneficial, position to discuss such matters. Still, when we ask our undergraduate students, "why don't you talk to your grandparents about sex?" they often respond with "they won't understand because they lived in a different time/are too conservative" or "it's just a little weird to think of my grandparents being affectionate … and very weird to think of them as sexual!" These comments evoke common stereotypes about older adulthood—intense conservatism and asexual behaviors—both of which are exaggerations reflective of ageist attitudes. We propose these ageist attitudes, as well as the communication which it incites or prohibits, to be amoral in the sense that it wrongly casts individuals in a negative light due (merely) to their group membership. Like all prejudicial attitudes, these prohibit both parties from having deeper, meaningful conversation, including those surrounding morality in non-age-related realms.

Despite this trend of grandchildren ignoring or avoiding grandparents' wisdom on taboo topics, we are hopeful that grandparent/grandchild communication—when expanded to include these meaningful discussions—can be a vessel for the moral message of looking at older adults positively and diversely, and thus treating their messages as *wisdom*. More specifically, as we discuss in the next section, the grandparent/grandchild bond can be a contact space for reducing stereotypes that come with seeing the other as "old" or "young" as we begin communicating as individuals. In this way, we have great hope that grandparents and grandchild can overcome these barriers and achieve great depth of understanding in even the most uncomfortable of topics. Again, such endeavors could assist in *both* parties' expansion of their moral selves.

The aforementioned studies reflect some of the ways that grandparents socialize their grandchildren's worldviews. Next we emphasize differences in how grandparents and grandchildren benefit from the quality and quantity of these interactions. While grandparents' esteem and relationship satisfaction corresponds heavily with *both* the amount and quality of contact with their grandchildren (Reitzes & Mutran, 2004), frequency of contact is relatively unimportant in the eyes of grandchildren (Roberto & Stroes, 1992). Therefore, in regard to moral development, it is likely that the *quality* of interactions emerges as the determining factor in the impact of grandparent-grandchild communication on grandchildren's sense of self. This "quality over quantity" theme is likely more evident as grandchildren grow into adulthood and their relationships with grandparents are less obligatory. At this turning point, intergenerational communication is more conversational than it is instructional. While the quality of communication and its inclusion of "life lessons" are shown to improve grandparent relationships and shape grandchildren's thinking, few have researched the specific communication practices of these exchanges (although see Nussbaum & Bettini, 1994). Because the aforementioned research suggests ways that the (closest) grandparent/grandchild bonds influence grandchildren's worldviews, we focus on these in our next section on intergenerational contact between a grandparent and a grandchild who share a deep family tie.

## GRANDPARENT-GRANDCHILD CONTACT AND INTERGENERATIONAL ATTITUDES

Because grandparents and grandchildren belong to separate social groups that are salient in society (i.e., old and young), they present a unique and fascinating context for shaping, maintaining, and/or changing worldviews as it relates to values and perspectives on aging. Their "young" versus "old" status may make it harder for some life lessons to "sink in" (e.g., "how could you possibly relate to my life—you are so old/young?"), but it also presents the opportunity for social change! In our society, much attention is given to identifying interactions and contexts in which racist and sexist attitudes are reduced. These efforts are often framed as a "moral imperative" and, as such, scholars and cultural critics attempt to identify processes and discourses that give rise to these prejudices as well as ways to ameliorate these attitudes. Our argument is that ageism and ageist attitudes should be given the same attention. Just as we have seen in many other contexts in which two social groups improve their attitudes about each other through positive, intimate communication, the grandparent-grandchild bond may be one in which positive communication bestows an important moral message—that older adults are vibrant, complex, interesting, diverse, and that growing older is something to be relished, not resisted. In other words, we propose that grandparents have the power to bestow a kind of anti-ageism upon their grandchildren. Before we address this more specifically, we summarize some of the fundamental theory behind this position.

Given that enduring grandparent-grandchild relationships are typically positive, this family relationship provides a context in which the nature of the communication may ameliorate or minimize some of these negative intergenerational attitudes, especially given that grandchildren tend to feel that the stereotypes for older adults do not apply to their grandparents (Franks et al., 1993). The theoretical foundation for the potential connection between grandparent-grandchild communication and intergenerational attitudes is grounded in social identity theory, intergroup contact theory and communication accommodation theory.

Based on the tenets of social identity theory (Tajfel & Turner, 1986), the grandparent-grandchild relationship can be characterized as an intergroup relational context given that each family member represents a salient social identity. Specifically, although they share a common familial identity, they also represent distinct age groups and, in some cases, may perceive and respond to each other as members of their respective age groups instead of responding to each other as individuals or as family members. Unfortunately, when individuals interact as members of social groups (instead of interacting as individuals), overgeneralizations and negative perceptions often occur. This is especially true for the younger adults, who are prone to use old age cues such as physical appearance (e.g., wrinkles, gray hair) and communication behaviors (slow speaking rate, simplified sentence structure) to access negative schemas for stereotypical older adult interactions (Ryan, Giles, Bartolucci, & Henwood, 1986). The process through which these attitudes have negative consequences for older adults' self-concept and communicative efficacy are outlined in the communication predicament of aging model (CPAM; Ryan et al., 1986). The CPAM posits the following links in consecutive order. Negative attitudes about aging drive younger adults' negative communication with older adults (e.g., patronizing talk, stereotypical and superficial content, secondary baby talk). These constrain conversations and inhibit the older adult's feelings of control and esteem. The predicament lies in the fact that the now debilitated older adult is less likely to make strong, important contributions to future conversations, which will only support the younger adult's stance that the older adult has little worth contributing. Thus, the cycle begins again, wherein lies the predicament.

In fact, this tendency among younger adults to stereotype older adults is perhaps best demonstrated by findings that less-than-satisfying interactions are often attributed to age difference, especially in the eyes of younger adults (Williams & Giles, 1996). We even see this trend in the context of family relationships, as grandchildren tend to equate grandparents' dissatisfying communication to their old age (Fowler & Soliz, 2013). One could ask, therefore, how can we have positive perceptions of enduring grandparent relationships yet still maintain negative intergenerational attitudes? Perhaps more importantly to our discussion about a bestowed *moral* lesson, in what ways can our experiences with grandparents improve our attitudes toward older adults (as a group) and aging?

Brown and Hewstone's (2005) elaboration of intergroup contact theory posits that age salience in the interactions must be considered to understand the nuances of this potential association between relationships with grandparents and intergenerational attitudes. Specifically, younger adults must see grandparents as *typical* and *representative* of older adults (as a collective social group) in order for them to make the cognitive link between their positive relationship with their grandparent and positive attitudes toward older adults and aging. Perceiving grandparents as an "older adult" may seem like an obvious and fairly trivial nuance. But, for many, grandparents are seen as older *family members* rather than older adults. As such, negative perceptions of older adults are not evident in the grandparent-grandchild relationship. Conversely—and unfortunately—positive experiences with grandparents may not be generalized to older adults as a whole *because* the grandchild does not perceive them as an older adult (i.e., they are not typical or representative). It is important to note that these perceptions of identity manifest in our communication as the nature of interactions in grandparent-grandchild relationship can represent age differences or perceptions of a more interpersonal relationship characterized by the shared family identity (Soliz & Harwood, 2006). Given its emphasis on interpersonal (i.e., personalized) and intergroup (e.g., age distinctions) dynamics, communication accommodation theory (Dragojevic, Gasiorek, & Giles, in press) has served as a guiding framework for communicative correlates of age salience and, in turn, understanding how grandparent-grandchild interactions correspond with intergenerational attitudes.

Harwood, Raman, and Hewstone (2006) identified various topics of conversation or nature of interactions associated with age distinctions. For instance, painful self-disclosures (i.e., complaining about health, bereavement: Coupland, Coupland,

& Giles, 1991), talking about the past, disapproval of morals and values, and perceptions that the grandparent is patronizing the grandchild are all behaviors that highlight age distinctions. Further, communicative barriers associated with physical issues (e.g., hearing) also cue age salience and associated stereotypes of the group. Conversely, storytelling and passing on desired advice or wisdom decreases perceptions of age distinction. Not surprisingly—and in-line with intergroup theorizing—age salience was found to be negatively associated with closeness in this relationship. As such, research linking grandparent relationships with intergenerational attitudes necessitates a focus on various communicative and relational dynamics.

In line with Hewstone and Brown's emphasized importance of age salience within positive intergroup interactions, Soliz and Harwood (2006) demonstrated that perceptions of shared family identity and age salience interplay to provide insight into potential benefits of grandparent-grandchild contact in that more personal and positive interactions (i.e., those characterized by high degrees of shared family identity) are associated with more positive perceptions of older adults and aging when the age identity is salient in the interactions. Further investigating the communication associated with these perceptions, comforting and supportive communication as well as desired self-disclosure (i.e., those that are comfortable and bring people together) increases perceptions of shared family identity whereas behaviors such as grandparents complaining, criticizing, and talking about topics seemingly irrelevant to younger adults highlight the age distinctions.

Soliz and Harwood's (2006) findings support the work by Harwood et al. (2006) and complement other intergenerational contact work. For instance, Tam, Hewstone, Harwood, Voci, and Kenworthy (2006) demonstrated how quantity and quality of contact with non-family older adults is associated with intergenerational attitudes. However, this association is mediated by self-disclosure as it reduces intergenerational communication anxiety (i.e., "What will I talk about with my grandparent?!?") thereby increasing empathy with grandparents and, in the end, more positive perceptions of the relationship. Harwood, Hewstone, Paolini, and Voci (2005) found similar results but also took into account the significance of frequency of grandparent-grandchild interaction (i.e., more frequent interactions are more beneficial for intergroup attitudes). Further, in addition to self-disclosure, Harwood and colleagues also identified grandchild perspective-taking and accommodation on the part of the grandparent (i.e., attuning their communication to the needs and wants of the grandchild). Similar to the Soliz and Harwood (2006) study, group salience played a moderating role in that the connection between grandparent-grandchild contact and intergenerational attitudes was evident when age salience was high. In other words, only when grandchildren actually see their grandparent as an older adult is there a relationship between interactions with a grandparent and attitudes toward older adults or aging.

Collectively, the findings from these studies and others (e.g., Soliz & Harwood, 2003) offer an interesting conclusion when considering implications for grandparent-grandchild relationships in terms of moral communication. Specifically, whereas conventional thought would point to personal (i.e., individualized), positive communication as the most beneficial for ameliorating negative attitudes toward older adults and aging, there is a benefit to the more negative communication, as it allows for a generalization to attitudes outside of the family. Obviously, however, these negative communications do not overshadow positive features of grandparent-grandchild interactions. In other words, there is a functional ambivalence (see Spitzberg & Cupach, 2007) to some more negative communication features when considering the attitudinal outcomes of these intergenerational interactions.

As we illuminate in the preceding discussion, the potential benefits of communication in grandparent-grandchild relationships as it relates to intergenerational attitudes is important on several fronts. This communication not only improves intergenerational attitudes in the proximal context but it also lays the foundation for "successful aging" (Giles et al., 2013). Specifically, age identity is one of the few identities in which we will become what was once our outgroup (i.e., younger adults become older adults). Thus, it reasons that negative attitudes toward older adults and aging—in other words, our "future selves" (Giles, Fortman, Honeycutt, & Ota, 2003)—will influence how we perceive aging and likely our well-being into older adulthood. In this sense, communication with grandparents implicates our attitudes about the latter end of the lifespan even when messages do not explicitly discuss attitudes and perceptions of aging and older adults. Given that the nature of these interactions (e.g., contact) is just as influential in changing attitudes as explicit, directive messages (e.g., being told how you should think about group x), understanding the transmission, alteration, or reification of worldviews (e.g., values, moral) relevant to older adults and aging necessitates a focus on general communication in the grandparent-grandchild relationship. In proposing this connection between grandparent contact and perceptions of aging and older adults, we expand the idea of what constitutes moral communication and, ideally, provide a broader perspective on what may influence our values. Whereas the preceding discussion represents an indirect aspect of moral communication, we now turn our attention to more direct, or explicit, types of messages with a focus on memorable messages.

## MEMORABLE MESSAGES: A QUALITATIVE INQUIRY

A "memorable messages" framework has been applied to a variety of contexts (e.g., relational, organizational) as it emphasizes those messages individuals receive that they believe to be instrumental in their development of self-concept and their general perceptions of the social world (e.g., Knapp, Stohl, & Reardon, 1981; Medved, Brogan, McClanahan, Morris, & Shepherd, 2006). Holladay (2002) applied this framework to the intergenerational relationships, demonstrating that memorable messages about aging had both positive and negative themes. For instance, some positive messages centered on aging as something to enjoy and embrace as there are many aspects of it that are rewarding. Conversely, more negative or critical messages centered on issues related to a decline in physical and cognitive abilities. The negative messages—quite fear-inducing, indeed—included likening aging to death, and even proposing the latter as the better "alternative." This study was important because it established that younger adults do indeed identify and remember salient messages passed on from older adults. More importantly, amidst a plethora of public messages condemning age as something to be avoided (though this is impossible—we all age!), there are positive messages being passed on by those that have aged. We build on this research by examining memorable messages to uncover the ways that older adults teach their younger adult grandchildren to frame their morality surrounding older people and aging.

RQ:     What types of memorable messages from grandparents, if any, do young adults identify as being instrumental in shaping their general outlooks on life?

## Participants and Procedures

As part of a larger study on intergenerational attitudes and communication, participants ($N$ = 52) completed an on-line questionnaire with a portion of the questionnaire focusing on relationships with grandparents. Participants represented the young adult age group ranging in age from 18–23 years old ($M$ = 19.63, $SD$ = 1.14; 27 female, 24 male). A majority of the participants indicated their race-ethnicity as "white" (85%) with the remaining participants indicating "Asian" or "Hispanic." Participants were recruited predominantly through an undergraduate research pool at a large, Midwestern university. A series of open-ended questions were used in the survey to elicit responses focusing on the relationships with grandparents and messages participants received that resonated with the grandchild. Additional questions then focused on one grandparent in particular. Specifically, participants selected a grandparent with whom they were emotionally close and a primary question asked specifically about messages related to worldviews:

"Please write down any memorable messages this grandparent passed down that have had an influence on your life and how you view the world."

Participants also explained why these messages were important for them in their responses to other open-ended questions.

## Analysis

Data were analyzed using an inductive approach in which themes of memorable messages emerged from the data, and were not reflections of an a priori taxonomy (Strauss & Corbin, 1994). For this process, as we read through each response to the open-ended questions about memorable messages, we highlighted any significant portions and made notes about potential similarities across these messages. Our coding of messages was based on our conceptualization of morality introduced in our chapter's opening in that we examined messages that included perspectives of "right and wrong," what is to be valued in life, what is to be valued in other people, and what is to be valued as we age. After this initial review, we identified convergence and similarity across the messages to make sure we were not missing important points shared by the participants. We classified all memorable messages into general categories (i.e., themes) and conducted a negative case analysis to determine if any non-classified responses warranted further consideration or reflected a new theme. In other words, if some messages were not categorized into the themes that were identified, we returned to these messages and developed new categories if warranted. After we identified the themes, we created descriptions and labels before identifying representative quotations as exemplars for each theme. Additional methodological detail is available from the first author. Though the themes emerged from the content itself, and were not driven by our search for (purely) moral themes, note the moral dimensions to the various themes described below.

## Findings

There were only three grandchildren who were unable to recall a specific message. This in and of itself is an important finding because, similar to Holladay's (2002) study, it demonstrates that there are important messages passed on to grandchildren. As was the case in this earlier study, several messages focused on contrasting older adulthood with death (e.g., "Growing old is better than the alternative."). These were likely intended to be amusing, in claiming that old age is a positive thing *only* because it involves being alive. However, most of the messages were positive and, rather than focusing on aging, provided important considerations for life in general. We identified four main themes. Some grandchildren (*n* = 6) reported multiple messages that represented different themes. Therefore, these themes should be interpreted as complementary rather than competing.

**Fulfilling Life.** Many messages centered on grandparents' advice on what makes a "full life" or a life "well-lived." For instance some grandparents focused on encouraging their grandchildren to take chances in life and take advantages of all opportunities afforded to them:

"To say there are no regrets in life is to fool yourself. How boring it would be without any regrets."

"You only go around once!"

"You only have a certain amount of time here, make the most of it. Live, love, and laugh."

These messages were sometimes laced with humor and were trivial, but still reflected the sentiment that life is something to enjoy and not take too seriously (e.g., "You are never too old for ice cream!"). Other messages in this theme centered on the importance of relationships and having an impact on others. Obviously, there are clear connections to the prosocial aspect of generativity discussed earlier in this chapter:

"It is easy to tell if a man lived a good life because all you have to do is look at the family he leaves behind when he dies. If the family is close and they love the Lord then that man lived the best life possible."

"At the end of my life, the amount of money and other things I had in my life mean nothing compared to the impact I had on other's lives."

A final aspect of this theme reflected messages about overall temperament in terms of dealing with life's challenges and opportunities or just the importance of being satisfied in life:

"Always try to look at the bright side of things because there's no point in getting angry over things you can't control.

"Appreciate what I have and not worrying [sic] about other things that are not important."

"Do anything that it is going to make you happy."

"Anger always works against us and you should try [your] best to never lose [your] temper."

**Grandparent-Grandchild Relationships.** Grandchildren reported on messages that discussed the importance of the grandparent-grandchild relationship. Although not an explicit message about life and worldviews, participants often framed this by indicating it gave them insight into the importance of this intergenerational relationship that represents moral issues such as relational values and familial obligations. Further, these messages highlight the importance of family relationships as a positive aspect of aging.

"Enjoy the time that you spend with all of your grandparents and cherish it, because you never know when that time will end."

"And bless all the children and the grandchildren."

Related to this, participants indicated that statements of caring, love, and pride were some of the most important memorable messages as they provided a solid relational foundation and demonstrated that it was important to be open with one's affection.

> "She never lets you leave without saying she loves you!"

> "Just always told me how much she loved me ... she was always proud of me even if I just completed a small task."

**Engaging Others.** Many grandparents passed on messages focusing specifically on relationships and interactions, some of these were about very personal and/or specific relationships. For instance, one participant indicated that her grandmother would tell her from a young age "to love my husband and care for him." However, most of the messages reflecting this theme were in reference to interactions and how you treat a general "other":

> "Make sure you meet people with an open mind."

> "Remembering things about people. Give to others always!"

> "Our lives are all about the impact we have on others."

Finally, while they received direct messages related to engaging others, participants also indicated that their perspectives were shaped, in part, by how they observed their grandparents interacting with others. This is evident in one grandchild's comment when she states, "Their patience and kindness really made a mark on how I view helping others." In short, these messages reflect aspects of altruism, generosity, empathy, and helpfulness.

**Pragmatics & Work Ethic.** A series of messages revolved around pragmatic advice (e.g., saving money and becoming an "economical person") or general aspects of responsibility and work ethic.

> "You are the oldest. You have to take care of your sisters."

> "No matter how insignificant your job might seem, always do your best and work your hardest."

> "Always work for what you want and do not rely on anybody else to get what you want or need out of life and always believe in yourself."

> "Compete like the dickens."

> "Always work hard. Believe in yourself"

## Discussion of Findings

The themes emerging from this inquiry complement Holladay's (2002) work by demonstrating that messages grandparents pass on to grandchildren are not only about aging, instead they represent issues of morality and values across a broad spectrum of life domains (e.g., finances, temperament, family). Moreover, in discussing these messages, grandchildren often made statements indicating that these messages were not "just" memorable, but truly instrumental in shaping their outlooks on life, including their approaches to relationships, challenges, and opportunities. Many of the messages were of the "should do" variety as they were characterized with words such as "always," "no matter what," "have to," and "make sure." In short, these were clearly directive and, as a whole, the themes emerging from these memorable messages represent a constellation of what it means to be a good person, characteristics of virtue (both in terms of how hard one works and how one treats others), the value of meaningful relationships, and an overall *vision* for how to live a fulfilling life. Research has shown that grandparents take a great deal of pride in grandparenting and this family role is often central to their identity (Harwood & Lin, 2000). One of the reasons is undoubtedly being able to shape subsequent generations (i.e., generativity). The findings make this influence evident in the recalled grandchildren's experiences with grandparents and, perhaps most importantly, reflect a range of domains for expressing morality and values.

As demonstrated in this discussion, memorable messages are likely an extension of and/or a method for socializing the attitudes, values, and beliefs addressed previously in this chapter. Although our questionnaire did not address the issue of whether or not grandchildren were likely to pass on these messages to future generations (or other friends and family), theorizing on memorable messages indicates that we likely pass on those that we believe are significant (Knapp et al., 1981). As such, memorable messages exist in an interactional moment but likely emerge from previous generations and are passed on to future ones.

We should note that these messages were received from grandparents for whom the grandchild felt emotionally close to or those in satisfying relationships with their grandchildren, another trend reminiscent of the other research highlighted in this chapter. As such, we are not suggesting that *all* grandparent-grandchild relationships are infused with these types of messages, nor that all are positive. As research has shown, there are less-than-ideal or negative grandparent relationships (Soliz & Lin, 2013) and those are often characterized by messages and/or behaviors that grandchildren are less likely to embrace or pass on to others. Given this, further inquiries on the grandparent-grandchild relationship would benefit from a modeling vs. compensation perspective. As demonstrated in Floyd and Morman (2000) work on father-son relationships, younger generations may embrace and enact some behaviors (or messages) from older generations (i.e., modeling).

Conversely, if they disagree with the message or, perhaps, do not identify closely with an older generation, grandchildren will attempt to enact behaviors that are in contrast to those of their grandparents (i.e., compensation) as shown in recent research on parent-child relationships (Odenweller, Rittenour, Myers, & Brann, 2013). Thus, our understanding of grandparents' role in moral development would benefit from inquiries into grandchildren's reactions to more anti-social (and, perhaps, socially undesirable) messages about life and aging. Overall, investigating the factors that differentiate modeling and compensation perspectives will shed additional light on the role of grandparents in passing down outlooks on life that are internalized by grandchildren and, thus, likely to be communicated for generations to come.

## CONCLUSION AND FUTURE CONSIDERATIONS

Our goal in this chapter was to highlight the significant, yet often overlooked, influence grandparents can have on the values and worldviews of their grandchildren. In doing so, we also hope to broaden the conceptualization of moral communication by introducing the idea that morality includes an orientation to the entire lifespan including perceptions of aging and attitudes toward older adults. Research has demonstrated both direct and indirect communicative pathways for grandparents' influence on these younger generations. Grandparents' specific, explicit "life lessons" and indirect pathways are likely to be equally influential. As outlined in the preceding discussion, interactions and relationships with grandparents can have a positive outcome for younger adults' intergenerational attitudes—even in the absence of explicit discussions about aging or older adulthood. These attitudes are associated with the overall demeanor that younger adults bring with them as they enter interactions with older adults. As such, positive interactions with grandparents have the capacity to engender constructive and beneficial intergenerational interactions. Likewise, intergenerational attitudes are likely associated with perceptions of "future selves" (see Giles et al., 2003). Specifically, if we have negative attitudes toward aging and older adults, then we are likely to have a negative self-concept and experience negative aspects of well-being (e.g., depression, anxiety) as we age and reach older adulthood. Thus, relationships and interactions with grandparents are instrumental in not only how we interact with others and the values we hold, but also positioning us to age "successfully." Finally, grandparents can indirectly socialize grandchildren by enacting behaviors that model specific values to the grandchildren (e.g., charitable giving, helping others).

Above and beyond those highlighted in this chapter, there are undoubtedly other roles and behaviors that are influential in shaping the life outlook of grandchildren. For instance, grandparents often play a supportive role in the lives of grandchildren during times of conflict or family strife such as serving as stable figures following parental divorce (Soliz, 2008), acting as a primary caregiver (i.e., custodial grandparenting) when parents are unable to serve this role (Hayslip & Kaminski, 2005), or assisting grandchildren with physical or mental health issues (Woodbridge, Buys, & Miller, 2011). It is likely that, through these actions and the communication surrounding these supportive roles, grandchildren glean insight into how we put others before ourselves—giving comfort and support to others in times of need. As we hope is evident at this point, our goal in this chapter is to not only highlight the influential role of grandparents in shaping the moral outlook and worldviews of younger generations but to also challenge the conceptualizations of moral communication that reflects direct, explicit messages to others. We believe both modeling behavior and our daily interactions and conversations shape our worldviews. This can occur even absent of a concerted effort on the part of each person in the relationship (e.g., a positive grandparent-grandchild relationship shaping more positive values on later-life).

We conclude with two caveats for digesting the information presented in this chapter. First, much of this chapter is written from the presumptive perspective that grandchildren and grandparents' relationships bookend the parents who are in the "middle" so to speak, but we addressed parents' role very minimally. Research has demonstrated that parental support of grandparent-grandchild relationship is an important facilitator for quality relationships (Soliz & Harwood, 2006). Following this logic, it is also likely that parents serve as filters to the messages passed on by grandparents that can either amplify and support or deflect and stifle this intergenerational transmission of worldviews. Second, our discussion has emphasized a top-down, unidirectional perspective on this relationship (i.e., grandparents influencing grandchildren). We suggest attentiveness to morality socialization that is *bidirectional* recognizing that grandchildren also have the capacity to influence the worldviews of grandparents. For instance, can grandchildren change values of grandparents and, if so, what factors (e.g., quality and quantity of interactions, nature of relationship) facilitate this upward socialization? We believe this is an area ripe for research and necessary to further our understanding of complex moral development in the family.

# REFERENCES

Albom, M. (1997). *Tuesdays with Morrie: An old man, a young man, and life's greatest lesson.* New York: Doubleday.

Arnett, J. J. (2004). *Emerging adulthood: The winding road from the late teens through the twenties.* New York: Oxford University Press.

Brown, R., & Hewstone, M. (2005). An integrative theory of intergroup contact. *Advances in Experimental Social Psychology, 37,* 255–343.

Brussoni, M. J., & Boon, S. D. (1998). Grandparental impact in young adults' relationships with their closest grandparents: The role of relationship strength and emotional closeness. *International Journal of Aging and Human Development, 46*, 267–286.

Chan, C. G., & Elder, G. H., Jr. (2000). Matrilineal advantage in grandchild-grandparent relations. *The Gerontologist, 40*, 179–190.

Cherlin, A. J., & Furstenberg, F. F., Jr. (1986). *The new American grandparent: A place in the family, a life apart.* New York: Basic Books.

Coupland, N., Coupland, J., & Giles, H. (1991). *Language, society and the elderly: Discourse, identity, and aging.* Oxford, UK: Blackwell.

Dragojevic, M., Gasiorek, J., & Giles, H. (in press). Communication accommodation theory. In C. R. Berger & M. L. Roloff (Eds.), *Encyclopedia of interpersonal communication.* New York: Wiley/Blackwell.

Erikson, E. (1963). *Childhood and society.* New York: Norton.

Fisher, T. D. (1986). Parent-child communication about sex and young adolescents' sexual knowledge and attitudes. *Adolescence, 21*, 517–527.

Floyd, K., & Morman, M. T. (2000). Affection received from fathers as a predictor of men's affection with their own sons: Tests of the modeling and compensation hypotheses. *Communication Monographs, 67*, 347–361.

Fowler, C. A., & Soliz, J. (2013). Intergenerational communication with familial and non-familial older adults: Developing a conceptual model of pro-social and disengaging responses to painful self-disclosures. *International Journal of Aging and Human Development, 77*, 163–178.

Franks, L. J., Hughes, J. P., Phelps, L. H., & Williams, D. G. (1993). Intergenerational influences on midwest college students by their grandparents and significant elders. *Educational Gerontology, 19*, 265–271.

Frensch, K. M., Pratt, M. W., & Norris, J. E. (2007). Foundations of generativity: Personal and family correlates of emerging adults' generative life-story themes. *Journal of Research in Personality, 41*, 45–62.

Geurts, T., Van Tilburg, T. G., & Poortman, A-R. (2012). The grandparent-grandchild relationship in childhood and adulthood: A matter on continuation? *Personal Relationships, 19*, 267–278.

Giles, H., Davis, S., Gasiorek, & Giles, J. (2013). *Successful aging: A communication guide to empowerment.* Barcelona: Editorial Aresta.

Giles, H., Fortman, J., Honeycutt, J., & Ota (2003). Future selves and others: A lifespan and cross-cultural perspective. *Communication Reports, 16*, 1–22.

Guerrero, L. K., & Afifi, W. A. (1995). Some things are better left unsaid: Topic avoidance in family relationships. *Communication Quarterly, 43*, 276–296.

Hagestad, G. O., & Uhlenberg, P. (2005). The social separation of old and young: A root of ageism. *Journal of Social Issues, 61*, 343–360.

Hart, H. M., McAdams, D. P., Hirsch, B. J., & Bauer, J. J. (2001). Generativity and social involvement among African Americans and White adults. *Journal of Research in Personality, 35*, 208–230.

Harwood, J., Hewstone, M., Paolini, S., & Voci, A. (2005). Grandparent-grandchild contact and attitudes towards older adults: Moderator and mediator effects. *Personality and Social Psychology Bulletin, 31*, 393–406.

Harwood, J., & Lin, M-C. (2000). Affiliation, pride, exchange, and distance in grandparents' accounts of relationships with their college-aged grandchildren. *Journal of Communication, 3*, 31–47.

Harwood, J., Raman, P., & Hewstone, M. (2006). Communicative predictors of group salience in the intergenerational setting. *Journal of Family Communication, 6*, 181–200.

Hayslip, B., & Kaminski, P. L. (2005). Grandparents raising their grandchildren: A review of the literature and suggestions for practice. *The Gerontologist, 45*, 262–269.

Heisler, J. M., & Ellis, J. B. (2008). Motherhood and the construction of "Mommy Identity": Messages about motherhood and face negotiation. *Communication Quarterly, 56*, 445–467. doi: 10.1080/01463370802448246

Hitlin, S. (2011). Values, personal identity, and the moral self. In S. J. Schwartz, K. Luyckx & V. L. Vignoles (Eds.), *Handbook of Identity Theory and Research* (pp. 515–529). New York: Springer.

Holladay, S. (2002). "Have fun while you can," "You're only as old as you feel," and "Don't ever get old!": An examination of memorable messages about aging. *Journal of Communication, 52*, 681–697.

Hummert, M. L., Garstka, T. A., Ryan, E. B., & Bonnesen, J. L. (2004). The role of age stereotypes in interpersonal communication. In J Nussbaum & J. Coupland (Eds.), *Handbook of Communication and Aging Research* (pp. 91–114). Mahwah, NJ. Lawrence Erlbaum.

King, V., Elder, G. H., & Conger, R. D. (2000). Church, family, and friends. In G. H. Elder & R. D. Conger (Eds.), *Children of the land: Adversity and success in rural America* (pp. 151–163). Chicago: University of Chicago Press.

Kite, M. E., Stockdale, G. D., Whitley, B. E., Jr. & Johnson, B. T. (2005). Attitudes toward older and younger adults: An updated meta-analysis. *Journal of Social Issues, 61*, 241–266.

Knapp, M., Stohl, C., & Reardon, K. (1981). Memorable messages. *Journal of Communication, 31*, 27–41.

Kornhaber, A. (1985). Grandparenthood and the "new social contract." In V. L. Bengtson & J. F. Robertson (Eds.), *Grandparenthood* (pp. 159–172). Beverly Hills, CA: Sage.

Lin, M.-C., Giles, H., & Soliz, J. (in press). Problematic intergenerational communication and caregiving in the family: Elder abuse and neglect. In L. N. Olson & M. A. Fine (Eds.), *Examining the darkness of family communication: The harmful, the morally suspect, and the socially inappropriate.* New York: Peter Lang.

McAdams, D. P., & de St. Aubin, E. (1992). A theory of generativity and its assessment through self-report, behavioral acts, and narrative themes in autobiography. *Journal of Personality and Social Psychology, 62*, 1003–1015.

McAdams, D. P., de St. Aubin, E., & Logan, R. L. (1993). Generativity among young, midlife, and older adults. *Psychology and Aging, 8*, 221–230.

Medved, C. E., Brogan, S. M., McClanahan, A. M., Morris, J. F., & Shepherd, G. J. (2006). Family and work socializing communication: Messages, gender, and ideological implications. *Journal of Family Communication, 6*, 161–180.

Nussbaum, J. F., & Bettini, L. (1994). Shared stories of the grandparent-grandchild relationship. *International Journal of Aging and Human Development, 39*, 67–80.

Odenweller, K. G., Rittenour, C. E., Myers, S. A., & Brann, M. (2013). Father-son family communication patterns and gender ideologies: Modeling and compensation analysis. *Journal of Family Communication, 13*, 340–257.

Peterson, B. E. (2002). Longitudinal analysis of midlife generativity, intergenerational roles, and caregiving. *Psychology and Aging, 17*, 161–168.

Pratt, M. W., Norris, J. E., Hebblethwaite, S., & Arnold, M. L. (2008). Intergenerational transmission of values: Family generativity and adolescents' narratives of parent and grandparent value teaching. *Journal of Personality, 76*, 171–198.

Reitzes, D. C., & Mutran, E. J. (2004). Grandparenthood: Factors influencing frequency of grandparent-grandchildren contact and grandparent role satisfaction. *Journal of Gerontology, 59*, S9–S16.

Roberto, K. A., & Stroes, J. (1992). Grandchildren and grandparents: Roles, influences, and relationships. *International Journal of Aging and Human Development, 34*, 227–239.

Ryan, B., Giles, H., Bartolucci, G., & Henwood, K. (1986). Psycholinguistics and social psychological components of communication by and with the elderly. *Language and Communication, 6*, 1–24.

Soliz, J. (2008). Intergenerational support and the role of grandparents in post-divorce families: Retrospective accounts of young adult grandchildren. *Qualitative Research Reports in Communication, 9*, 72–80.

Soliz, J., & Harwood, J. (2006). Shared family identity, age salience, and intergroup contact: Investigation of the grandparent-grandchild relationship. *Communication Monographs, 73*, 87–107.

Soliz, J., & Harwood, J. (2003). Perceptions of communication in a family relationship and the reduction of intergroup prejudice. *Journal of Applied Communication Research, 31*, 320–345.

Soliz, J., & Lin, M.-C. (2013). Friends and allies: Communication in grandparent-grandchild relationships. In K. Floyd & M. Mormon (Eds.), *Widening the family circle: New research on family communication,* (2nd ed., pp. 35–50). Thousand Oaks, CA: Sage.

Spitzberg, B. H., & Cupach, W. R. (2007). *The dark side of interpersonal communication* (2nd ed.). Mahwah, NJ: Lawrence Erlbaum Associates.

Strauss, A., & Corbin, J. (1994). Grounded theory methodology: An overview. In N. K. Denzin & Y. S. Lincoln (Eds.), *Handbook of qualitative research* (pp. 273–285). Thousand Oaks, CA: Sage.

Tajfel, H., & Turner, J. C. (1986). The social identity theory of intergroup behavior. In S. Worchel & W. Austin (Eds.), *Psychology of intergroup relations* (pp. 7–24). Chicago: Nelson-Hall.

Tam, T., Hewstone, M., Harwood, J., Voci, A., & Kenworthy, J. (2006). Intergroup contact and grandparent-grandchild communication: The effects of self-disclosure on implicit and explicit biases against older people. *Group Processes and Intergroup Relations, 9*, 413–430.

Thiele, D., & Whelan, T. (2008). The relationship between grandparent satisfaction, meaning, and generativity. *International Journal of Aging and Human Development, 66*, 21–48.

Thompson, B., Koenig Kellas, J., Soliz, J., Thompson, J., Epp, A., & Schrodt, P. (2009). Family legacies: Constructing individual and family identity through intergenerational storytelling. *Narrative Inquiry, 19*, 106–134.

Williams, A., & Giles, H. (1996). Intergenerational conversations: Young adults' retrospective accounts. *Human Communication Research, 23*, 220–250.

Wiscott, R., & Kopera-Frye, K. (2000). Sharing the culture: Adult grandchildren's perceptions of intergenerational relations. *International Journal of Aging & Human Development, 51*, 199–215.

Woodbridge, S., Buys, L., & Miller, E. (2011). "My grandchild has a disability": Impact on grandparenting identity, roles and relationships. *Journal of Aging Studies, 25*, 355–363.

# CHAPTER FOUR

# *Just* Marriage

DOUGLAS KELLEY*

"I always have to initiate." "You never help with the kids." "I can't get a word in edgewise!" "THAT'S NOT FAIR!" Couples, almost instinctively, know when their relationship, or parts of their relationship, is out of balance, unequal, unfair. One lens with which relational partners view their marriages is justice (Canary & Stafford, 2007; Kelley, 2012a; 2012b). The recognition of relationship dynamics, such as equity, inequality, power, bargaining and distribution, attribution, and guilt, reveal a justice ethic that is present in the communication interactions of personal relationship partners (Bierhoff, Buck, & Klein, 1986; Greenberg & Cohen, 1982; Stafford, 2003).

While various forms of justice are manifest in personal relationships, distributive justice, often conceptualized as equity (Adams, 1965; Homans, 1961, 1974; Cohen & Greenberg, 1982), has been identified as a significant feature of intimate relationships. For example, Canary and Stafford (1992; Stafford & Canary, 2006) have identified equity as a significant component of marriage maintenance, though there has been some debate as to the role of distributive justice in married partners' decisions to maintain their relationships (Canary & Stafford, 1992, 2007; Ragsdale & Brandau-Brown, 2005, 2007; Stafford & Canary, 2006). In addition, it has been suggested that procedural justice is the key component in analyzing whether any given dispute resolution is just (Thibaut & Walker, 1975).

---

*Special thanks to Daniel Kelley and Emily Johnson for their work on this project.

The focus of this essay is to examine couples' interpersonal forgiveness narratives (one type of relational maintenance strategy; Fincham, Hall, & Beach, 2005) for evidence of justice talk. Specifically, I provide an overview of justice in personal relationships emphasizing how individuals develop a justice motive and relationship partners negotiate a relationship justice ethic (or moral code). I focus discussion on distributive justice and equity, as well as what I term processual justice (procedural, interactional, and relational aspects of justice). I then highlight the relationship between justice and forgiveness, strongly suggesting that forgiveness plays a significant role in responding to perceived relational injustice (Exline, Worthington, Hill, & McCullough, 2003) and restoring the moral balance of the relationship (Kelley, 2012a). To this end, I examine 60 forgiveness transcripts, from couples married between 30 and 80 years, to determine how justice is expressed in partners' discussion of their relationships. Content analysis reveals the words partners use to frame their relationships along dimensions of justice. Implications of viewing relationships from a justice perspective are discussed, as well as potential applications to younger couples.

## JUSTICE AND HUMAN DEVELOPMENT

Justice is an essential element of human social experience and, consequently, of all significant relationships. Lerner (2002) frames the significance of justice:

> In Western societies, justice has a special status superseding all other norms and values. The requirements of justice have the power to legitimize and, at times, to demand the sacrifice of liberty, lives, and happiness. No other secular norm or value has comparable power. (p. 10)

Just world theory (Batson, 2002; Bierhoff et al., 1986; Lerner, 1980) posits that individuals develop a justice motive based on early childhood experiences. This justice motive emerges as individuals observe a "perceived consistency between outcomes and contributions" (Bierhoff et al., 1986, p. 179) and develop a *personal contract* (Batson, 2002; Lerner, 2002) that essentially holds, all things being equal, that enacting certain behaviors will result in obtaining certain outcomes. And, not only that behaviors will result in certain outcomes, but *should* result in certain outcomes. The *shouldness* of these expectations forms the basis of a moral worldview. Batson (2002) believes that it is a short developmental step from formulating the personal contract to, "need[ing] to believe in a just world, a world in which people get what they deserve and deserve what they get" (Batson, 2002, p. 91; Lerner & Goldberg, 1999). Once children realize similarities between themselves and others, particularly as it relates to other individuals behaving in certain ways in order to achieve certain goals, it becomes necessary to believe that others most often get what they deserve. Threats to this belief undermine one's sense of justice, the connection between behavior and expected outcomes, and the ability to function as moral beings. As such, individuals learn to behave in ways that maintain their moral perception of the world, and that behavioral adherence or deviation from this standard results in appropriate outcomes for that action. A number of research studies have demonstrated that this need to believe that people most often get what they deserve is so strong that individuals often reject innocent victims in order to maintain a sense of a just world and maintain one's ability to move toward one's long-term goals (see Hafer, 2002, for a review of this literature).

Interestingly, the justice motive does not guarantee *just* behavior. Whereas the justice motive naturally *emerges* from one's observations of the world, a second motive, the motive to behave consistently with justice principles, is *received* (Batson, 2002). Batson (2002) emphasizes that moral prescriptions are learned (received) from others (also see, Waldron, Kloeber, Goman, Piemonte, & Dahaher, 2014) and, as such, one must continually choose whether or not to act in a manner consistent with one's personal ethic.

As individuals develop significant personal relationships they not only follow their personal ethic, but they negotiate a unique relationship ethic. Personal relationships are built upon implicit and explicit negotiations that define each relationship (Burgoon & Hale, 1984). A significant aspect of these negotiations is the development of a relationship moral code (Kelley, 2012a, 2012b; Waldron & Kelley, 2008). Using forgiveness episodes as an example, Vince Waldron and I (2008) argue that relational partners negotiate the moral standards of their relationship based on community and personal values, and that part of the goal of this negotiation is to ensure justice at the relationship and individual-interaction levels. Hill et al. (2005) recognize that "justice norms that help regulate behavior are developed as guidelines for fair interactions that are mutually beneficial" (p. 479) and suggest that these guidelines give partners a sense of confidence and predictability regarding the relationship's future. In this sense, justice norms are an expression of the relationship's moral code (Kelley, 2012a).

## TYPES OF JUSTICE IN PERSONAL RELATIONSHIPS

Justice has most often been conceptualized as distributive and procedural (Cohen & Greenberg, 1982; Folger, 1977; Hill, Exline, & Cohen, 2005; Deutsch, 2006), although justice may also be understood as retributional, reparative (Darley, 2002; Deutsch, 2006), and relational (Kelley, 2012a). Because the focus of this essay is the expression of justice in marriage relationships and I am describing data from fairly happy long-term couples, all of whom are describing forgiveness processes, the following discussion emphasizes distributive, procedural, and relational justice, with only a brief description of retributive justice to provide a context for the other justice responses.

## Retributive Justice

Retributive (or retributional, Darley, 2002) justice is most closely associated with punishment for perceived injustice, "the interpersonal world has been put out of order, and it must be restored by punishment of the transgressor" (Darley, 2002, p. 316). Thus, retributive justice only comes into play after a perceived transgression. Deutsch (2006) states that retribution can serve a number of functions, including: strengthening of a weakened moral code; catharsis for the injured party; deterrence from future injustices; reeducation and reform of the transgressor; restoration of loss, possibly in the form of restitution. When one chooses to forgive, one typically lays aside one's right to retributive justice (Waldron & Kelley, 2008).

## Distributive Justice

Distributive justice is primarily related to allocation of resources, or alternatively, allocation of workload, responsibility, obligation, or harm. Distributed elements may be physiological, economic, social or other conditions that influence an individual's well-being (Deutsch, 1985). In essence, distributed justice focuses "on the attainment of parity in the distribution of societal goods and harms" (McClelland & Opotow, 2011, p. 123). Three principles guide distribution of these elements: equity, equality, and need (Deutsch, 1985, 2006, 2011). The equity principle reflects peoples' desire to receive benefits or rewards in proportion to their contribution or effort or costs incurred. In marriage one might assess equity by comparing partner reward:cost ratios. For example, a husband who experiences 5 units of happiness to the 3 units of effort he puts into the relationship has an equitable relationship with his wife who experiences 10 units of happiness for the 6 units of effort she puts in (5: 3 = 10: 6). Deutsch (2006) suggests that equity is most prominent in situations where principles of economic productivity are primary. In marriage, one might see equity as important whenever one uses an economic lens through which to view a relationship (e.g., the exchange of relationship currencies or resources).

The equality principle asserts that both members of the relationship should share equal benefits. In the preceding example, the husband and wife have an equitable relationship, but not an equal relationship. They have matching ratios, but they don't receive equal benefits from the relationship; the wife receives 10 benefits, while the husband only receives 5. It may be that equality is most sought after when couples' primary relationship lens is closeness and cohesiveness (Deutsch, 2006). For example, marriage partners likely want to feel a sense of equality regarding how much they love each other or how close they feel to one another.

The need principle assumes distributive justice is achieved when distributions are made in proportion to individuals' need. For example, a husband caring for his wife as she receives chemotherapy for breast cancer may not be experiencing an equitable reward-cost ratio with his wife or equal benefits in the relationship. Yet, he may experience no sense of injustice because he perceives his wife's need to be the greatest at the moment. Thus, need may be the driving perspective when personal welfare and growth are preeminent goals for the couple (Deutsch, 2006).

One problem in assessing distributive justice in marriage relationships is the fact that all three principles often work in the relationship simultaneously (Deutsch, 2006) and may mutually influence one another. A second problem is how to reasonably assess equity, equality, or needs. What seems like a favorable (or unfavorable) outcome to one person, may not seem so to another (Hill et al., 2005). To return to the example of the husband caring for his wife who has breast cancer, the husband might consider his relationship as equitable because he views caring for his wife as primarily a reward, not a cost, and equal because he and his wife have developed a deep mutual sense of intimacy during this period. Clearly these personal evaluations of the situation will vary by individual and, as such, make assessments and judgments about justice in personal relationships quite complex.

## Processual Justice

I am using the term *processual justice* for this section because procedural justice, interactional justice, and relational justice are all based on a general sense of fairness in the process of relating, as opposed to fairness in the distribution of resources, efforts, or outcomes. I believe using processual justice as an overarching concept also simplifies the following discussion and reporting of my data analysis.

**Procedural justice.** Whereas distributive justice is outcomes based, procedural justice reflects the sense of fairness of the procedures used to distribute outcomes or deal with other decision making within a relationship. Central to understanding procedural justice is fair distribution of control (Thibaut & Walker, 1975). Studies show that fair practice is more important to most people, than the actual allocation of resources (Deutsch, 2006; Hill et al., 2005; Lind & Tyler, 1988). Thibaut and Walker (1975) go so far as to propose that, "The distribution of control constitutes the basic variable or dimension for analyzing, comparing, and assessing the justice of all forms of dispute resolution, legal or otherwise" (p. 2).

Deutsch (2006) suggests that procedural justice is important to people for a number of reasons. First, in situations wherein fair distribution is difficult to determine, fair procedures are the surest way to hope for fair distribution in the present and future. In addition, people tend to be more committed to institutions that have perceived fair procedures. One might assume this is the case in marriage, as well. And, finally, people can better handle disappointing outcomes when treated with respect and dignity. In essence, the quality of interpersonal interactions, as it reflects a sense of equity or equality between partners, may be one of the driving forces behind much of the procedural justice effect: "What is also important is *how* the distribution outcome and procedures are communicated" (Hill et al., 2005, p. 479).

Another driving force behind procedural justice may be perceptions of equity or equality of control (Cohen & Greenberg, 1982). Referencing Thibaut and Walker's (1975) conceptualization of procedural justice as "an optimal distribution of control" (p. 2), Cohen and Greenberg (1982) presume this to mean that the decision making procedure is distributed *justly* among those whose outcomes are dependent on it. So, married couples who feel they have equal "voice" in decision making regarding issues important to them are likely to think they are in a just relationship.

**Relational justice.** A final category worth discussion is relational justice (Kelley, 2012a; Schemmel, 2011). In the same way that certain interaction characteristics may influence justice perceptions (Hill et al., 2005), certain relationship qualities may influence the perception of fairness. Lind (2001, 2002) states that perceptions of fair treatment are likely to orient individuals in a socially focused direction. He argues that fairness judgments form a heuristic to guide our choices, because event-by-event evaluations require too much cognitive effort. Relationships characterized by fair procedures and interactions are likely to be viewed as fair or just relationships without continued evaluation of every individual event. As such, relationship characteristics such as equal commitment and mutual respect, may influence perceptions that a relationship is just. In the same way that happy married couples adhere to a personal, positive relationship mythology to maintain their relationships, by downplaying the negative and focusing on the positive (Bradbury & Fincham, 1990; Holtzworth-Munroe & Jacobson, 1988; McNulty, O'Mara, & Karney, 2008), couples may interpret fairness within their marriage relationships in light of their global perception as to whether they are meeting their personal relationship justice ethic.

## EQUITY, JUSTICE, AND FORGIVENESS IN MARRIAGE

Distributive justice has been shown to affect the stability of intimate relationships (Joyner, 2009). To this end, Canary and Stafford's (1992, 2007) research agenda has focused on equity-driven relational maintenance strategies that function to create fair relationships. Canary and Stafford (2007) state that, "Equity theory constitutes a general theory of fairness that applies to any type of relationship, including marriage" (p. 62) and that, "Most people do want to be treated fairly and to treat others in a similar manner" (p. 67).

Canary and Stafford's work is based on the premise that individuals are more highly motivated to maintain equitable relationships, than inequitable relationships (Canary & Stafford, 1992; Stafford & Canary, 2006). As such, it has been posited that overbenefited (higher reward: cost ratio) and underbenefited (lower reward: cost ratio) partners are less emotionally satisfied (Sprecher, 1986) and, thus, less inclined to exhibit maintenance behaviors. In other words, marriages that are not characterized by fairness, are less inclined to be actively maintained.

Canary and Stafford's work is consistent with fairness heuristic theory (Lind, 2001, 2002) which posits that fairness serves as a heuristic to guide individuals toward egoistic, self-interest-focused directions or group-oriented (relationship-oriented), socially focused directions (Lind, 2002). The primary motivation to pursue fairness, according to Lind (2002) is to avoid the threat of exploitation and rejection by relational partners. Although most of Lind's work has been in organizational settings, his theory and findings are certainly consistent with the notion that perceptions of fairness are associated with emotional satisfaction, trust, and closeness and, as such, should be associated with the display of relationship maintenance behaviors designed to maintain or re-establish fairness.

**Forgiveness and justice.** The ability of forgiveness to strengthen, maintain, or restore the moral order of the relationship after a relational transgression (Kelley, 2012a, 2012b; Waldron & Kelley, 2008) makes it a significant maintenance strategy (Fincham et al., 2005; Hodgson & Wertheim, 2007) related to negotiating marital justice. Because relationship transgressions often involve injustice/unfairness (Hargrave & Sells, 1997; Kelley, 2012b), forgiving behaviors are frequently intended to maintain or restore equity, or fairness, in marital relationships. Hargrave and Sells (1997) describe the process, as follows:

> Relational ethics is rooted in the idea that people have an innate sense of justice that demands balance between what they are entitled to receive from a relationship and what they are obligated to give in order to maintain relational existence. When people engage in relationships that have a balance of give (obligations) and take (entitlements) over a period of time, the innate sense of justice is satisfied and trustworthiness is established in the relationship. However, when there is a consistent or severe imbalance between the relational give and take, the sense of justice is violated and individuals feel cheated or overbenefited by the relationship ... The work of forgiveness ... is defined as effort in restoring love and trustworthiness to relationships." (pp. 42–43)

Trustworthiness, from Hargrave and Sells's perspective, is regained by the restoration of justice. Consistent with justice motive theorizing (Batson, 2002; Bierhoff et al., 1986; Lerner, 1980), Hargrave and Sells emphasize restoring the balance between obligation and entitlement, or give and take. This "balance" may be maintained or restored through distributive or processual justice processes. In marriage there may be fair distribution of gain (from finances, to emotional support, to time) and effort (from watching the kids, to initiating "relationship" talks, to healthy self-sacrifice). There may also be fair process.

As described previously, processual justice represents any form of justice that is focused on *just process*. Marriage partners gauge their relationship justice based on procedures, interaction characteristics, and relational qualities. First, procedural elements like relationship decision-making procedures (e.g., clear decision-making guidelines such as mandatory partner consultation on purchases over $50, possible career moves, and implementing discipline structure with the children; or, equitable decision-making roles), represent one form of processual justice. Interestingly, procedural justice was originally conceptualized as *voice*; essentially, that one has a "say" in decision-making, even if one doesn't get one's desired outcome (Hill et al., 2005; Thibaut & Walker, 1975). Second, because the nature of one's interpersonal interactions is closely connected to how individuals view procedural justice (Hill et al., 2005), certain interaction characteristics can be counted as a form of processual justice. This means that communication elements such as being spoken to with respect may be associated with couples' relationship justice ethic. A partner spoken to with respect may be more likely to trust that his or her partner's decision making will be in the best interest of each partner and the relationship. The final form of processual justice, perceived relational qualities, influences perceptions of relational interactions and the overall sense of whether the relationship is just. For example, believing that "We each want the best for the other," creates a context such that even when direct equality or equity cannot be achieved, the partners perceive that a given decision was as fair as it could be, given the circumstance.

The previous discussion of Deutsch's (2006, 2011) descriptions of equity, equality, and need may provide additional insight as to how couples seek justice in their relationships. To paraphrase Deutsch, equity might typically be the standard and goal when partners view a situation with an economic lens, when gains and effort are somewhat measureable or product or resource based. Equality might show itself as most important when closeness or intimacy is the highest priority. And, need, might be most prominent in situations characterized by personal growth and welfare.

## SCOPE OF THIS STUDY

While development of a justice motive is part of the human experience, one of the tasks of partners in long-term relationships is to negotiate a moral ethic for the relationship, including how justice is to be construed. This negotiation likely involves implicit and explicit processes, and takes into account both distributive and processual aspects of justice. The current exploratory study examines interviews from long-term married partners to determine whether married partners operate in a manner consistent with holding a justice motive (Lerner, 2002) and how language usage reflects couples' perceptions of relationship fairness.

## METHOD

To explore language use that reflects couples' perceptions of justice in marriage, the research team examined written transcripts from in-depth, semi-structured interviews with 54 heterosexual, married couples. The mean length of marriage was 44 years, with all couples being married at least 30 years to their current spouse. Interviews lasted between 60–120 minutes and were conducted in participants' homes in three phases. Phase One began with both partners together and asked for general information about their marriage and the identification of forgiveness events in the marriage. Phase Two entailed interviewing each partner individually about her or his recollection of the identified forgiveness events. In Phase Three the couple was brought back together to gain any additional insights they had to offer about long-term marriage, and to offer final encouragement to them as a couple. In particular, it was assumed that questions focusing on motivation to forgive or not forgive, and couple descriptions of how the forgiveness process develops over time, would provide evidence for couples' awareness of justice or injustice in their relationship. (For more detail on this sample and the semi-structured interview script, see Waldron & Kelley, 2008.)

### Data Analysis

Content analysis was conducted in order to identify terms related to justice in participants' talk about their marriages (Krippendorff, 2004). Both manifest and latent content were examined. Manifest content was examined by generating a list of justice-based words drawing from the extant literature and an online thesaurus (Thesaurus Rex, Dictionary.com). As we searched terms and read them in context, we added additional terms to the search that were used by couples to reflect their perception of justice in the relationship. For example, we searched obvious terms such as justice, fair, equity, and equality, but other terms also that had the potential of being used in connection with relationship justice or fairness, such as balance and power, words that were particularly related to distribution, such as more and less, and even words that at times reflect a relationship quality associated with being treated fairly, such as respect. Using Microsoft Word, each transcript was searched for each word, or form of the word. For example, searching for "fair" would reveal fair, unfair, and fairness. After a research assistant located each word in the transcript, latent content was examined by reading the word in context and making a determination as to whether use of the term reflected a relational justice ethic. A second coder also read for latent content. Coders were instructed that a relational justice ethic could contain any of the following elements: distribution of resources, effort, or outcomes; processual elements such as procedures (e.g., rules about how decisions are made), interaction characteristics, and relational qualities, such as respect. For example, searching the term "balance" resulted in finding statements, such as, "We just had to balance the check book" and "He'll do something and I do something and that is the balance." Clearly, only the latter statement carries latent meaning related to distribution of effort in the relationship. There was disagreement between the coders on four cases; for example, one coder had identified "50/50" as a justice issue, however, after discussion with the other coder they agreed that the husband was actually stating that he never considered things as having to be 50/50. After discussion 100% agreement was achieved.

## FINDINGS

A total of 46 possible justice-based words or phrases were searched in the transcripts. Of these, seventeen words were used in a manner that reflected a justice ethic (as described previously as distributed or processual). The seventeen words were used 44 times, across 39 separate instances, and 24 couples' transcripts. The following descriptions only report occurrences of words that indicated a justice perspective. Couple identification numbers follow quotations.

### Distributive Justice Words in the Transcripts

The following words represented perceived justice in the distribution of outcomes or effort in the relationship.

**Fair.** *Fair* occurred once in the transcripts. This particular instance exemplifies a sense of unequal distribution of type of work. The wife stayed at home with eight children while her husband worked multiple jobs, yet they were financially tight. She wanted also to be able to work outside the home. She states, "And of course, you hear this and you go along with it, and you go along with it, go along with it. But I just thought this was not fair, you know" (005). This particular example also exemplifies the interrelationship between justice types. The emphasis on "hearing" and "go along with it" hints at a perceived loss of voice (procedural justice) for this issue in the relationship.

**Fifty-fifty.** *Fifty-fifty*, or a similar ratio indicating equality or inequality, occurred twice in the transcripts. The following quote is from a husband who didn't realize, for the first few decades of their marriage, that his wife was carrying most of the load of the relationship, "She gave, uh, you know, 75% or 100%. And I didn't. I wouldn't back down ... With us, there was no 50/50. She gave the most, uh, for the first ten or fifteen years we was married, probably" (A018).

**Unselfish.** *Unselfish* occurred once in the transcripts. Unselfishness carries undertones of Deutsch (2006) assertion that *need* is one way of judging equitable distribution. As one wife mentions regarding how she and her husband have helped each other at various times in their marriage, "Unselfish. I have always, ever since I've been married, thought ... and I've tried to teach the kids that, it's a sign of maturity when you begin to care more about the other person" (195). There may be a temptation to view this statement as reflecting inequity and inequality, yet the wife in this marriage apparently sees justice and altruism as compatible concepts. Consistent with this perspective, Stanley et al. (2006) report a positive relationship between healthy self-sacrifice and marital satisfaction.

**Jealousy.** *Jealousy* occurred once in the transcripts. After having their baby, a wife reports her perception of her husband's experience regarding a shift from equity to inequity: "If you set a goal and you work for it, you're not mad at each other. You're working for that house or that car, or you know, then if you have a baby and the mother spends more time with the baby and the guy is jealous" (A018). In this instance, jealousy reflects the husband's perception of inequity regarding distribution of the wife's time.

**More.** *More* occurred once in the transcripts. More and *less* are clear indicators of distribution of resources. In the following case, love is the resource being shared by the couple: "That's another thing, I think sometimes she loves me more than I love her. I mean, you know, the way she loves. I think that, so I'm saying to myself, well, 'Wow, she loves me,' then I must be okay and so I'll return the favor, you know." Interestingly, even though the husband perceives himself as over-benefited, he is motivated to restore balance, or fairness, to the relationship by returning love, in like kind, to his wife.

**Respect.** *Respect*, as related to justice, was used by ten different marital partners. I have chosen to list respect as both evidence of distributive and procedural justice. Regarding distributive justice, at times respect was discussed in regard to concrete qualities or ideas, or as something the partners had presumably in equal amounts. As such, it was not so much a reflection of process as of some element that one or both partners held. In the following quote from a husband, both partners *have* respect for the other, and both are perceived as *having* legitimate ideas: "But you know, there's another quality that I made a note on here and that is that we have respect for each other. You know? We respect each other as a person and we have respect for each other's ideas" (1001).

**Equality.** *Equality* occurred in the transcripts once. Whereas *equal* appears below under the heading processual justice, here equality refers to particular actions (caring for someone when they are sick) that are distributed according to partner's need: "If we are sick on occasion, which doesn't happen very often, um, I think that the equality of caring is there, is great on both sides" (192).

**Accommodation.** *Accommodation* occurred once in the transcripts. While long-standing patterns of unidirectional accommodation may reflect a lack of fairness in a relationship, the following quote illustrates how accommodation is used for fair distribution between partners when resources are distributed in accordance with partner need: "We always accommodated each other within our means. I think that's so important" (A023). In addition, the fact that both partners accommodate within their means hints at accommodation as a processual issue, as well.

## Processual Justice Words in the Transcripts

The following words were used in a manner that reflected perceptions of just process in the relationship.

**Equal.** The word *equal* occurred twice in the transcripts. I offer both quotes as each brings a different nuance to the notion of equality. The wife of the first couple discusses a move to equality that primarily reflects the nature of their interpersonal interactions; but, her use of the term "give" may also represent the distribution of *time*: "I think that communication has changed a lot, in that, only because I'm the talker and Jack has learned to talk and discuss and so we give each other equal time" (A026).

The second couple reflects Deutsch's (2006, 2011) contention that equality is most salient when representing closeness in the relationship: "And I've learned to back down to where it has gotten a bit more equal, I think. Now. Uh, you just do it as time goes by, you know? You care more for the person. I think you just grow more to the person. You care more for them. You see what they do and how much they care for you and it changes that way" (A018).

**Respect.** As was mentioned previously, *respect* was used by ten different married partners in the transcripts. Although, at times, respect represented distributive justice, often it described interactional characteristics or relational qualities that presumed a sense of equality or fairness in the relationship. For example, one husband emphasized that respect created a foundation for healthy communication in their relationship, "I have a ton of respect for her, and I've always had it and I always will have it. And, so I think that fits into that foundation that we were talking about. I just, when she says something. I don't poo poo it, or kick it aside, or, and I don't think she does with me either." (1561).

**Balance.** *Balance* occurred twice in the transcripts. Balance represented how equity in effort or roles was achieved. The following quote from a wife demonstrates how compromise can be used to achieve fair effort: "We compromise. He does something and I do something and that is the balance" (A081). Another wife saw balance in taking complementary roles, "It's the balance. And he's a very handy man and he does so many things. But I do everything at home" (A081).

**Honesty.** *Honest* occurred twice in the transcripts. As a processual justice issue, the following quote from a husband, describes honesty as part of the communication process and then links this to a distributive justice issue regarding effort: "Well, I think the main thing would be to be honest and if you're honest in everything, you know, you can't go wrong … If your partner isn't willing to pitch in and help then it probably wasn't meant to be" (A026). This simple statement illustrates that perceptions of procedural fairness and certain interaction qualities can create trust in a just outcome (Lind, 2001, 2002).

**Civility.** *Civility* occurred three times in the transcripts. Civility indicated procedural/interactional justice, much like honesty. The following comment from a husband represents other participant comments on the importance of civility in communication, "We will talk about it sometime the next day, but it's in a very civil manner and we never, ever fight for more than 24 hours over the same subject" (277).

**Commitment.** *Commitment* occurred in five partner transcripts. As with honesty and civility, having a shared, equal, commitment seems to imply trusting that the relationship will be fair. The following quotes from two husbands focus on the equality of the commitment: "Well, once we got married, we were committed. We had a commitment to each other and it was very important" (447) and "We were both very much committed to the marriage" (A015). A third husband pulls together procedural and relational justice issues: "It's not just one thing that sets off making a marriage work. Being committed, being honest, the willingness to work at what you're doing" (A026). One might be tempted to see work as a distributive justice concept (equal effort), however, the emphasis here is a "willingness" to work. Again, this supports Deutsch's (2006) notion that equality is present when the focus is on closeness and cohesiveness. Believing there is equal commitment creates a relational justice ethic that likely influences partner perceptions of procedural and interactional justice in the relationship.

**True/Untrue.** *True and untrue* each appeared once in the transcripts. These terms indicate adherence to, or violation of, established fair-relationship standards. In essence, they suggest a relationship between the idea of mutual fidelity and relationship justice: "And so, we never had those extra-marital relationships. She never did either. We've been true to each other" (A080) and "Without her I could not have overcome the mistake I made being untrue to her, and I could not have overcome the alcoholism" (A032).

**Mutual agreement.** *Mutual agreement* occurred three times in the transcripts. Agreement represented a fair procedure wherein couples didn't act on major decisions without consulting one another and being in agreement: "Because we do talk just about everything we do. We just, we talk it over and we come to a mutual agreement before we execute on it, to go on to whatever that was" (414).

**Understood.** *Understood* occurred twice in the transcripts. Perception of mutual understanding was considered an element that facilitated fair practice. In the following quote, the husband indicates that once understanding is achieved, the problem is gone: "So, once it's [the conflict] understood and we talk about it and you see it the way the other person meant it, or didn't mean it or something, then it's gone" (414).

## DISCUSSION

This study supports the notion that married couples conceptualize their relationships in terms of justice. It appears that married partners do operate in a manner consistent with holding a justice motive (Lerner, 2002) and that perceptions of relationship fairness affect how couples conduct their marriage relationships (Canary & Stafford, 2007; Lind, 2002). Moreover, the findings reveal the kinds of language couples use to express their perceptions of justice. Examination of couples' language use provides important insights for researchers, practitioners, and couples.

For analysis of data, I looked for words that reflected couples' perceptions of justice as distributed resources, effort, or outcomes, and words that focused on justice as it relates to more processual elements, such as procedures or rules that ensure fair practice, communication elements that demonstrate equity, such as speaking to one another with respect, and relational elements wherein couples saw qualities in their relationship as contributing to just outcomes. Married partners' language gave evidence of both distributive and processual justice. Distributive justice was exemplified by words and terms, such as: fair, fifty-fifty, unselfish, jealousy, more, respect, equality, and accommodation. These terms were used in narratives to describe whether resources or effort was equitably distributed in the relationship. For example, one husband's statement that, "there was no *fifty-fifty*. She gave the most ...," demonstrated his recognition that for the first decade of the marriage his wife put more effort into the relationship. Certain terms, such as *fair*, gave more direct evidence of a relational moral standard. "I just thought this was not fair," represented one wife's perception that opportunities to work outside the home were not fairly distributed.

Processual justice was demonstrated in couples' use of the following terms: equal, respect, balance, honesty, civility, commitment, true/untrue, agreement, and understood. These terms represented partners' perceptions of just qualities typical in their marital interactions or of the marriage itself. A husband's statement that he and his wife are "reasonably civil to each other most of the time" laid the groundwork for why he and she seldom need apology in their relationship. "Respect each other as a person," was a relationship quality cited by many as part of creating a relationship foundation wherein one could trust one's partner regarding decision-making, effort, and communication. These words are critical to shaping a broader understanding of processual justice. Perceptions of justice are deeply embedded within the nature of relationships, not merely "fair" procedure. Trusting the process, one's partner, and the quality of the relationship has a significant impact on one's perception as to whether the relationship, or interactions and decisions within the relationship, is fair or is as fair as can be expected given situational contingencies.

Couples' narratives also demonstrated the complex relationship between processual and distributive justice. A number of partner statements included both processual and distributive elements. For example, as one wife discussed how finances were not being handled fairly, her statement, "And of course, you hear this and you go along with it, and you go along with it, go along with it," implies that there was a lack of equal voice in the process. In addition, certain words (or form of the words) were used both in a distributive and processual manner. For example, equal (equality) was discussed by one wife in a distributive manner as she focused on giving an equal *amount* of caring in the relationship, and in a processual manner by a husband who focused on the fact that over time they learned to do conflict in a manner in which there was more equality in the relationship.

The integral relationship between procedural and distributive justice observed in this data is consistent with Cohen and Greenberg's (1982) observation that fair practice often involves equal distribution of decision-making power. This was demonstrated in couples' descriptions of their relationships in a variety of ways. For example, the process-oriented element, agreement, demonstrated how informal or formal decision making procedures kept decision-making power equitably distributed, "We talk it over, and we come to *mutual* agreement before we execute on it." Balance was another process element that was discussed in terms of equitable distribution. For example, balancing the relationship by using complementing roles or compromise was cited by participants as one way to do relationships fairly. Complementary roles balance the distribution of responsibility and effort. As one wife stated, she and her husband found balance in that he was handy and did "so many things" and she primarily does "everything at home." Compromise is a process that balances partners' experience of relationship rewards and costs. In this way, couples' descriptions of balancing demonstrated how many process-based forms of justice can be conceptualized as distribution.

The nature of the current data set likely affected outcomes of this study. For example, although these couple interviews were conducted to look at forgiveness themes, we found that most couples didn't talk about the importance of forgiveness until we raised the issue with them. Likewise, the longevity of these relationships may have affected the salience of justice for married partners in these relationships. Couples married over 30 years and who are generally stable and often show evidence of satisfaction in their relationships (e.g., free laughter together and holding hands during the interview), may be less cognizant of justice issues in their relationships. Presumably, justice (or lack thereof) would be a more prominent phenomenon for couples who are under stress or separated. As Bierhoff et al. (1986) suggest, individuals' early development of a justice motive manifests itself as the belief that certain behavior results in certain outcomes. Perceived violations of the expectations that accompany this belief likely reduce the relational satisfaction of relational partners (Kelley & Burgoon, 1991). Practitioners and couples should be aware that justice language may not often appear in couple talk until there has been some violation of what was expected by one or both partners. Then, justice may be an issue that has to be dealt with, "How can we make this situation more fair?"

It is also unclear how the justice motive may change over time due to normal developmental processes and maturation. For example, might young couples be more inclined to desire immediate justice rather than allow justice to develop over time? Previous analysis of the long-term marriage data analyzed for this study revealed many participants discussing how, over the years, they learned to accept differences between themselves and their partners—not because of changed behavior, but because their perception changed. During one interview the husband showed his thumb and forefinger held close together and stated, "People change about this much." He expressed that he and his wife's behavior had changed little over forty years of marriage, however, they learned to accept many of their differences. This is consistent with Cohen and Greenberg (1982) and Batson (2002) who state that as we grow and mature we hold the justice motive along with the recognition that there is not a simple, singular cause-and-effect mechanism between behavior and consequence (When I do the "right" thing, I don't always get the "right" result). Consequently, it would be interesting to examine justice effects in younger marriages. When do individuals begin to shift their perceptions regarding the likelihood of receiving fair treatment? In addition, researchers need to examine justice talk in all forms of cohabiting couples. For example, certain research indicates that equal division of household labor varies between heterosexual relationships and gay and lesbian relationships (Gotta et al., 2011), which raises questions about how the justice motive functions across various relationship types.

Future research should also take into account gender effects regarding the justice motive. Numerous researchers have examined or called for the examination of gender effects related to justice, equity, and equality (Bierhoff, Buck, & Klein, 1986; Kulik, Lind, Ambrose, & MacCoun, 1996). In the present study, of the 39 different instances where words were used to describe justice aspects of the relationships, 17 were made by the wife in the relationship, and of the words used by women most were focused on processual justice issues. For example, wives predominately mentioned equality of caring, being unselfish, maintaining a balance in the relationship, accommodation, and understanding.

## PERSONAL PONDERINGS

The current study reminds researchers, relationship theorists, and relationship practitioners that the "justice lens" is one significant way to view intimate personal relationships. It also reminds us that couples' conceptions of justice are broader than we might typically think. Relationship partners hold a deep sense of relationship *fairness* that is expressed explicitly ("That's not fair"!) and implicitly ("We balance each other."). Partners' sense of fairness is both outcome based (distribution) and process based (procedural, interactional characteristics, and relational qualities) and often experienced or viewed in terms of equity, equality, and need. Because justice judgments likely affect perceptions of the relationship as well as goals for future interactions, recognition of how justice is perceived or communicatively negotiated in one's personal relationships is essential. As Lerner (2002) states regarding the social impact of justice perceptions, "No other secular norm or value has comparable power" (p. 10).

I would like to end with a personal reflection. The other day (during the various weeks of writing this chapter) my wife, Ann, and I were having a "discussion." In this discussion she raised an issue regarding our relationship wherein she thought something was "wrong." "Aha!" I thought. "A moral issue. How timely since I'm writing about this." In the spirit of this chapter I suggested, "You see this as wrong because it's not fair." She said, "No. It's wrong because that's not the way you treat people." Me: "You don't treat people that way because it's not fair." Ann: "Why does it have to be fair? You just don't treat people like that." Ann's responses reflect some recent thinking by Carol Gilligan (2014), wherein she writes about an "ethic of care." In her article she proposes that many men eventually realize they have betrayed love, and many women realize that their selflessness (actually, also a betrayal of love) is morally problematic. Gilligan states, "The ethic of care guides us in acting carefully in the human world and highlights the costs of carelessness. It is grounded less in moral precepts than in psychological wisdom, underscoring the costs of not paying attention, not listening, being absent rather than present, not responding with integrity and respect" (p. 103). In this same vein, elsewhere I have been writing about social justice and arguing that true justice can only be achieved through love. Only full love (not sentimentality, but rather deep commitment, emotional connection, and healthy altruism; Kelley, 2012b) can construct a just future and just relationships that have longevity. This chapter is intended to broaden our ideas about justice in personal relationships. Justice may involve equal distribution and the processes that insure fair play. But, justice is very much about the types of loving relationships, and communities and cultures we are creating.

## REFERENCES

Adams, J. S. (1965). Inequity in social exchange. In L. Berkowitz (Ed.), *Advances in experimental social psychology* (Vol. 2, pp. 267–299). New York: Academic Press.

Batson, C. D. (2002). Justice motivation and moral motivation. In M. Ross & D. T. Miller (Eds.), *The justice motive in everyday life* (pp. 91–106). Cambridge: Cambridge University Press.

Bierhoff, H. W., Buck, E., & Klein, R. (1986). Social context and perceived justice. In H. W. Bierhoff, R. L. Cohen, & J. Greenberg (Eds.), *Justice in social relations* (pp. 165–186). New York: Plenum Press.

Bradbury, T. N., & Fincham, F. D. (1990). Attributions in marriage: Review and critique. *Psychological Bulletin, 107*, 3–33.

Burgoon, J. K., & Hale, J. L. (1984). The fundamental topoi of relational communication. *Communication Monographs, 51*, 193–214.

Canary, D. J., & Stafford, L. (1992). Relational maintenance strategies and equity in marriage. *Communication Monographs, 59*, 243–267.

Canary, D. J., & Stafford, L. (2007) People want—and maintain—fair marriages: Reply to Ragsdale and Brandau-Brown. *Journal of Family Communication, 7*, 61–68.

Darley, J. (2002). Just punishments: Research on retributional justice. In M. Ross & D. T. Miller (Eds.), *The justice motive in everyday life* (pp. 314–333). Cambridge: Cambridge University Press.

Deutsch, M. (1985). *Distributive justice: A social-psychological perspective.* New Haven: Yale University Press.

Deutsch, M. (2006). Justice and conflict. In M. Deutsch, P. T. Coleman, & E. C. Marcus (Eds.), *The handbook of conflict resolution: Theory and practice* (pp. 43–68). San Francisco: Jossey-Bass.

Deutsch, M. (2011). Justice and conflict. In P. T. Coleman (Ed.), *Conflict, interdependence, and justice: The intellectual legacy of Morton Deutsch* (pp. 95–118). New York: Springer.

Exline, J. J., Worthington, E. L., Hill, P., & McCullough, M. E. (2003). Forgiveness and justice: A research agenda for social and personality psychology. *Personality and Social Psychology Review, 7*, 337–348.

Fincham, F. D., Hall, J. H., & Beach, S. R. H. (2005). "Til lack of forgiveness doth us part": Forgiveness and marriage. In E. Worthington Jr. (Ed.), *Handbook of forgiveness* (pp. 207–226). New York: Routledge.

Folger, R. (1977). Distributional and procedural justice: Combined impact of "voice" and improvement on experienced inequity. *Journal of Personality and Social Psychology, 35*, 108–119.

Gilligan, C. (2014). Moral injury and the ethic of care: Reframing the conversation about differences. *Journal of Social Philosophy, 45*, 89–106.

Gotta, G., Green, R-J., Rothblum, E., Solomon, S., Balsam, K., & Schwartz, P. (2011). Heterosexual, lesbian, and gay male relationships: A comparison of couples in 1975 and 2000. *Family Process, 50*, 353–376.

Greenberg, J., & Cohen, R. L. (1982). *Equity and justice in social behavior.* New York: Academic Press.

Hafer, C. L. (2002). Why we reject the innocent victims. In M. Ross & D. T. Miller (Eds.), *The justice motive in everyday life* (pp. 109–126). Cambridge: Cambridge University Press.

Hargrave, T. D., & Sells, J. N. (1997). The development of a forgiveness scale. *Journal of Marital and Family Therapy, 23,* 41–63.

Hill, P. C., Exline, J. J., & Cohen, A. B. (2005). The social psychology of justice and forgiveness in civil and organizational settings. In E. Worthington Jr. (Ed.), *Handbook of forgiveness* (pp. 477–490). New York: Routledge.

Hodgson, L. K., & Wertheim, E. H. (2007). Does good emotion management aid forgiving? Multiple dimensions of empathy, emotional management of forgiveness of self and others. *Journal of Social and Personal Relationships, 24,* 931–949.

Holtzworth-Munroe, A., & Jacobson, N. S. (1988). Toward a methodology for coding spontaneous causal attributions: Preliminary results with married couples. *Journal of Social and Clinical Psychology, 7,* 101–112.

Homans, G. C. (1961). *Social behavior: Its elementary forms.* New York: Harcourt, Brace & World.

Homans, G. C. (1974). *Social behavior: Its elementary forms* (Rev ed.). New York: Harcourt Brace Jovanovich.

Joyner, K. (2009). Justice and the fate of married and cohabiting couples. *Social Psychology Quarterly, 72,* 61–76.

Kelley, D. L. (2012a). Forgiveness as restoration: The search for well-being, reconciliation, and relational justice. In T. Socha & M. Pitts (Eds.), *Positive interpersonal communication* (pp. 193–210). New York: Peter Lang.

Kelley, D. L. (2012b). *Marital communication.* Cambridge: Polity.

Kelley, D. L., & Burgoon, J. K. (1991). Understanding marital satisfaction and couple type as functions of relational expectations. *Human Communication Research, 18,* 40–69.

Krippendorff, K. (2004). *Content analysis: An introduction to its methodology.* Thousand Oaks, CA: Sage.

Kulik, C., Lind, E. A., Ambrose, M., & MacCoun, R. (1996). Understanding gender differences in distributive and procedural justice. *Social Justice Research, 9,* 351–369.

Lerner, M. J. (2002). Pursuing the justice motive. In M. Ross & D. T. Miller (Eds.), *The justice motive in everyday life* (pp. 10–40). Cambridge: Cambridge University Press.

Lerner, M. J. (1980). *The belief in a just world: A fundamental delusion.* New York: Plenum.

Lerner, M. J., & Goldberg, J. H. (1999). When do decent people blame victims? The differing effects of the explicit/rational and implicit/experimental cognitive systems. In S. Chaiken & Y. Trope (Eds.), *Dual process theories in social psychology* (pp. 627–640). New York: Guilford.

Lind, E. A. (2001). Fairness heuristic theory: Justice judgments as pivotal cognitions in organizational relations. In J. Greenberg & R. Cropanzano (Eds.), *Advances in organizational justice* (pp. 56–89). San Francisco, CA: New Lexington Press.

Lind, E. A. (2002). Fairness judgments as cognitions. In M. Ross & D. T. Miller (Eds.), *The justice motive in everyday life* (pp. 416–432). Cambridge: Cambridge University Press.

Lind, E. A., & Tyler, T. R. (1988). *The social psychology of procedural justice.* New York: Plenum.

McClelland, S. J., & Opotow, S. (2011). Studying injustice in the macro and micro spheres: Four generations of social psychological research. In P. T. Coleman (Ed.), *Conflict, interdependence, and justice* (pp. 119–145). New York: Springer.

McNulty, J. K., O'Mara, E. M., & Karney, B. R. (2008). Benevolent cognitions as a strategy of relationship maintenance: "Don't sweat the small stuff" … but it is not all small stuff. *Journal of Personality and Social Psychology, 94,* 631–646.

Ragsdale, J. D., & Brandau-Brown, F. E. (2005). Individual differences in the use of relational maintenance strategies in marriage. *Journal of Family Communication, 5*, 61–75.

Ragsdale, J. D., & Brandau-Brown, F. E. (2007). Asked but not answered: A second reply to Stafford and Canary. *Journal of Family Communication, 7*, 69–73.

Schemmel, C. (2011). Distributive and relational equality. *Politics, Philosophy, & Economics, 11*, 123–148.

Sprecher, S. (1986). The relation between inequity and emotions in close relationships. *Social Psychology Bulletin, 49*, 309–321.

Stafford, L. (2003). Maintaining romantic relationships: Summary and analysis of one research program. In D. J. Canary & M. Dainton (Eds.), *Maintaining relationships through communication* (pp. 59–78). Mahwah, NJ: Lawrence Erlbaum.

Stafford, L., & Canary, D. J. (2006). Equity and interdependence as predictors of relational maintenance strategies. *Journal of Family Communication, 6*, 227–254.

Stanley, S. M., Whitton, S. W., Sadberry, S. L., Clements, M. L., & Markman, H. J. (2006). Sacrifice as a predictor of marital outcomes. *Family Process, 45*, 289–303.

Thibaut, J. W., & Walker, L. (1975). *Procedural justice: A psychological analysis*. Hillsdale, NJ: Erlbaum.

Waldron, V. R., & Kelley, D. L. (2008). *Communicating forgiveness*. Los Angeles: Sage.

Waldron, V. R., Kloeber, D. K., Goman, C., Piemonte, N., & Danaher, J. (2014). How parents communicate right and wrong: A study of memorable moral messages recalled by emerging adults. *Journal of Family Communication, 14*, 274–397.

# CHAPTER FIVE

# Morality AND Family Communication When Coping WITH Cancer

CARLA L. FISHER & BIANCA WOLF

We are increasingly presented with health messages about how one "should" go about living a healthy life or attend to an illness, assigning responsibility to individuals as moral agents of their bodies (Sontag, 1978). When individuals become ill, at any point in the lifespan, attributions of responsibility for their health status can insinuate failure on their part to live properly or correctly (Broom & Whittaker, 2004). They can feel pressured to cope (or survive) in the "right" way. Likewise, their families feel morally obligated to respond in the "right" way by facilitating and not inhibiting their loved one's survival. Patients and families not only negotiate such moral commitments within their family where norms of "right or wrong" behavior are first developed, but also simultaneously navigate societal norms that apply "moral and psychological pressure" on how they should be coping (de Raeve, 1997, p. 249). Ultimately, these moral discourses about managing illness might both enhance and challenge illness experiences.

More attention is being paid to helping families develop healthy communication approaches to manage illness, but rarely is morality considered an important factor in how they cope. Likewise, even though morality may drive how one copes (or what one deems to be the right way to manage illness), their behavior may not be aligned with the "right" health outcomes. In this chapter we explore this intersection of morality, family coping, and health by examining how moral discourse shapes the ways that families cope with a life-threatening illness like cancer.

Rather than impose a pre-existing definition of morality, it is imperative to understand how families frame coping as moral behavior, in other words, right or wrong, good or bad, adaptive or maladaptive, healthy or unhealthy. At the same time, we recognize that coping can both facilitate and inhibit well-being. Thus, even though a family may perceive a coping approach as morally "right," from a clinical perspective it may not necessarily correspond to what's "right" for one's health. In other words, is it health-promoting (enhances mental, physical or social health) or helpful to their loved one's disease adjustment and stress management from the patient's perspective? Coping behavior and various systems of moral meaning may at times be at odds with one another as families attempt to manage illness-related stress. By exploring this, we can better appreciate how and why families cope in the ways that they do and explicate those discourses or systems of meaning that give relevance to their behaviors as morally correct. In doing so, we can then reconsider the relational and health implications of coping done "right" or "wrong" and ascertain whether the "right" ways to cope are inherently better ways to cope.

Using lifespan theoretical underpinnings, we shed light on the impact of families' communicative constructions of "right and wrong" ways to cope with cancer. A lifespan perspective enables us to appreciate the complexity of morality and coping with illness by recognizing not only how it develops within familial culture but how it may function differently in various phases of life, by generations socialized in variant socio-historical contexts, and by individuals of distinct gender (Fisher, 2014; Miller-Day, 2011; Pecchioni, Wright, & Nussbaum, 2005; Rolland, 1994). With this in mind, we narrow our focus to an intergenerational bond that plays a central role in coping, the parent-child relationship. In light of societal-level moral discourse that holds women largely responsible for the welfare of families, we contextualize further and examine mother-daughter communication (Seelbach, 1977). We examine how they fare with a more common cancer type, breast cancer, a disease that 1 in 8 women born today will develop during their lifetime (Jemel et al., 2003).

To carefully attend to morality on both societal and familial levels, we begin with a lifespan conceptualization of morality in coping behavior. We illustrate the intersection of moral discourse and health in a relational context, including moral discourse surrounding cancer and women's roles. We then identify lifespan theories that help us understand how families make sense of their moral obligations to one another by engaging in what they perceive to be the "right" way to cope with cancer.

## THE INTERSECTION OF MORALITY AND ILLNESS COPING: CONCEPTUALIZING COPING AS RIGHT OR WRONG, HEALTHY OR UNHEALTHY

Lazarus (1993) defines coping as a process by which individuals manage stress. In line with a lifespan approach, he contends that by conceptualizing coping as a process we can better focus on how coping changes across time in response to the situation in which it occurs and highlight how coping differs across the disease trajectory, life stages, and generations. This approach further allows us to understand the quality of the behavior and associated outcomes—their potentially adaptive properties. As Lazarus suggests, "there may be no universally good or bad coping processes, though some might more often be better or worse than others" (p. 235).

From this view, researchers have become increasingly interested in linking coping approaches with better health outcomes on psychological, physical, and social levels. In fact, scholars focused on psychological health have concluded that certain forms of coping (e.g., emotion-focused, problem-centered, and less avoidant) improve psychosomatic outcomes (e.g., less distress, depression, and anxiety) for survivors and their loved ones (Dukes Holland & Holahan, 2003; Kershaw, Northouse, Kritpracha, Schafenacker, & Mood, 2004; Stanton, Danoff-Burg, & Huggins, 2002). Some experts contend that these coping approaches are linked to healthy physiological effects (e.g., decreased stress hormones; better immunological functioning; less fatigue or pain) (Luecken & Compas, 2002). Moreover, social scientists suggest that particular coping orientations (e.g., communal) or behaviors (e.g., openness) result in strengthened relationships (Afifi & Nussbaum, 2006).

Still, much of this research fails to collect lay understandings and assessments of coping as defined and enacted by patients and their family. We also do not know how patients and families figure morality into their approaches, consistent with and/or in resistance to dominant cultural moral discourses about cancer survivorship. For instance, adaptive constructions of coping are consistently linked to "thinking positively," both in popular culture and research, thereby perpetuating positive behavior as a social moral norm for surviving cancer (Wilkinson & Kitzinger, 2000). As a result, patients and families are presented with clear ideas about how coping should be done, which ironically can result in increased distress when they cannot consistently maintain positivity as a coping technique (Gray & Doan, 1990). Moreover, it may not always be helpful or the "better" way to cope. Research conducted by the first author shows that while positive communication is common in the context of mother-daughter breast cancer coping, it is not always helpful to their ability to manage disease-related stress, meaning it can lead to women feeling silenced by preventing them from releasing distressing emotions (Fisher, Miller-Day, & Nussbaum, 2013).

Moral discourse about coping is also gendered. Dominant social discourse supports an ideology where women are largely expected to fulfill the role of nurturer, caregiver, and kinkeeper (Cancian & Oliker, 2000). As such, a moral obligation is inferred for women to enact these roles, particularly during times of illness, including their own. In fact, mothers diagnosed with breast cancer report pressure to cope according to conflicting role expectations of being a good mother and a good patient (Elmberger, Bolund, & Lutzen, 2005). The pressure to perform both roles correctly (i.e., in the first, to not burden their family through failed performance and in the second, to rectify their disease status through all ends of treatment) produces coping predicaments by which women cannot successfully achieve either (Thorne, 1990).

While patients and their families are influenced by these moral societal-level norms designating right or wrong ways to cope as women and in the context of cancer, such norms are also cultivated in their family environments. Theorists taking a lifespan perspective of family behavior offer useful insights on how morality might develop in a family and, in turn, influence their coping communication.

## THE INTERSECTION OF MORALITY AND FAMILY BEHAVIOR

From a lifespan perspective, coping with health and illness is an interactive, relational experience, impacted by each partner's communication expectations and norms that are first developed in their family environment (Afifi & Nussbaum, 2006). These norms of behavior help direct members as to how they "should" behave thereby instituting expectations about the right or wrong way to communicate. In particular, how a family develops norms of attachment and solidarity can have implications for not only how they manage stressful health experiences like cancer, but also how they "should" cope together as a family.

### Developing Attachment and Solidarity

Well-known lifespan theorists Bowlby (1979) and Ainsworth (1989) established attachment theory based on how an infant and primary caregiver (often a mother) develops a secure relational basis through interaction. Within this parent-child relational context, they learn essential supportive, nurturing behaviors. As a result, attachment is considered to be a stress-reducing resource for both across the lifespan (Posada & Lu, 2011). The more intense and healthy the attachment (referred to as "secure" and associated with feelings of connectedness, closeness, trust, availability) the more resources (e.g., social support) to buffer them from stress (Afifi & Nussbaum, 2006). The theory has helped explain norms of attachment that inform moral obligations to one another throughout the lifespan, including adult children's felt obligation for aging parents' well-being (Cicirelli, 1983). Recently, researchers have argued that attachment is important to consider to ensure women with breast cancer are adjusting in a healthy manner (i.e., diagnosed women with healthier or secure familial attachments manage emotions better) (Tacón, Caldera, & Bell, 2001).

Related to attachment is how families develop solidarity, a layered concept of cohesion, closeness, affect, and maintaining communication. According to intergenerational solidarity theory, families develop norms and rules for behaving and providing resources to one another that encourage and maintain solidarity in the family (Bengston & Harootyan, 1994). Family behavior critical for developing solidarity includes frequency of contact and affection to enhance closeness and trust (versus estrangement), being available, exchanging help between generations, and establishing expected roles. Like attachment, solidarity may inform why children feel a sense of obligation to their parents as they age. Family norms of solidarity may also be gendered. Women, particularly mothers and daughters, are often expected to enact behaviors of solidarity, like providing care consistent with their role as "kinkeepers," an obligation of "filial responsibility" (Seelbach, 1977). Theorists have suggested that families without solidarity norms may encounter more strain during challenging times (Afifi & Nussbaum, 2006). Thus, like attachment, family solidarity may also shape families' moral discourses about how they "should" cope together.

Though this theory has not guided cancer coping scholarship, recently, the concept of solidarity was integrated into a model of healthy family coping and breast cancer survivorship. Breast cancer is regarded as an illness that is more likely to result in long-term survivorship, as the five-year survival rate is high for women diagnosed in stages 0–II (American Cancer Society, 2014). Accordingly, attention is needed not only on how families cope but how their communication impacts survivorship in the long-term. The health-related family quality of life (HR-FQoL) model is grounded in several frameworks, including intergenerational solidarity theory, to explain how family interaction impacts quality of life during coping and survivorship (Radina, 2013). One aspect of family communication to consider is behavior cultivating emotional closeness or solidarity.

The lifespan theoretical constructs of attachment and solidarity provide insight into coping approaches that might be most adaptive and, therefore, important for families to develop. At the same time, though, it is important to consider how these micro-level moral assumptions first developed in the family intersect with macro-level social moral discourse about the right way to manage illness. While social norms of coping may at times complement moral obligations developed in the family (e.g., gendered roles of providing care), morality at the social and familial levels might also create difficult tensions individuals must learn to negotiate or redefine. Lifespan theories shed light on how family and social moral discourses collectively shape mother-daughter coping behavior and, at the same time, allow us to recognize that moral challenges could also result.

## RESEARCH FOCUS

To explore this, we returned to previous research conducted independently by both authors on family coping with breast cancer across the lifespan. Per Morse (2002), to fully understand the complexity of illness, we should triangulate findings from studies using different approaches. To guide this secondary analysis we posed the following inquiry with the goal of examining mothers' and daughters' coping as communicative behavior informed by familial and social moral discourse about the right way to cope:

RQ: What moral approaches to coping do mothers and adult daughters engage in after a breast cancer diagnosis?

## METHODS

This study involved secondary analyses of narrative data collected from two larger data sets on family coping after a breast cancer diagnosis. Both studies utilized unique theoretical frameworks and diverse methodology providing the potential to deepen our understanding of morality in coping by examining the same phenomena captured with a different lens (Morse, 2002). The first author utilized a grounded theory approach to analyze and triangulate narrative data sought via interviews, diaries, and diary-interviews. Using Carstensen's (1991, 1992) socioemotional selectivity theory, she examined the emotional support, openness, and avoidance of mothers and daughters (see also Fisher & Nussbaum, in press; Fisher, 2014). The second author interviewed family members to capture narratives of coping following diagnosis and analyzed that data for dominant discourses that rendered the coping processes intelligible for families. She used communal coping theory (Afifi, Hutchinson, & Krouse, 2006; Lyons, Mickelson, Sullivan, & Coyne, 1998) to examine coping as a joint (familial) effort as well as relational dialectics theory (Baxter & Montgomery, 1996) to attend to relationally negotiated meanings of phenomena. While the participants could select any member to participate, the majority chose their mother or daughter.

### Sampling & Procedures

For the present study, data were analyzed from a total of 109 in-depth interviews (57 diagnosed women and 52 of their mothers or adult daughters), 10 two-week diaries (5 dyads), and 8 diary-interviews. Following IRB approval by the university's Internal Review Board, sampling was purposive and recruitment sought in a number of ways (e.g., university newswire; medical clinics; state cancer registry; support groups). Five diagnosed women elected more than one daughter to partake in either original study and an additional five women participated without a partner. Mean age of diagnosed women was 51 ($SD$ = 10.82, Range 30–80). The majority were in midlife (56.1%) with 16% in emerging or young adulthood (aged 18–39) and 28% in later life (60 or older). Mean age of their mother or daughter was 36 (*SD* = 18.20, Range 18–83). The majority were emerging/young adults (71%). Most were Caucasian and lived in the Northeast or Midwest. About half of participants were married and most had a college-level education. Of those diagnosed, 60% were in treatment or had treatment within 12 months and about 40% had treatment within five years. Women varied in treatment experiences (some had only a lumpectomy whereas others underwent radiation, chemotherapy, a mastectomy, and reconstruction) and also varied in stage at diagnosis (65% diagnosed in stages 0–II, 35% in stages III or IV). Four women were experiencing a recurrence.

Most interviews were face-to-face at a comfortable location chosen by participants, in a relational research lab, or conducted over the phone. Interviews ranged from 30 minutes to more than 2 hours but generally took about 90 minutes. Verification strategies (e.g., thinking theoretically, theoretical sampling and adequacy, investigator flexibility) were employed in both studies throughout the research process to ensure the design and findings were trustworthy and rigorous (Morse, Barrett, Mayan, Olson, & Spiers, 2002). The data sets were each originally orthographically transcribed resulting in more than 3,000 pages of text and were managed using SPSS, Microsoft Excel, and Atlas.ti.5.2.

## Analysis

Coding and analysis were conducted using the constant comparative method outlined in Glaser and Strauss's (1967) and Strauss and Corbin's (1998) grounded theory approach. Themes are presented as action statements or phrases in the text and Table 1 using Banning's (2003) "ecological sentence synthesis" approach to ensure findings can be easily transferred into interventions (Sandelowski & Leeman, 2012). Details of procedures are available from the first author.

Data were analyzed inductively to identify both explicit and implicit traces of morality in families' coping approaches, using sensitizing constructs from lifespan theories of attachment (e.g., secure family norms of availability, expression, and support) and solidarity (e.g., felt obligation to provide support/care). We paid special attention to analyzing described communication as embedded in discourses of moral coping, in other words, coping described by participants as right or wrong. For example, if women stated that they heard or were told that maintenance of a positive attitude is something one "should do" (indicating a social moral command) or implied positivity as a preferred coping behavior within their family, we marked both sites as behavior indicative of their own/familial or social moral codes for coping. At times their language was explicit (i.e., using terms like "should" or "right") and in other instances, the women articulated morality in their explanation of why they coped in such a manner (e.g., enacting an approach because the alternative was deemed wrong or detrimental to one's health). After all data were coded, themes were refined to identify moral discourses (both at the familial and

Table 1. Mother–Daughter Moral Approaches to Coping with Breast Cancer.

| Mothers and daughters describe the following moral approaches to coping, | that are characterized by these communicative behaviors, | and grounded in these moral understandings. | This approach aids coping as noted below | but creates these morally-problematic outcomes: |
| --- | --- | --- | --- | --- |
| facilitating positivity and eliminating negativity | offering reassurances; providing encouragement; reframing negativity; eliminating negative talk | staying positive is essential to survival; positivity is a family norm; being positive is a philosophy of life | providing faith/hope; being uplifting; symbolizing that their loved one was doing okay | pressures one to be positive all the time; infers that the loved one does not understand what the other is going through; prevents one from releasing fears or concerns |
| talking (or not) about end of life | discussing fears & concerns about death or recurrence; sharing uncertainty about the future; discussed once if at all, then avoided | talking about death is taboo and equated with negativity | releasing fears; making plans | one does not have the opportunity to plan or dispel fear |
| engaging in solace behaviors | being affectionate; listening; being there | expected role of a woman in society (kinkeeper; caretaker) expected role of woman in her family; normal role change for daughter and mother | providing a sense of constant support, companionship, health advocacy, & feeling of connection; conveying nurturance & concern; enhances feeling loved; cultivating a more egalitarian dynamic | it encroaches upon one's space, sense of control, or autonomy |

social levels) that women used to describe why they coped in a particular manner. Some coping approaches seemed motivated by both levels of morality whereas others were linked to only one level (e.g., familial values). We reviewed each theme of moral coping for their health implications (i.e., psychological, physical, relational) to garner a better sense of families' morally driven perceptions of the right way to cope and whether they are health-promoting.

## FINDINGS

The following themes illustrate mothers' and daughters' moral approaches to coping after diagnosis. Characteristics of each theme are italicized to illustrate communicative behaviors encompassing each moral coping approach, moral discourse (at familial and/or social levels) that shaped their descriptions or explanations for enacting these approaches, and associated health implications.

### Facilitating Positivity and Eliminating Negativity

Diagnosed women and their mothers and daughters described a moral approach to coping that centered on the need to stay positive and, often at the same time, eliminate negativity. Staying positive was a means of coping with various stressors women encountered (e.g., changes in body image and self-esteem after surgery and hair loss; debilitating treatments and side effects; managing uncertainty). Women framed positivity morally as the "right" way to deal with cancer in that the opposite behavior (*not* being positive) would negatively impact health or survival.

This moral coping approach involved a number of communicative strategies. These included *offering reassurances* (e.g., saying "Everything will be okay"). Women *provided encouragement* to instill hope and faith (e.g., sharing survivor's stories to "pump up" their mother/daughter), particularly when diagnosed women "talked negatively" meaning they expressed sadness, anger, or fear. Mothers and daughters also engaged in positivity *by reframing situations and feelings* to highlight the "positive side" of things. Thus, this coping approach was defined in relation to an absence or denial of negativity. At times, diagnosed women tried to *eliminate any negative talk.* As a diagnosed mother recalled, "If I would talk about it in a negative way, she would not be happy about that. She wants that positive attitude."

Although families expressed difficulty in engaging in positivity, they often described doing so in step with broader social discourses of morality. Some women adamantly claimed it was a *necessary approach to facing cancer and key to survival.* As one mother of a diagnosed daughter stated, "If you had a positive attitude, you could come through a lot things. And without one, sometimes they just didn't make it." For many, positivity was viewed as a *philosophy of life*. For others it was described as a *family norm or as a fundamental part of their family system*. Thus, positivity was also described at the familial level of morality in that these values encouraged certain behavior (positive communication) and discouraged behavior that violated this norm. One woman explained: "It's both of us ... We always try to take something good out of it. Let's just look at it, see where it's taking us, where can we go with it, and hopefully we come out a better person after it." Similarly a diagnosed mother described her daughter's positivity as representative of their family's values and central to her own coping:

> She just believed that I had the strength to do this ... "Believe. You know, just believe in yourself." It was like the word in the house ... That's what she would tell me. It was almost like it came full circle ... what you preach and what you teach comes back.

Many diagnosed women described this approach to coping as helpful in their adjustment. One diagnosed daughter explained,

> If I say, "Oh my gosh! I got to go through this test. I hope everything's okay. Oh my gosh! I hope [the cancer] doesn't come back!" And she'll be like, "Don't even worry! Everything's going to be fine. You'll be fine. If it is something, we'll deal with it." ... Sometimes I just need to hear that.

The therapeutic effect of positivity seemed particularly important to diagnosed mothers. When daughters communicated positively, mothers described this as *uplifting*. For mothers with younger daughters (late adolescents and emerging adults) this approach conveyed to them that their *daughter was faring okay*. It made them more comfortable with how the daughters were coping, which was particularly important given they were quite concerned about their daughter's well-being. One irony of this pattern is that both diagnosed mothers and daughters often performed positivity as part of their exhibited solace behaviors (explicated subsequently) to help one another feel better, regardless of whether either was actually experiencing positivity.

This latter observation pointed to those cases where positivity was not always helpful, particularly when it was enacted to deny, eliminate, or replace negativity. This resulted in diagnosed women feeling *pressured to be positive all the time*, behavior for them that was not realistic in the stressful nature of cancer. Excerpts from one dyad highlight this dark side of positivity. The diagnosed mother articulated this pressure:

> They [family] wanted me to be positive. And I know there's something to that. You know you always hear them say if you have a positive attitude you may have a more positive outcome [laughs], which only fed my negativity. Because I told myself, I'm so negative that for sure I'm gonna die.

Likewise, her daughter explains how she and other family members denied any space for their own negativity:

> I felt like I had to overcompensate with positivity. And we've talked about this, we've been like, "Mom, we had to be so positive because you were so negative," like, we couldn't even face the reality necessarily because we had to compensate for your negativity [laughs].

Furthermore, when a positive moral coping approach was not functional, diagnosed mothers and daughters described this behavior as minimizing their concerns, which coincided with them feeling that their daughter/mother *did not understand or appreciate what they were going through*. As one diagnosed young-adult daughter stated, "As long as it's just talking positive and not crossing over [my feelings], it's helpful. Once [she] crosses over something then it's not helpful." In this case, the daughter recalled her mother minimizing her concerns about recurrence saying "Sometimes she goes, 'You don't really have to worry about that because you're young and your doctors are on top of things.'" The same negative effect of positivity resulted when it *inhibited women from dispelling negative feelings*. As one diagnosed mother stated, "Let me get it out of my system!" Thus, even though positivity seemed to be viewed as a moral standard of behavior in the family, in order for this approach to be health-promoting (meaning it was perceived as helpful), it was critical that it did not result in women feeling pressured or silenced.

## Talking (or Not) about End of Life

Women also described a moral coping approach that involved facing the end of life. This approach had strict boundaries in that typically women were allowed to (or attempt to) only discuss mortality once or it was avoided altogether. Facing death was more of a pressing issue for women diagnosed in later stages (e.g., III or IV), experiencing a recurrence or metastatic cancer, or when diagnosed early in life. Mothers and daughters described this coping approach as moral behavior because talking about death was both taboo in society and negative (thus, in line with the previous theme, detrimental to one's health). Some women also described moral assumptions at the familial level in that talking about mortality was perceived as bad behavior.

This moral coping approach encompassed a variety of behaviors that included *sharing fears or concerns about death or recurrence* (e.g., "I don't want to die."), *expressing uncertainty about the future* (e.g., contemplating future risk), *making plans for the future* (e.g., having a funeral) as well as *sharing concerns about one's future with family* (e.g., would they see their children grow up). Most women indicated that this was not a coping approach they thought should be frequently enacted. Some viewed it as a phase they needed to "get through" (facing mortality) whereas others characterized it as an opportunity to make plans. Still, many avoided this form of coping in their mother-daughter bond altogether.

Ultimately, women expressed that even though they did have concerns about their own or their loved one's mortality, they consciously evaded the issue *viewing it as either a negative form of talk or a taboo topic.* Hence, this moral coping approach was somewhat related to the previous theme in that talking about end of life was deemed negative (or the opposite of facilitating positivity). For some families, it was a forbidden topic. As a young daughter of a diagnosed mother recalled, "Pretty much immediately, either my mother or father or both of them said, 'Nobody's talking about dying.'" For daughters of diagnosed mothers, this topic seemed especially difficult as it went against the norm of the hierarchy of their family bond. As one daughter explained, "It's not really a conversation I think any child wants to have with their parents." Likewise, younger diagnosed women (in their thirties) described fearing death but rarely, if ever, sharing it with their mothers. Instead these daughters stated that it was something they had to deal with on their own because they believed that talking about such issues with their mother would *cause them stress.* In other words, it was deemed unhealthy to talk about in this bond and, therefore, wrong.

This coping approach was linked to the prior approach of positivity. Mothers and daughters, in particular, may have felt morally obligated as women in the family to maintain a "positive" atmosphere. In other words, to be a "good" mother or daughter meant to always uphold hope, even if it meant sacrificing honesty or individual needs (e.g., dispelling fears or making end-of-life decisions). Ultimately, talking about mortality did not mesh with the moral standard of maintaining positivity in the family.

## Engaging in Solace Behaviors

Women also engaged in numerous communicative behaviors that collectively embody "solace behaviors" as a moral coping approach (Barbee, Derlega, Sherburne, & Grimshaw, 1998). Solace behaviors are enacted to attend to one's emotional needs by allowing for the expression of emotion and intimacy, behaviors that cultivate attachment and solidarity. While women seemed to morally frame solace communication as right/wrong according to their (or their mother/daughter's) needs, this was also enmeshed in broader scripts of social appropriateness (i.e., what one should say and do as the "right" things for others who are sick), expectations (a woman's role), and familial norms of behavior.

Solace behaviors included *showing affection, listening,* and what mothers and daughters' called *"being there."* These behaviors seemed to enhance both diagnosed women and their mothers' and daughters' disease adjustment or function in a health-promoting manner. For instance, women showed affection for one another through nonverbal behavior (e.g., smiles, kisses, hugs, cuddling, holding hands, rubbing one's bald head) as well as verbal expressions (e.g., saying or texting "I love you" often or when getting off the phone or saying goodbye). Affection seemed to be helpful in their coping because it conveyed to them that they were *loved and supported.* This form of coping seemed especially poignant to diagnosed mothers with younger daughters. Affection was described as not a "norm" of their daughter's behavior and sometimes viewed as a role change in that the daughter provided support for the first time. As one mother explained, "She never really gave me a hug or kissed me or said "I love you" before this all happened." Thus, in these cases, this new moral standard of behavior seemed to *strengthen their relational connection.* Listening behavior was similarly helpful in women's adjustment and coping by making them feel supported and loved. Often times listening was a silent form of support or means of being a "sounding board." As a diagnosed daughter explained, "She didn't always have all the right words or sometimes she didn't even answer me. She just listened to what I had to say, and that was okay."

"Being there," as women referred to it, involved a number of behaviors to convey love, support, and concern for one another. This included calling and visiting more and trying to "be there" in some way. For some mother-daughter pairs "being there" was *companionship or as caretaker* at home, and for others, it was as a *partner or advocate* at medical appointments. Being present at appointments often served dual coping functions: support for diagnosed women and inclusion in the experience for their mother/daughter. One daughter explained of her mother's appointments: "I know that she wanted someone to go with her, and I also kind of wanted to be there, kind of almost comfort for her but also comfort for myself knowing what was actually happening and going on." Ultimately, being there seemed to be behavior that conveyed solidarity and attachment for one another, both the patient and her mother/daughter. As such, it may have also been linked to a familial moral standard of the right thing to do in the context of illness.

Some daughters "dropped everything" and moved back in to take care of their mothers. This form of solace coping seemed to ensure diagnosed women *did not feel alone,* thereby solidifying solidarity and attachment in their bond which was health-promoting. As a diagnosed daughter said, "I could always count on her." They thought this behavior "made it easier" as they always had their mother or daughter "by my side," whether physically there or not. Thus, at times "being there" was a verbal expression repeated across the course of the disease that *conveyed a sense of trust and reliance* they would "be there." As a mother of a diagnosed daughter shared, "Many times I've said, 'You've got me, and I've got you.'" "Being there" also allowed diagnosed women's mothers and daughters to feel needed and observe that their loved one was doing okay. They too felt a need to "be there" for their own sense of well-being. Oftentimes for mothers of younger diagnosed daughters, they needed to "mother" their daughters. While conveying trustworthiness and reliance may have functioned as moral values or qualities of a "good" mother-daughter bond, what seemed clear was these behaviors were perceived as helpful to both diagnosed women *and* their mother/daughter in managing disease-related stress.

Solace behaviors like showing affection, listening, and being there for one another seemed linked to the mothers' and daughters' established attachment and connection and the central *role of women as kinkeepers and caretakers in the family.* Many described this solace communication as something they assumed their mother/daughter wanted them to do or that it was "the right thing to do." For some families, it was identified as a *family norm*—to be there for one another. As a daughter stated about her mother, "That's just her." For others, it was perceived as *the woman's role as mother.* Diagnosed daughters believed that allowing their mother to "be there" helped the mother feel more at ease with the daughter's condition and well-being. For daughters of diagnosed mothers, it was also a *relational role change* that seemed tied to their need to "mother" their mother for the first time.

While solace coping seemed to largely function in a helpful manner for both diagnosed women's and their mother/daughter's adjustment, at times this approach was not helpful. This outcome was tied to struggles for *independence, space,* and *control.* For instance, diagnosed daughters needed to set the tone for how their mothers would "be there." When mothers did not respect that (e.g., talking to a doctor without the daughter; sharing a daughter's disclosures outside the family), tension resulted. Women also described the importance of their autonomy and space. As one diagnosed daughter explained after her mother's extended stay, "I'm ready to have my space back!" Similarly, diagnosed mothers wanted control over how much their daughter knew about their cancer experiences and mentioned a need for privacy. As a mother explained, "I don't want everyone to know how I feel ... or always tell what I'm thinking ... [My daughter] doesn't need to know everything. Sometimes she thinks she should." For mothers and daughters, issues of autonomy, privacy, and control may have been moral standards they wanted each other to respect in their relationship.

## DISCUSSION

This is the only study that we know of to explore how social and local discourses of morality inform mother-daughter coping processes with breast cancer. We located three primary moral approaches by which women appeared to cope: facilitating positivity and eliminating negativity; talking (or not) about end-of-life issues; and enacting solace behaviors. One compelling observation is that these coping approaches appear to function in *both* adaptive and maladaptive ways in relation to helping women manage disease-related distress. Thus, identifying moral discourses in coping does not simplify our understanding of when it is adaptive but rather offers us a more nuanced understanding of coping behaviors that are *both* right and wrong, good and bad, healthy and unhealthy. Furthermore, our findings highlight how family morality cannot be divorced from broader social discourses of morality. Ultimately, while family coping behavior may be morally motivated and perceived as the "right" thing to do, such communication may not always function in a helpful (or healthy) manner.

## Connecting Morality with Helpful and Unhelpful Mother-Daughter Coping Behavior

The findings help illustrate how mother-daughter coping behavior is embedded within a moral discourse of right or wrong at both the familial and societal levels. While at times moral discourse can inform healthy coping behavior, it can also complicate it. Families may have cultivated their own norms of behavior (as has been identified in lifespan theorizing about solidarity and attachment) but may also find it difficult to enact *flexible* coping behaviors when they are not reinforced by broader moral discourses at the societal level.

For instance, two moral coping approaches, being positive and engaging in solace behaviors, were described by mothers and daughters as core behaviors of their family culture. In line with intergenerational solidarity theory, mothers and daughters in part relied on familial norms in their coping experiences. For many women being positive was a philosophy of life or family perspective maintained across their history. Moreover, "being there" is suggestive of communication central to cultivating solidarity and was also referred to as the right thing to do or linked to their loved one's typical behavior or family role. Such behaviors may also be explained by lifespan attachment theory which posits that the intimate connection formed early in the lifespan will hold strong across their history, particularly during trying times, thereby helping them cope and emerge resilient. That sense of attachment may be amplified when a family member's life is threatened and act to bind the family together as is seen with mothers' and daughters' enactment of solace behaviors. Thus, these moral coping approaches are linked with norms of family behavior that might, in part, govern how members should face a crisis.

Reliance on one's family norms and rules certainly provides guidance in how to care for one another and cultivate a sense of normalcy or peace. Yet, at times, these norms may need to be flexible, such as in the case of allowing for the expression of negativity. Social moral discourse about positivity may further complicate their coping by inhibiting their ability to be flexible in this manner. Noted earlier, positivity is a dominant theme running through social discourse on breast cancer (particularly within the breast cancer movement) as well as medical messages of coping with cancer (Wilkinson & Kitzinger, 2000). Women are inundated with messages that convey the deadly consequences of their failure to remain positive. Therefore, it is no surprise that women in our study exemplified this moral discourse in their coping, particularly if positivity was a developed familial norm for facilitating attachment and solidarity. Even though women who engaged in this approach often found it to be helpful, this was not always the case. Familial and social discourse of positivity may collectively be instilling pressure on both patients/survivors and loved ones to perform positivity to the relative neglect of appreciating their stress, fears, and negative thoughts.

In the case of solace behavior or "being there," larger social discourses related to gender expectations and role performance within family might explain women's tendency to enact behaviors consistent with social stereotypes of women as nurturing caregivers and kinkeepers (Cancian & Oliker, 2000). In fact, the second author of this chapter identified gendered and role-based discourses present in family member talk of coping to be one primary reason as to why women with breast cancer demonstrate individual coping with their illness and deny communal coping processes with their family (Wolf, in press). Women invoked a discourse of "Responsible Womanhood" as they excluded spouses, children, and other family members from medical visits, making treatment decisions on their own, withholding information, and declining social support from loved ones. In the current study, the mother-daughter pairs displayed generally complementary solace behaviors, but this may be related to them being same sex/gender family members. Moreover, gendered expectations may complicate how mothers and daughters can "be there" for one another in the most helpful way (e.g., allowing a diagnosed daughter to be in control of how her mother can be there for her, even though as a mother she might want to or need to fulfill her gendered role).

Likewise, familial and social discourse complicates the mother-daughter moral coping approach of talking (or not) about death. Women's sense of attachment and commitment to one another is likely solidified in life-threatening circumstances. Yet, this enhanced attachment may also inhibit the desire or willingness to face end of life, or for these families, lead them to avoid addressing issues tied to the uncertainty of one's future (e.g., mortality, risk of disease recurrence, making end-of-life decisions). While this is certainly morality embedded on the familial level, it is undoubtedly influenced by broader cultural discourses that influence relational behaviors surrounding the discussion of death. It is clear that talk of death in Western society is considered taboo (Book, 1996). Death talk is viewed negatively and considered impolite, inappropriate, and something to be feared, including within the context of breast cancer (Kenen, Arden-Jones, & Eeles, 2004). Unfortunately, this communicative taboo often hinders information exchange, medical decision making, and relational coping. In essence it results in a communication "impasse" for families who need to address the end of life (Lannamann, Harris, Bakos, & Baker, 2008). Ironically, social assumptions of the "right" behavior (not talking about death) may ultimately perpetuate wrong behavior or less humane or supportive communication.

The women in this analysis exhibited coping behaviors that are entrenched in a web of moral discourses that demonstrate how constructions of coping as right or wrong might not always facilitate "better" ways of coping. However, our findings are limited given these may be particularly specific to mothers and daughters or for understanding how women cope in the family. We offer some guidance in extending these findings with future research.

## Considerations for Future Research That Addresses Gender

Given that both social and familial moral discourse about coping address gendered constructions of right and wrong behavior, additional research on how morality shapes male coping behavior is warranted. To explore this, data from the second author's original study did include a small subset of diagnosed women and their son/father ($n = 6$). Although the sample is small, we found that sons displayed somewhat different moral coping approaches. Sons/fathers emphasized solace behaviors by "being there" for primarily key diagnostic, surgical, and treatment appointments but not for day-to-day contact. Sons/fathers also made a point to make regular phone calls and be present at family functions, but their solace behavior did not typically include expressions of affection or listening (emotionally focused behavior) as was exhibited by daughters. In line with related research and previously elaborated gender discourses, it is likely that moral approaches to coping and associated expectations differ based on family role and sex/gender (Wolf, in press).

## Practical Implications: Engaging in Moral Coping Effectively

We hope our findings help illustrate how coping in what families perceive as the "right" way may not always be the best way. Based on our data, it appears that both personal and social moral commitments may motivate behavioral choices during the coping process. We hope that by recognizing families' sometimes conflicted moral obligations, as was expressed in their narratives, we could potentially enhance their care. This study highlights the need for health care professionals to listen for these conflicting obligations. Providers can help patients and their family better understand complicated feelings of anger, sadness, or guilt. They can also help families articulate their moral assumptions and discover different, and perhaps liberating, moral rationales that function in a more health-promoting manner. With this mind, we also end by offering a few principles we hope aid families in developing healthy moral coping approaches:

- Family norms or rules of behavior provide guidance on how to bind together and cope effectively. Yet, flexibility is also important. Families who facilitate solidarity and attachment through positivity need to be willing to allow for the disclosure of negative emotions to ensure their loved one can have concerns expressed and validated.
- Family communication that facilitates both attachment and solidarity (showing affection, listening, spending time together, calling more, providing companionship, being a caretaker or health advocate, and voicing that you will "be there") are all ways to enhance relational connection and feelings of cohesiveness critical to coping. At the same time, it is important to be mindful of each other's need for autonomy, space, control, and privacy.
- Facing mortality is natural though not without difficulty. It can be an opportunity to release fears, make plans, and ensure one's wishes are always at the forefront of any end-of-life decision. Dealing with uncertainty about the future does not have to be negative and, rather, might be a time to reconnect or enhance intimacy.

## REFERENCES

Afifi, T. D., Hutchinson, S., & Krouse, S. (2006). Toward a theoretical model of communal coping in postdivorce families and other naturally occurring groups. *Communication Theory, 16*, 378–409.

Afifi, T. D., & Nussbaum, J. F. (2006). Stress and adaptation theories: Families across the lifespan. In D. O. Braithwaite & L. A. Baxter (Eds.), *Engaging theories in family communication: Multiple perspectives* (pp. 276–292). Thousand Oaks, CA: Sage.

Ainsworth, M. D. (1989). Attachment beyond infancy. *American Psychologist, 44*, 709–716.

American Cancer Society. (2014). *Cancer facts and figures: 2014*. Atlanta: American Cancer Society, Inc. Retrieved from: http://www.cancer.org/acs/groups/content/@research/documents/webcontent/acspc-04251.pdf

Banning, J. H. (2003, July). *Ecological sentence synthesis*. Available at http://mycahs.colostate.edu/James.H.Banning/PDFs/Ecological%20Sentence%20Syntheis.pdf

Barbee, A. P., Derlega, V. J., Sherburne, S. P., & Grimshaw, A. (1998). Helpful and unhelpful forms of social support for HIV-positive individuals. In V. J. Derlega & A. P. Barbee (Eds.), *HIV and social interaction* (pp. 83–105). Thousand Oaks, CA: Sage.

Baxter, L. A., & Montgomery, B. M. (1996). *Relating: Dialogues & dialectics*. New York: Guilford.

Bengston, V. L., & Harootyan, R. A. (1994). *Intergenerational linkages: Hidden connections in American society*. New York: Springer.

Book, P. L. (1996). How does the family narrative influence the individual's ability to communicate about death? *OMEGA—Journal of Death and Dying, 33*, 323–341.

Bowlby, J. (1979). *The making and breaking of affectional bonds*. London: Tavistock.

Broom, D., & Whittaker, A. (2004). Controlling diabetes, controlling diabetics: Moral language in the management of diabetes type 2. *Social Science & Medicine, 58*, 2371–2382. doi:10.1016/j.socscimed.2003.09.002

Cancian, F. M., & Oliker, S. J. (2000). *Caring and gender*. Lanham, MD: Rowman & Littlefield.

Carstensen, L. L. (1991). Selectivity theory: Social activity in lifespan context. *Annual Review of Gerontology and Geriatrics, 11*, 195–217.

Carstensen, L. L. (1992). Social and emotional patterns in adulthood: Support for socioemotional selectivity theory. *Psychology and Aging, 7*, 331–338.

Cicirelli, V. G. (1983). Adult children's attachment and helping behavior to elderly parents: A path model. *Journal of Marriage and the Family, 45*, 815–822.

De Raeve, L. (1997). Positive thinking and moral oppression in cancer care. *European Journal Cancer Care, 6*, 249–256.

Dukes Holland, K., & Holahan, C. K. (2003). The relation of social support and coping to positive adaptation to breast cancer. *Psychology and Heath, 18*, 15–29.

Elmberger, E., Bolund, C., & Lutzen, K. (2005). Experience of dealing with moral responsibility as a mother with cancer. *Nursing Ethics, 12*, 253–262.

Fisher, C. L. (2014). *Coping together, side by side: Enriching mother-daughter communication across the breast cancer journey*. New York: Hampton Press.

Fisher, C. L., Miller-Day, M., & Nussbaum, J. F. (2013). Healthy doses of positivity: Mothers' and daughters' use of positive communication when coping with breast cancer. In M. Pitts & T. J. Socha (Eds.), *Studies in positive communication* (pp. 98–113). New York: Peter Lang.

Fisher, C. L., & Nussbaum, J. F. (in press). Maximizing wellness in successful aging and cancer coping: The importance of family communication from a socioemotional selectivity theoretical perspective. *Journal of Family Communication*.

Glaser, B. G., & Strauss, A. L. (1967). *The discovery of grounded theory: Strategies for qualitative research*. New York: Aldine de Gruyter.

Gray, R. E., & Doan, B. D. (1990). Heroic self-healing and cancer: Clinical issues for the health professions. *Journal of Palliative Care, 6*, 32–41.

Jemel, A., Murray, T., Samuels, A., Kaplan, A. G., Miller, J. B., Stiver, I. P., & Sorrey, J. L. (2003). Cancer statistics, 2003. *CA: A Cancer Journal for Clinicians, 53*, 5–26.

Kenen, R., Arden-Jones, A., & Eeles, R. (2004). We are talking, but are they listening? Communication patterns in families with a history of breast/ovarian cancer (HBOC). *Psycho-Oncology, 13*, 335–345.

Kershaw, T., Northouse, L., Kritpracha, C., Schafenacker, A., & Mood, D. (2004). Coping strategies and quality of life in women with advanced breast cancer and their family caregivers. *Psychology & Health, 19*, 139–155.

Lannamann, J. W., Harris, L. M., Bakos, A. D., & Baker, K. J. (2008). Ending the end-of-life communication impasse. In L. Sparks, H. D. O'Hair, & G. L. Kreps (Eds.), *Cancer, communication, and aging* (pp. 293–318). Cresskill, NJ: Hampton.

Lazarus, R. S. (1993). Coping theory and research: Past, present, and future. *Psychosomatic Medicine, 55*, 234–247.

Luecken, L. J., & Compas, B. E. (2002). Stress, coping, and immune function in breast cancer. *Annals of Behavioral Medicine, 24*, 336–344.

Lyons, R. F., Mickelson, K. D., Sullivan, M. L., & Coyne, J. C. (1998). Coping as a communal process. *Journal of Social and Personal Relationships, 15*, 579–605.

Miller-Day, M. (Ed.). (2011). *Family communication, connections, and health transitions: Going through this together*. New York: Peter Lang.

Morse, J. M. (2002). Qualitative health research: Challenges for the 21st Century. *Qualitative Health Research, 12*, 116–129.

Morse, J. M., Barrett, M., Mayan, M., Olson, K., & Spiers, J. (2002). Verification strategies for establishing reliability and validity in qualitative research. *International Journal of Qualitative Methods, 1*(2), Article 2. Retrieved May 23, 2007, from http://www.ualberta.ca/~ijqm/Motram, 2003.

National Cancer Institute (2014). *SEER Cancer fact sheets: All cancer sites*. Bethesda, MD: NCI. Retrieved from: http://seer.cancer.gov/statfacts/html/all.html

Pecchioni, L. L., Wright, K., & Nussbaum, J. F. (2005). *Lifespan communication*. Mahwah, NJ: Lawrence Erlbaum.

Posada, G., & Lu, T. (2011). Child-parent attachment relationships: A lifespan perspective. In K. Fingerman, C. A. Berg, J. Smith, & T. C. Antonucci (Eds.), *Handbook of lifespan development*, (pp. 88–116). New York: Springer.

Radina, M. E. (2013). Toward a theory of health-related family quality of life. *Journal of Family Theory & Review, 5*, 35–50.

Rolland, J. (1994). *Families, illness, and disability: An integrative treatment model*. New York: Basic.

Sandelowski, M., & Leeman, J. (2012). Writing usable qualitative health research findings. *Qualitative Health Research, 22*, 1404–1413.

Seelbach, W. C. (1977). Gender differences in expectations for filial responsibility. *The Gerontologist, 17*(5 Part 1), 421–425.

Sontag, S. (1978). *Illness as a metaphor*. London: Allen Lane.

Stanton, A. L., Danoff-Burg, S., & Huggins, M. E. (2002). The first year after breast cancer diagnosis: Hope and coping strategies as predictors of adjustment. *Psycho-Oncology, 11*, 93–102.

Strauss, A., & Corbin, J. (1998). *Basics of qualitative research: Techniques and procedures for developing grounded theory*. Thousand Oaks, CA: Sage.

Tacón, A. M., Caldera, Y. M., & Bell, N. J. (2001). Attachment style, emotional control, and breast cancer. *Families, Systems, & Health, 19*, 319.

Thorne, S. (1990). Mothers with chronic illness: A predicament of social construction. *Health Care Woman International, 11*, 209–221.

Wilkinson, S., & Kitzinger, C. (2000). Thinking differently about thinking positive: A discursive approach to cancer patient's talk. *Social Science and Medicine, 50*, 797–811.

Wolf, B. W. (in press). Do families cope communally with breast cancer, or is it just talk? *Qualitative Health Research*.

# PART TWO

# Moral Messages AND Conversations

# CHAPTER SIX

# Negotiating Morality Through Poetic Justice

LESLIE A. BAXTER, SARAH N. PEDERSON &
KRISTEN M. NORWOOD

## NEGOTIATING RELATIONAL MORALITY THROUGH
## POETIC JUSTICE

Every culture is characterized by moral guidelines that provide an ideal for the
relationship between the self and other. Haste and Abrahams (2008) explain, "Underlying them [moral theories or guidelines] are not just values, but assumptions
about the relationships that underpin human interdependence in that society and
therefore underpin the codes that sustain the moral order" (p. 384). This interpersonal moral order, or *ethic of community* (Shweder, Much, Mahapatra, & Park,
1997), not only guides interpersonal relating, but arises from it, as it is "through
dialogue we acquire and negotiate the frames and lenses to view, value and legitimate our experience" (Haste & Abrahams, p. 382).

Our chapter addresses how relationship parties negotiate norms and expectations of what is moral and ethical relating through the enactment and retelling of
certain revenge scenarios. On first blush, it might seem peculiar to find a chapter
that focuses on revenge in a volume devoted to moral communication in good relationships. Interpersonal scholars often presume that relating parties are motivated
to function cooperatively (Grice, 1989) to sustain the moral aspects of the social
order and the social interests and identities of both parties (Brown & Levinson,
1987; Goffman 1959, 1967). This presumption, of course, is the scholarly equiva-
lent of the infamous Golden Rule, which says "Do unto others as you would have

done unto you." Within this presumption, revenge is understood as an unethical and immoral act of aggression that violates the social order more generally and one facet of that social order in particular—norms of morality.

However, parties frequently violate The Golden Rule, acting without moral regret in untoward ways that result in harm to others. In these lacunas of immorality, revenge can be understood as the enforcement arm of The Golden Rule; in inflicting punishment on a wrongdoer, moral reform could occur, returning the social order to its baseline of social cooperation (Forschler, 2012). Revenge, in short, is a complicated communicative practice, as it fits under the scholarly umbrella of the "dark side" of interpersonal communication (Spitzberg & Cupach, 2007) yet is a dark cloud with a silver lining (p. 6) in that it has potential to restore a relationship's social and moral order. Specifically, a kind of revenge that holds this potential, and is the focus of this chapter, is *poetic justice*. We argue that this particular communicative practice is a way to exact justice in a socially appropriate manner and to restore the social and moral order between relating partners. It is potentially a powerful way to socialize others to what is morally expected of them.

The development of moral reasoning—a concern for fairness, justice, and preventing harm to others—is a complex process that involves both psychological and social factors. From a psychological perspective, moral reasoning requires a number of sophisticated cognitive and emotional capacities, including but not limited to perspective-taking or the capacity to imagine from the other's point of view. As Mead (1934) astutely observed in his classic discussion of the "I" and the "me," self-consciousness, including the capacity to reflect on the morality of one's actions, depends on a person's ability to take into account the perspective of generalized and particularized others:

> The attitudes of the others constitute the organized "me," and then one reacts toward that as an "I." ... [I]t is due to the individual's ability to take the attitudes of these others in so far as they can be organized that he gets self-conscious. (p. 175)

Acquiring an understanding of others' expectations is a profoundly social process, eloquently described by Mead as a "conversation of gestures" (p. 175). A developing child gradually internalizes the social and moral order of his or her society through interactions with others. Encounters with both family members and peers are important in this process of becoming a moral self (Smetana, 2011). Poetic justice, a socially appropriate form of revenge, can be a useful tool in the arsenal of conversational gestures to socialize a person in how to behave as a moral self.

## REVENGE AS DARK- AND LIGHT-SIDED

Scholars have largely conceptualized revenge as an exclusively dark-sided phenomenon, typically viewing it as uncivilized and irrational—an unbecoming, undesirable and deviant behavior (Barreca, 1995; Tripp & Bies, 1997; Tripp, Bies, & Aquino, 2002). Indeed, unchecked revenge can be regarded as an immoral act of aggression. However, revenge also has a light side in its potential for restoring the social and moral order in the face of misconduct.

Goffman's (1959, 1967, 1971, 1974) theory of the interaction order is a useful framework through which to think about the light side of revenge. Although Goffman's work is extensive and diffused, Smith (2006) cogently argues that the notion of the interaction order is the key master concept around which all else coheres; he cites Goffman's (1983) posthumous address on this construct to the American Sociological Association as his intended final word on the corpus of his life's work. In particular, the theoretical concepts of the *remedial interchange, face,* and *frame* are particularly useful in understanding the potential role of revenge in restoring the moral order of social life. Goffman (1971) argues that informal social interaction—the interaction order—is guided by social norms, that is, expectations for action. Many of these norms exist for the sake of convenience, but others provide guidelines for how to enact *good* interactions, or those that respect, protect, and save face for others. Such moral norms are "supported by social sanctions, negative ones providing penalties for infractions, positive ones providing rewards for exemplary compliance" (Goffman, 1971, p. 95).

When an offender acts in a manner that violates this kind of social norm, thereby disrupting the moral order, this act of wrongdoing is ideally followed by a repair sequence known as the *remedial interchange*, the purpose of which is to restore face for individuals involved as well as the moral order. The interchange begins with a *challenge*, that is, calling attention to the misconduct. If the interchange moves toward repair and restoration, the offender ideally advances an *offering* (e.g., an account or an apology) that recognizes his or her misconduct, which is met with an *acceptance* of the offer (e.g., an expression of forgiveness), and a gesture of *gratitude* by the offender that his or her offer was accepted. Sometimes, the remedial exchange is short and to the point, for example:

> Offended: "Hey, you didn't fill the car up with gas." (Challenge)
> Offender: "I know. I ran out of time. I'm sorry." (Offering of account and apology)
> Offended: "That's OK, that's happened to me before." (Acceptance of offering)
> Offender: "Thanks for understanding. I owe you one." (Expression of gratitude)

Other times, the remedial interchange is more complex. The simple example above presumes that the mere act of challenge is sufficient motivation for the offender to apologize and thereby restore the social and moral order. But sometimes, a mere "calling out" might not suffice, and sanctioning might be needed to increase the offender's motivation to reform. The enactment of revenge is a kind of social sanction that deploys punishment in order to motivate the offender to alter his or her future actions such that they are morally appropriate. Thus, we can think of revenge as an intensified form of challenge.

A small corpus of work has focused on the instrumental functionality of revenge as an enforcement mechanism of the social and moral order. In their study of workplace revenge, Tripp et al. (2002) argue that revenge can function positively in organizations by protecting subordinates against the abuse of power by authority figures; that is, revenge becomes light in its function of sustaining the social and moral order that guides informal, civil interaction in the workplace. Research that supports the functionality of revenge has been conducted primarily in workplace settings to the relative neglect of personal relationships (Bies, 1987; Bies & Tripp, 1995; Bies, Tripp, & Kramer, 1997; Morrill, 1996; O'Leary-Kelly, Griffin, & Glew, 1996; Tripp & Bies, 1997). However, some research in personal relationships has investigated the potential remedial value of revenge. Yoshimura (2007), for example, investigated revenge goals, finding that revenge acts were motivated by an overarching instrumental goal of control over the perpetrator in order to regulate his or her actions. Boon, Deveau, and Alibhai (2009) focused more specifically on provocations for revenge in romantic relationships and found that most revenge acts between romantic partners were motivated by a rule violation, such as infidelity (arguably not merely a rule violation but an act of immorality), and that the most common reason reported for revenge acts was to bring about change in the romantic partner's behavior. Gollwitzer and colleagues (Gollwitzer & Denzler, 2009; Gollwitzer, Meder, & Schmitt, 2011) found that revenge acts in personal relationships were perceived as most beneficial when the initial offender understood his/her punishment and learned a lesson regarding appropriate relational behavior.

These studies underscore the instrumental value of revenge in altering the other's behavior. However, this positive or "light side" of revenge appears to be short-lived in memory; revenge tends to be framed negatively in hindsight and is accompanied by remorse and apprehension (Carlsmith, Wilson, & Gilbert, 2008; Yoshimura, 2007). This emotional fallout, of course, perpetuates a view of revenge as a dark-sided phenomenon.

Not only are revenge acts framed negatively in hindsight, they are also framed negatively in their inception as they are often seen as prompted by volatile and negative emotions. For instance, Stouten, De Cremer, and van Dijk (2006) found that negative emotions are often the instigators of revenge. Furthermore, revenge acts often feature dehumanizing elements that deny the offender's personhood, especially when the offender is seen as lacking emotional feelings of remorse (Leidner, Castano, & Ginges, 2013).

## POETIC JUSTICE AS APPROPRIATE REVENGE

Although revenge can manifest a "light side" by functioning as a corrective for another's moral misconduct, it is a kind of social action that also implicates the *face* of the avenger, that is, "the positive social value a person effectively claims for himself"

(Goffman, 1967, p. 6). On the one hand, if the offended person does nothing, he or she is subject to having an identity as a victim. The mere act of seeking revenge positions the victim as agentic. But revenge is not without moral ambivalence. As Victor Hugo so eloquently expresses it in *Les Misérables*, "Every blade has two edges, he who wounds with one wounds himself with the other." An avenger could enact retribution but end up contaminated nonetheless—morally wounded in seeking punishment through retaliation. The key to revenge is to position it as something other than inappropriate aggression. Social sanctions, Goffman (1971) reminds us, are normatively regulated with social expectations about what is appropriate and inappropriate, just as all social actions are so regulated. When revenge is accomplished artfully, with an ironic twist in which the wrongdoer receives punishment in a way that is a direct causal consequence of his wrongdoing, we have the kind of revenge that is the focus of this chapter: poetic justice (Berglar, 1946). The social advantage of poetic justice might be its ability to absolve the avenger from perceived responsibility for the particulars of the punishment; responsibility for the punishment rests with the wrongdoer and not the avenger. In poetic justice, avengers gain justice, thereby demonstrating that they are not victims, and, ideally, teaching the offender a moral lesson, but they are able to accomplish this without themselves becoming morally suspect.

However, in order for poetic justice to restore the social and moral order in a manner that protects the face of the avenger, the wrongdoer and third party observers must correctly frame the revenge act as an ironic form of revenge. Goffman (1974) argues that the concept of *frame* is helpful in understanding how interactants make sense of any given slice of interactional activity. A frame is "a schemata of interpretation" that "allows its user to locate, perceive, identify, and label" (p. 21) interactional activity in order to infer its meaning. If parties do not frame the punishment implicated in poetic justice as ironically caused by the wrongdoer, the avenger is positioned to lose face as an antisocial and perhaps immoral aggressor. Furthermore, the wrongdoer might fail to understand that the revenge is a symbolic act of remedial challenge, thereby jeopardizing, as well, the potential for lesson learning and behavioral change.

Although poetic justice has long been the object of study among literary critics, it has received scant attention by researchers. To date, only one study has examined the layperson's perspective. Tripp et al. (2002) asked study participants to describe two stories of workplace revenge that they had either participated in or observed. Both stories were required to be about occasions when the participant or somebody else "decided to 'get even' with another person at your workplace" (p. 969). The first story was required to fit this criterion: "You feel really good telling others about the incident. Indeed, if you were to tell this story at a bar or over dinner, people might view the actions as wonderful or engaging" (p. 969). The second story had to meet this criterion: "You feel really bad telling others about the incident. Indeed, if you were to tell this story at a bar or over dinner, people might view the actions as unseemly or ugly" (p. 969). The first story prompt was designed to elicit an occurrence of poetic justice, whereas the second story prompt was designed to elicit a contrast example of non-poetic revenge. The researchers identified three qualities that differentiated the first from the second story: (1) altruism, that is, display of concern for the general welfare of others at work; (2) poetic qualities, that is, the dispensing of justice the "way one might wish it to be" (p. 970); and (3) symmetry of two types—symmetry of consequences, in which the avenger caused an equal amount of harm to the wrongdoer, and symmetry of method, in which the method of getting even resembled the method by which the wrongdoer hurt the victim. Overall, symmetry emerged as the most important of these qualities. Symmetry of consequence is also known as retributive justice (e.g., Witvliet, Worthington, Root, Sato, Ludwig, & Exline, 2008), that is, revenge proportional to the wrongdoing. This eye-for-an-eye measured response has a long social history that can be traced to Hammurabi's Code and the early Judeo-Christian tradition.

Although the Tripp et al. (2002) study is a significant contribution in understanding poetic justice, it did not examine how poetic justice is enacted in personal relationships outside of a workplace setting. Unlike workplace relationships, which are grounded in role-based and contractual relationships, personal relationships are voluntary associations whose currency is mutual affection and support. As Simmel (1950) noted in his writings in the early twentieth century, and Owen (1984) confirmed in his study of themes in relational communication, personal dyadic relationships are particularly fragile and subject to dissolution, which in turn encourages partners to be relationally sensitive to one another's needs. Although family relationships might be viewed as less voluntary than friendships and romantic relationships (Hess, 2000; Scharp, 2014), they are still deeply situated in ideas of affection and support. Acts of revenge could rupture the emotional delicacy of personal relationships in ways different from workplace relationships. Relational sensitivity might emerge as a salient feature of poetic justice enactments in personal relationships, unlike the less intimate, role-based relationships of the workplace. A relationship between workmates can continue, for example, even if the members are emotionally disaffected; it is their roles that bind them. To understand the complexities of how poetic justice is enacted in the more intimate personal relationships, we conducted a critical-incident study of poetic justice among young-adult friendship, romantic, and familial relationships.

## THE STUDY

### Methods

**Participants.** Participants for the study were recruited from undergraduate communication courses at a large Midwestern university. College students provided a convenient sample, of course, but such a sample also provides a snapshot of moral development with respect to poetic justice at a crucial age when participants are leaving home and adolescence behind and entering adulthood. Consistent with Internal Review Board (IRB) approval requirements, students who participated in the survey or the alternative assignment were awarded extra credit in their courses. Completed surveys were returned from 131 participants; 46 participants returned surveys which asked about poetic justice among family, 42 participants returned surveys which asked about poetic justice among friends, and 43 returned surveys which asked about poetic justice among romantic partners. Participants were mostly female (69.7%) and Caucasian (91.7%) with an average age of 20.26 years (SD = 1.13; range 18–25).

**Materials.** The questionnaire informed participants that the researchers were interested in learning about both poetic and non-poetic justice. Because we sought to focus participant attention on the details of enactment, participants were provided with a general definition of poetic justice that did not pre-judge its constituent features: *For our study, "poetic justice" can be thought of as sweet revenge; that is, revenge accomplished in an especially appropriate or ironic way. "Non-poetic justice" can be thought of as the opposite; that is unsweet revenge that is accomplished in an inappropriate or nonironic way.* Although a variety of kinds of revenge might be regarded as "sweet" or "unsweet," we stipulated that the basis of this assessment was to be the appropriateness and irony of its enactment. Following this general information, the survey employed a critical-incident technique (Erlandson, Harris, Skipper, & Allen, 1993) to gather qualitative descriptions of poetic and non-poetic justice. We asked participants to provide a detailed account of a revenge incident that they deemed as poetic justice and a revenge scenario that they deemed as non-poetic justice for the relationship type to which they were randomly assigned (friendship, romantic relationship, family relationship). Although both incidents were situated in the same relationship type for a given participant, the specific relationship could vary; for example, one friendship might have been the context for the poetic justice incident whereas a different friendship might have been the context for the non-poetic revenge incident. The incident type (poetic or non-poetic justice) was counterbalanced in its order of presentation across participants to prevent an ordering effect.

Participants were asked to answer a series of questions after providing an open-ended description of each incident, including an identification of their role in the incident (the initial wrongdoer, the avenger, or a third party who either witnessed the revenge or was told about the revenge second hand) and their reflections on what qualified the incident of revenge as either poetic justice or not.

Although we have no systematic way to determine whether participants found it difficult to recall and reflect on instances of (non)poetic justice, our subjective impressions of the data suggest that they had vivid and detailed memories of such phenomena.

**Data Analysis.** Because of the paucity of research on poetic justice, we employed mixed qualitative and quantitative methods in order to gain descriptive insights into how poetic justice is communicatively accomplished. Once surveys were collected, the descriptions of the incidents of poetic and non-poetic justice were transcribed. Then, the researchers individually read through the transcripts, performing independent, open coding of the salient features of poetic justice and non-poetic justice (Lindlof & Taylor, 2002). The researchers were coding for characteristics of revenge that made it poetic justice or not, both etically and emically, that is, what characteristics they could discern from the incidents and what the participants explicitly marked as qualities of poetic justice and non-poetic justice. A given incident potentially could contain multiple features. After performing separate coding analyses, the researchers came together to discuss and refine categories in order to create final coding categories to be included in the coding manual. Two of the researchers were trained to the coding manual using a randomly drawn 30% of each incident type. Each identified feature was coded for its presence or absence in a given participant account. Coder reliability was assessed using both Cohen's kappa and Krippendorff's alpha (Hayes, 2005). Reliabilities for all of the emergent coding categories were quite high, with only one of the relevant computed reliability indices less than 1.00 (and this was an acceptable .83). Coding discrepancies were resolved through discussion. These two coders were randomly assigned to the remaining incidents which they coded independently.

Preliminary analyses were conducted to determine if the data could be pooled for male and female respondents and for respondents with different types of involvement in the revenge situation. Based on the statistically nonsignificant results of these chi squared analyses, the data were pooled. Findings were also compared for friendship, romantic, and familial relationships using a series of chi squared analyses; with one exception described below, no significant differences emerged and data were collapsed across relationship type.[1]

## Results

Overall, the features of non-poetic justice are mirror opposites of the features that characterize poetic justice. We organize our presentation of results around the features that, when present, characterized poetic justice and when absent, characterized revenge as non-poetic justice. Five primary features were identified in the data.[2]

**Symmetry of form.** Poetic justice was most frequently described as revenge characterized by symmetry of form, identified in 80.9% of incidents. That is, the revenge act was characterized by a similarity with respect to the method of the original act of perceived harm doing and the method of the revenge act. Illustrative of this category is this instance from a female participant who was the avenger against her boyfriend:

> My former boyfriend in high school, Philip, provoked the revenge because we would fight and then he'd say "We're on a break." But never actually telling me that out loud, he thought it was a given. So during those "2-day breaks" he would hook up (make out) with another girl. One time after a fight, I decided that Philip and I would be on a break. My 2 girlfriends and I snuck out and met up with 3 guy friends. I ended up making out with Philip's neighbor who was 2 years older than me. The next day Philip called me on the phone asking me about me and his neighbor. He was so mad. Philip was so angry on the phone, but all I could do was laugh and ask him how it felt to find out something like that. After that we didn't fight and "go on breaks." It was sweet because Philip got a taste of his own medicine and it just made it so much better because it was his neighbor. Because every girl he hooked up with was someone I was acquainted with.

To this participant, the revenge was poetic because it matched in form the initial act of harm doing—"hooking up" with an acquaintance of the romantic partner after a fight was exactly what the boyfriend had done to her.

By contrast, non-poetic enactments of revenge featured an asymmetry of form, identified in 71% of reported incidents. Illustrative is this description of revenge in a friendship, which the participant heard about second-hand:

> I heard that a guy I know through a friend was dating this girl. He played this one guy in a game of beer pong and beat him pretty bad, trash talking the whole time. In response to this, the guy who lost and was berated by the guy with the girlfriend, proceeded to find his girl at the bar, and got her very drunk and took her back to his place and they had sex. The guy, while having sex with the girlfriend, took a cell phone picture and sent a message to the guy who beat him in beer pong. He obviously was very upset in receiving this message, and broke up with his girlfriend. The fact that trash talk and victory in beer pong would push that other person to take advantage of his girlfriend with alcohol is very inappropriate and not ironic at all. Basically, the whole act was malicious and ridiculous.

To this participant, the revenge act was non-poetic because the form of the revenge—having sex with the girlfriend while she was under the influence of alcohol—was regarded as malicious and inappropriate when contrasted against the fairly innocuous precipitating event.

**Symmetry of consequence.** This category was conceptualized as similarity in the quantity and/or quality of harm between what was experienced by the victim of the original harm doing and what was experienced by the wrongdoer through the enactment of revenge, and it emerged in 68.7% of the critical incidents. Such symmetry is illustrated in this account told by a person who witnessed the revenge but was neither the avenger nor the wrongdoer:

> I have 2 brothers and in high school they shared 1 car. My brother Matt would always bring the car home with no gas. So when Joe would go to use the car he would always have to go straight to the gas station. He would always ask Matt nicely then yell at him to get gas but he never would. Finally at the end of the summer Joe was on his way to a job interview and the car died from no gas and he missed the interview and lost the job. Joe left for school a couple of weeks later. Then Matt started complaining about a terrible smell coming from his car, but he couldn't find where it was coming from. It was the worst smell in the world. It got to the point where he couldn't drive it. After a few weeks, Joe called and told Joe to look in the first aid kit in the back. Before he left for school, Joe put a frozen package of chicken in it, and the smell was rotten, spoiled meat ... Matt caused Joe so much frustration about the gas and made it hard for Joe to use the car but then Joe made it hard for Matt to use the car ... So I think it was perfect he did something that made it hard for Matt to drive the car.

This revenge enactment illustrates symmetry of outcome—the harm to the original victim was matched by the same harm to the wrongdoer: frustration in finding it difficult to drive the car.

By contrast, asymmetry of consequence was frequently reported as a feature of non-poetic revenge, emerging in 57.3% of reported incidents. Representative is this account in which a participant described a three-act sequence consisting of harm-doing, revenge, and counter-revenge against the revenge act. During this participant's senior year of high school, a group of friends vandalized with toilet paper the house and cars of the participant and other friends. The participant and friends reciprocated, but this produced yet another round of revenge by the original wrongdoers:

> After we TPed the guys, they did it back to us but not just with toilet paper ... They put flour and water on our cars which chipped the paint and put people's garbage in our yards along with road signs. The neighbors were very upset with how the yards looked and even cops came to ask us about the signs. This is unsweet because they took it too far and what was once a harmless joke turned into something serious.

What qualified this incident as non-poetic revenge was the asymmetry of consequences: the inconvenience of cleaning up a sea of toilet paper versus serious damage to cars and yards.

**Benefit to others.** This category captures a revenge enactment in which at least one person benefits from the enactment; 41.2% of incidents featured this outcome. An example is provided in this account provided by the target of the revenge act:

> Well, when I was 17 I slept over at my friend's house ... and I got really really drunk ... When I got home my mother asked me ... if I was drunk and I denied and then she asked

what I was drinking and I had blurted out vodka; then immediately ran to the bathroom to puke. Then I rested most of the day to sober up. When I was sober enough I was experiencing the most intense hangover I've ever had. My mom came down to the basement where I had the lights off and told me I had to mow the lawn. To this day, I have never heard a more annoying or louder noise than the tractor's engine. I wish I could describe this evil sound, but even thinking about it now makes me cringe. After my near death experience, I wanted nothing to do with alcohol ... My dad found this hilarious and he loved watching me mow the lawn that wretched day.

Although one might regard this as merely an example of a mother teaching her son a lesson about his drinking practices, the participant regarded it as an act of poetic justice. His drunken behavior and its resultant sickness were an offenses to the mother, and she enacted poetic justice by asking him to complete his assigned chore of mowing the lawn. The participant explicitly pointed to the father's gratification in appreciating the humor of the revenge as a reason why it was poetic.

Non-poetic revenge was characterized by harm to other(s) and was identified in 44.3% of incidents. This feature is identified by the participant in the following account involving college roommates:

One of my roommates wrote on another one of my roommate's face when he was passed out, with a marker. So my roommate that got written on decided to get him back by pretty much destroying his room. He wrote on his walls and threw his clothes about the room. He also punctured an Axe bottle and threw it in his room, which made his room smell and the rest of the apartment ... His revenge affected the whole apartment because he made it smell. So he didn't just hurt the one roommate, he affected all of us.

What made this incident non-poetic to this participant was that all of the roommates suffered, not just the original perpetrator of the wrongdoing.

**Lesson learned by wrongdoer.** This category refers to revenge enactments in which the original wrongdoer learned his or her lesson and the harmful practice ceased. In order for there to be a lesson learned, the wrongdoer needed to "connect the dots," and see the original act of harm as an antecedent cause of the revenge; that is, the wrongdoer needed to see the revenge act as an instance of revenge embedded in the whole fabric of an antecedent-consequent sequence. A total of 30.5% of the participants identified this feature in their incident accounts. Illustrative of this category is this account provided by an avenger against her father:

When my dad's car has little gas left, he will sometimes take my car, leaving me with his empty tank ... In order to teach my dad a lesson, I decided to hide my keys when I knew he would opt to use my car ... I hid my keys ultimately to teach my dad a lesson and communicate the idea that this was an action that needed to stop. He received the message successfully and did not incur any serious costs in the process.

To this participant, the revenge was poetic because her father realized the whole sequence of events in which his action of leaving his daughter with an empty gas tank resulted in the hidden keys. He learned the lesson that actions have consequences, the key to poetic justice for this daughter.

Non-poetic revenge featured, but only to a limited extent (3.1% of incidents), the failure of the wrongdoer to learn a lesson from his or her actions. Illustrative is this account of an incident between two brothers, provided by a participant who was neither the wrongdoer nor the avenger:

> This guy just bought these new shoes that he really wanted for a long time and when he finally got them his brother stole them and wouldn't tell him where they were. A week later this kid who bought the shoes punched his brother in the face but never told him it was because of the shoes he just said he was being a jerk. There was an argument and they resolved it by saying that they were acting like jerks but never said what they were specifically talking about. It was unsweet because the revenge wasn't tied to the original act of revenge and didn't make the other person realize that they should stop acting a certain way.

To this participant, the act of revenge was non-poetic justice because the avenger failed to make the wrongdoer realize the antecedent-consequence sequence.

**Absence of relational harm.** This category refers to revenge enactments that did not result in harmful consequences for the relationship between the wrongdoer and the victim. This feature varied in salience by relationship type. Whereas 60% of poetic justice incidents reported for familial relationships featured the absence of relational harm, only 29% of romantic relationship incidents and 24% of friendship incidents featured this quality ($X^2$ (2) = 12.08; $p$ = .002).

Typically, relational harm was avoided by framing the revenge act as playful. Although revenge is an act of aggression, its framing as playful transformed the enactment into an instance of fun. Representative of this category is an account provided by a third party about a revenge enactment between siblings:

> My oldest brother initially provoked the act of revenge. He was visiting my older sister at college and he ended up getting [a ticket]. My brother was good at getting away with things but since my sister had to loan him the money for the ticket she got to tell him what to do for a long time. Since Emily had bailed Tony out of his ticket she had the power to tell mom and dad or to have Tony do whatever she wanted ... One sweet act of revenge was when she made him karaoke in front of a huge crowd of her friends ... I guess it was hilarious to watch him make a fool of himself ... Emily and Tony laughed about it and they both had a good time since they were spending time together ... It was appropriate because no one really got hurt and it was all in good fun and something they still joke about to this day.

To this participant, the poetic nature of the revenge enactment rested in the fact that it was "in good fun" and is, to this day, a source of playful amusement among the siblings.

By contrast, non-poetic justice featured harm to the relationship between the wrongdoer and the avenger. This feature was not equally salient across relationship types ($X^2$ (2) = 17.51; $p$ < .001). Only 5.7% of familial incidents were characterized by the presence of relational harm compared to 48.9% of romantic and 29.6% of friendship relationships. Typical of accounts coded with this feature is the following third-party account:

> Two girls were friends and one of them betrayed the other by telling a few people a secret shared between the two. The betrayed friend … went after her ex-friend's ex-boyfriend to get back at her. So she started dating her ex-friend's ex-boyfriend and although they are still together—a year later—her intentions were unsweet revenge. Because no matter what a friend does to you, *intentionally* going after their ex-boyfriend with the purpose to hurt the other person is not sweet revenge. (*emphasis in original*)

What classified this incident as non-poetic justice to the participant was a revenge act that violated the essential fabric of a relationship. To this participant, no transgression was worth intentional harm and the destruction of the friendship.

## REFLECTIONS

Taken as a whole, the five constituent features of poetic justice appear to maintain the face of the avenger, absolving him or her from a contaminated identity as a victim or as an aggressor. *Symmetry of form*, the most frequently identified feature, clearly functions to implicate the wrongdoer in his or her punishment. In matching the form of the revenge with the form of the original offense, the avenger can reasonably claim to others (including the wrongdoer) that the offender established the very terms of the revenge. Relatedly, the second most frequently identified feature, *symmetry of consequence*, also functions to buffer the avenger from the criticism of inappropriate aggression with respect to the intensity of the punishment. Symmetry of consequence also clearly displays retributive justice, a proportional or matched response to the original offensive act, one which earns just retribution to the person wronged, thereby avoiding an identity as a victim.

The features of *benefit to others* and *absence of relational harm* appear to buffer the avenger from a criticism that the revenge is an antisocial act, thereby further protecting the avenger from a spoiled identity. Because the revenge act is a contained and measured response, it limits the collateral damage to others and to other facets of the relationship between the offender and the offended beyond the immediate domain of misconduct. In fact, benefit to others goes beyond mere neutrality to a positive claim about how others profit from the revenge enactment. If executed well, the face implications of poetic justice are clear: the avenger is a moral agent who is acting in a prosocial, not antisocial, manner.

The fifth feature of poetic justice, *lesson learned by wrongdoer*, is demonstrated by evidence that the wrongdoer has correctly understood the revenge as a response to his or her misconduct. This demonstration could unfold either indirectly or directly. Indirectly, the avenger simply noted a change in behavior by the wrongdoer such that future occasions of the misconduct did not occur. Directly, the lesson learned involved an explicit offering by the wrongdoer as part of the remedial interchange, that is, providing the offended with restitution or with an account and apology to which the avenger could respond with acceptance. In contrast to retributive justice, which holds potential to restore the social and moral order through deterrence (i.e., the threat of future punishment should misconduct continue), an explicit offering by the wrongdoer displays restorative justice (e.g., Witvliet et al., 2008). Restorative justice shows explicit evidence of reflexivity and remorse by the wrongdoer, perhaps involving restitution in some form.

In order for poetic justice to restore the social and moral order without threatening the face of the avenger, the participants must properly frame the activity. The wrongdoer and third parties must perceive the symmetry of form and consequence of the revenge action in order to discern its irony as an instance of poetic justice. Others (including the wrongdoer) need to understand the prosocial quality of benefits to others and the absence of relational harm in order to foreclose a judgment of the avenger as antisocial. The absence of relational harm, for example, frequently involved a framing of the revenge enactment as play, allowing the wrongdoer to see the intention for the revenge as non-hostile. The play frame has been noted by other scholars (e.g., Baxter, 1992) as a way to do serious relational work while foreclosing negative attributions.

Future research can productively move forward in several directions. First, this study was limited to recalled incidents of poetic justice and its opposite from the perspective of one person—either the wrongdoer, the avenger, or a third-party observer. Researchers could triangulate perceptions of all of the parties implicated in a given enactment of poetic justice to determine the likelihood that participants see poetic justice similarly. For example, family members could be asked in a laboratory environment to talk about recalled poetic justice instances, allowing perspectives to be compared. Such triangulation would allow scholars to identify which of the poetic justice features are more or less challenging in producing framing convergence.

The incidents in our data set were snapshots lacking a longitudinal perspective. We do not know, for example, if poetic justice (and revenge more generally) is a strategy of last resort that is employed only after other, seemingly more prosocial tactics, have first been tried and failed. At one level, poetic justice can be viewed as a kind of social influence in which the avenger is attempting to persuade the wrongdoer to change his future behavior. Social influence research suggests that persuaders become less prosocial after being rebuffed by targets (e.g., Hample &

Dallinger, 1998). Researchers need to determine when, if at all, repeated efforts at remediation lead parties to turn to revenge more generally and poetic justice in particular.

Researchers could also benefit from a developmental perspective on poetic justice. Poetic justice is a communicative act of some nuance, requiring avengers to have considerable communication skill in message production and wrongdoers/observers to display considerable skill in message reception. It might be that the ability to recognize, appreciate, or enact poetic justice is one that comes with a certain level of maturity or age. Tripp et al. (2002) studied poetic justice in workplace settings, indicating that working-age adults engage in poetic justice as a means of restoring the social and moral order. In our sample of college students, participants were capable of recalling instances of poetic justice, recognizing its constituent features, and distinguishing it from non-poetic revenge. If young adults are familiar with and have even enacted poetic justice, when did they develop the ability to frame revenge as poetic justice? And when do social actors gain the communicative sophistication needed to execute all of the features that collectively constitute poetic justice? According to Tappan (2006), moral development is the process by which people gradually appropriate the moral mediational tools of words, language and forms of discourse. Perhaps it is the case that persons are not morally developed enough in early childhood to understand certain revenge scenarios as poetic justice. There were instances of poetic justice reported by participants that had occurred years before, during late childhood or adolescence. Is it the case that instances like these were recognized at the time as poetic justice, as participants indicated they had been? Or, is it possible that they became framed as poetic justice in hindsight, after participants reached a certain level of moral development at which they became capable of framing a complex relational phenomenon as such?

Understanding how our moral compasses are developed throughout the lifespan would enrich our knowledge of good relationships and moral communication. Notably, poetic justice itself seems to qualify as a mediational tool of moral development in two ways. First, our participants reported that teaching wrongdoers moral lessons was an important feature of poetic justice, implying that by experiencing poetic justice, we learn how to be relationally moral. Second, it was indicated by our participants that stories of poetic justice are shared among members of social networks. Presumably, in addition to possible entertainment value, narratives of poetic justice function to inform and remind listeners of the right and wrong ways to interact. Cultural narratives carry moral and explanatory value and are used in interpersonal dialogue for specific purposes; among those is self-positioning and the resolution of moral dilemmas (Haste & Abrahams, 2008).

Poetic justice narratives might constitute one genre of cultural narratives that are highly important to our moral development (Haste & Abrahams, 2008). Often, in children's books and films there is an antagonist who bullies the protagonist. That antagonist often "gets what's coming" to him or her in the end, while the protagonist manages to keep his or her "nose clean," while still enjoying the bully's fate (e.g., *The Little Rascals*). This recurring theme indicates that poetic justice might serve as a cultural narrative of morality. Haste and Abrahams argue, "'Development' comprises increasing sophistication in the use of such narratives and in the *processes* of dialogue and interaction" (p. 379, emphasis in original). It might be that the more morally developed one is, the more inclined one is to restore moral order through the use of poetic justice rather than other means, and the more inclined one is to teach others to be moral through the use of poetic justice narratives. There were instances in our study in which participants reported poetic justice scenarios that purportedly happened to third parties, friends of friends, that might be, in actuality, the stuff of urban legend. Rather than diminish the moral force of the story, if this is true it seems to support our argument that poetic justice narratives serve an important function in maintaining the social and moral order.

Poetic justice also should be examined in the context of power structures. Under what conditions of relational power is poetic justice enacted or appreciated? Perhaps those in a power-up position can exact revenge without the negative social sanctions that might be directed to power-down individuals. Poetic justice thus might be enacted disproportionately by those most in need of face protection from social criticism as antisocial aggressors; that is, power-down individuals. In this sense, poetic justice might function as an indirect form of resistance to domination (e.g., Scott, 1990). Tripp et al. (2002) did find poetic justice particularly useful for protecting those with less power from negativity from those with more power. Noteworthy is the fact that in our study participants reported sometimes teaching their parents lessons through poetic justice, but always with a playful tone. This indicates that, perhaps, we are never morally developed enough in the lifespan to be immune to moral reminders. It also might indicate that in some relationships, where there is a power differential, poetic justice should be carried out and framed more carefully and to emphasize lightheartedness to reduce face loss and relational harm to those involved.

Interestingly, only one of the features of poetic justice, *absence of relational harm*, was differentially salient by relationship type. In particular, this feature was more salient in instances of poetic justice between family members than among either friends or romantic partners. As noted above, mainstream American culture regards family relationships as nonvoluntary compared to other close relationship forms (e.g., Hess, 2000) or at least challenging to dissolve (Scharp, 2014). Absence of relational harm might be more salient in family relationships than in other relationships because parties perceive that they must live with the consequences of the poetic justice for the rest of their lives.

Our arguments about the possible functions associated with the features of poetic justice merit empirical research to determine their reasonableness. For example, the utilitarian function of remedial correction might be more or less salient than the face protection function. Poetic justice could productively be compared with other forms of revenge to determine if there are any differences in either utilitarian outcomes or face-saving. For example, does retributive justice, outside of a poetic justice frame, produce different behavioral outcomes by the wrongdoer and different face threats to the avenger?

Poetic justice is a complex communicative practice that nicely exemplifies Spitzberg and Cupach's (2007) observation that the "dark side" and the "light side" of communication often do not function in a binary manner. Poetic justice, as a form of revenge, is a dark-sided act of retaliation in directing punishment toward a wrongdoer. However, the features that laypersons attribute to poetic justice allow us to understand it as a prosocial act that absolves the avenger of socially contaminated identities of *victim* or *aggressor*, while holding potential to restore the social and moral order through either deterrence or restorative justice.

## REFERENCES

Barreca, R. (1995). *Sweet revenge: The wicked delights of getting even.* New York, NY: Harmony Books.

Baxter, L. A. (1992). Forms and functions of intimate play in personal relationships. *Human Communication Research, 18,* 336–363. doi:10.1111/j.1468-2958.1992.tb00556.x

Berglar, E. (1946). Poetic justice and its unconscious background. *Medical Record, 1,* 548–550.

Bies, R. J. (1987). The predicament of injustice. The management of moral outrage. In L. L. Cummings & B. M. Staw (Eds.), *Research in organizational behavior* (Vol. 9, pp. 289–239). Greenwich, CT: JAI Press.

Bies, R. J., & Tripp, T. M. (1995). The use and abuse of power: Justice as social control. In R. Cropanzano & M. Kacmar (Eds.), *Politics, justice, and support: Managing social climate at work* (pp. 131–146). Westport, CT: Quorum Press.

Bies, R. J., Tripp, T. M., & Kramer, R. M. (1997). At the breaking point: Cognitive and social dynamics of revenge in organizations. In R. A. Giacalone & J. Greenberg (Eds.), *Anti-social behavior in organizations* (pp. 18–36). Thousand Oaks, CA: Sage.

Boon, S. D., Deveau, V. L., & Alibhai, A. M. (2009). Payback: The parameters of revenge in romantic relationships. *Journal of Social and Personal Relationships, 26,* 747–768. doi:10.1177/0265407509347926

Brown, P., & Levinson, S. G. (1987). *Politeness: Some universals in language usage.* New York, NY: Cambridge University Press.

Carlsmith, K. M., Wilson, T. D., & Gilbert, D. T. (2008). The paradoxical consequences of revenge. *Journal of Personality and Social Psychology, 95,* 1316–1324. doi:10.1037/a0012165

Erlandson, D. A., Harris, E. L., Skipper, B. L., & Allen, S. D. (1993). *Doing naturalistic inquiry: A guide to methods.* Newbury Park, CA: Sage.

Forschler, S. (2012). Revenge, poetic justice, resentment, and The Golden Rule. *Philosophy and Literature, 36,* 1–16. doi:10.1353/phl.2012.0021

Goffman, E. (1959). *The presentation of self in everyday life.* New York, NY: Anchor Books.

Goffman, E. (1967). *Interaction ritual: Essays on face-to-face behavior.* New York, NY: Anchor Books.

Goffman, E. (1971). *Relations in public.* New York, NY: Harper Colophon Books.

Goffman, E. (1974). *Frame analysis: An essay on the organization of experience.* Cambridge, MA: Harvard University Press.

Goffman, E. (1983). The interaction order. *American Sociological Review, 48,* 1–17.

Gollwitzer, M., & Denzler, M. (2009). What makes revenge sweet: Seeing the offender suffer or delivering a message? *Journal of Experimental Social Psychology, 45,* 840–844. doi:10.1016/j.jesp.2009.03.001

Gollwitzer, M., Meder, M., & Schmitt, M. (2011). What gives victims satisfaction when they seek revenge? *European Journal of Psychology, 41,* 364–374. doi:10.1002/ejsp.782

Grice, H. P. (1989). *Studies in the way of words.* Cambridge, MA: Harvard University Press.

Hample, D., & Dallinger, J. M. (1998). On the etiology of the rebuff phenomenon: Why are persuasive messages less polite after rebuffs? *Communication Studies, 49,* 305–321. doi:10.1080/10510979809368541

Haste, H., & Abrahams, S. (2008). Morality, culture and the dialogic self: Taking cultural pluralism seriously. *Journal of Moral Education, 37*(3), 377–394. Retrieved from: www.tandfonline.com/.../03057240802227502

Hayes, A. F. (2005). *Statistical methods for communication science.* Mahwah, NJ: Lawrence Erlbaum.

Hess, J. A. (2000). Maintaining nonvoluntary relationships with disliked partners: An investigation into the use of distancing behaviors. *Human Communication Research, 3,* 458–488. doi:10.1111/j.1468-2958.2000.tb00765.x

Leidner, B., Castano, E., & Ginges, J. (2013). Dehumanization, retributive and restorative justice, and aggressive versus diplomatic intergroup conflict resolution strategies. *Personality and Social Psychology Bulletin, 39,* 181–192. doi:10.1177/0146167212472208

Lindlof, T. R., & Taylor, B. C. (2002). *Qualitative communication research methods* (2nd ed.). Thousand Oaks, CA: Sage.

Mead, G. H. (1934). *Mind, self, & society: Vol. 1 of the works of George Herbert Mead* (Ed. by C. W. Morris). Chicago, IL: University of Chicago Press.

Morrill, C. (1996). *The executive way: Conflict management in corporations.* Chicago, IL: University of Chicago Press.

O'Leary-Kelly, A. M., Griffin, R. W., & Glew, D. J. (1996). Organization-motivated aggression: A research framework. *Academy of Management Review, 21,* 225–253. Retrieved from: http://www.jstor.org/stable/258635

Owen, W. F. (1984). Interpretive themes in relational communication. *Quarterly Journal of Speech, 70,* 274–287. doi:10.1080/00335638409383697

Scharp, K. (2014). *(De)constructing "family": Communicatively accomplishing estrangement between adult children and their parents.* Unpublished doctoral dissertation, University of Iowa.

Scott, J. C. (1990). *Domination and the arts of resistance.* New Haven, CT: Yale University Press.

Shweder, R., Much, N., Mahapatra, M., & Park, L. (1997). The "big three" of morality (autonomy, community, divinity) and the "big three" explanations of suffering. In A. M. Brandt & P. Rozin (Eds.), *Morality and health* (pp. 119–172). London, UK: Routledge.

Simmel, G. (1950). *The sociology of Georg Simmel* (Trans. & Ed., Kurt Wolff). New York, NY: The Free Press.

Smetana, J. G. (2011). *Adolescents, families, and social development: How teens construct their worlds.* New York NY: Wiley/Blackwell.

Smith, G. (2006). *Erving Goffman.* New York, NY: Routledge.

Spitzberg, B. H., & Cupach, W. R. (2007). Disentangling the dark side of interpersonal communication. In B. H. Spitzberg & W. R. Cupach (Eds.), *The dark side of interpersonal communication* (2nd ed., pp. 3–28). Mahwah, NJ: Lawrence Erlbaum Associates, Inc.

Stouten, J., De Cremer, D., & van Dijk, E. (2006). Violating equality in social dilemmas: Emotional and retributive reactions as a function of trust, attribution, and honesty. *Personality and Social Psychology Bulletin, 32,* 894–907. doi:10.1177/0146167206287538

Tappan, M. B. (2006). Mediated moralities: Sociocultural approaches to moral development. In M. Killen & J. Smetana (Eds.), *Handbook of moral development* (pp. 351–374). Mahwah, NJ: Lawrence Erlbaum.

Tripp, T. M., & Bies, R. J. (1997). What's good about revenge: The avenger's perspective. In R. J. Lewicki, R. J. Bies, & B. H. Sheppard (Eds.), *Research on negotiation in organizations* (Vol. 6, pp. 145–160). Greenwich, CT: JAI Press.

Tripp, T. M., Bies, R. J., & Aquino, K. (2002). Poetic justice or petty jealousy? The aesthetics of revenge. *Organizational Behavior and Human Decision Processes, 89,* 966–984. doi:10.1016/SO749-5978902)00038-9

Witvliet, C. V. O., Worthington, E. L., Root, L. M., Sato, A. F., Ludwig, T. E., & Exline, J. (2008). Retributive justice, restorative justice, and forgiveness. *Journal of Experimental Social Psychology, 44,* 10–25. doi:10.1016/j.jesp.2007.01.009

Yoshimura, S. (2007). Goals and emotional outcomes of revenge activities in interpersonal relationships. *Journal of Social and Personal Relationships, 24,* 87–98. doi:10.1177/0265407507072592

## NOTES

1. For details of the comparisons described in this paragraph, contact the lead author at leslie-baxter@uiowa.edu.
2. Additional "miscellaneous" features also emerged but are not reported here due to space limitations.

# CHAPTER SEVEN

# The Morality OF Revealing Others' Secrets

ANITA L. VANGELISTI & ERIN C. NELSON

*Through the study of secrecy, we encounter what human beings want above all to protect: the sacred, the intimate, the fragile, the dangerous, and the forbidden*

—BOK, 1983, p. 281

Secrets are often shared, then re-told, and even shared again. In fact, when people are told a secret about someone else, it is not uncommon for them to disclose the secret to a third party. In some cases, the reasons people divulge a secret about someone else are frivolous or self-serving. Individuals reveal the secret because it is entertaining, because it fits into a particular conversation, or because it affords them social status. In other cases, the reasons are much more serious. People may disclose a secret in an effort to protect someone from harm or even in an effort to save someone's life. When people choose to divulge a secret about someone else, they make judgments about whether to disclose and whether the reasons they might disclose are good ones. Because revealing secrets can have substantial influences on individuals and their personal relationships, the criteria that people use in deciding whether to divulge secrets—and the way they evaluate those criteria—are important.

The purpose of the current chapter is to examine the moral assessments associated with revealing secrets about other people. First, the morality involved in

AUTHOR NOTE: The authors are indebted to Vincent Waldron and Douglas Kelley for their invaluable feedback on this chapter.

divulging others' secrets is discussed. Then, criteria for revealing secrets are examined. The findings of a study exploring secrets about others that individuals noted they disclosed for "good reasons" are presented. Finally, some of the factors that may influence people's moral evaluations concerning reasons for revealing others' secrets are discussed.

## THE MORALITY OF SECRETS

Bok (1983) suggested that revealing secrets is a moral act. Decisions to divulge secret information involve moral issues because, as Bok notes, secrets "concern the protection of what we are, what we intend, what we do, and what we own" (p. 20). Secrets, in other words, safeguard individuals' identity, their goals, their actions, and even their possessions. They involve information that people see as important. Even secrets that focus on seemingly trivial issues (e.g., a child deciding not to tell her father what her favorite color is) may involve salient relational concerns (e.g., the child's desire for more autonomy or her effort to garner attention from her father). As a consequence, decisions to disclose a secret about another person have moral ramifications. More specifically, decisions to reveal a secret are moral when the revelation is perceived as having a positive or negative effect on the well-being of individuals or their relationships.

Some of the moral concerns associated with secret revelation are evident in the effects that divulging a secret has on the *individuals* involved. Disclosure can influence the person who tells the secret, the individual who is the focus of the secret, and the person who is the recipient of the secret information. The individual who tells the secret may gain a sense of power, competence, or moral virtue by disclosing the information. At the same time, he or she may feel guilty or anxious about the revelation. The person who is the focus of the secret may lose a sense of control and may face tasks associated with retooling his or her identity or, if the secret was burdensome, he or she may experience a degree of relief.[1] The individual who receives the information may gain status because of the new knowledge or may feel anxiety about how to respond to what he or she has learned. In each of these cases, revealing secret information influences individuals' psychological or emotional well-being.

Deciding to divulge secret information about another also can affect a number of different interpersonal *relationships*. Most obviously, it can influence the relationship between the person who tells the secret and the person who is the focus of the secret. If both parties are aware that keeping the secret was important, and if both are aware of the disclosure, any trust that characterized their relationship may be damaged. The association between the individual who is the focus of the secret and the person who receives the information also may change. The previously withheld information may affect one or both person's identity, it may change the goals of one or both individuals, and it may affect the way both parties behave toward each other. Further, and in addition to any effects that the content of the secret may have on their relationship, the understanding that a secret was kept, in the first place, may affect the way they interact. Another relationship that can be influenced by the disclosure is the one between the person who revealed the information and the individual who received it. In some cases, the bond between these two parties may be strengthened because they share information that was previously unshared. In other cases, such as when the disclosure was unwelcome, this relationship may become more strained. Divulging a secret, in short, can have a number of different positive and negative effects on relationships. Decisions to disclose secret information, thus, often have moral ramifications.

Because the impact of divulging secrets is so far reaching, the decisions people make about disclosing secrets—and the moral implications of disclosure—can be very complex (Caughlin, Scott, Miller, & Hefner, 2009; Caughlin, Vangelisti, & Mikucki-Enyart, 2013). Those who are contemplating disclosure may not only consider the aforementioned individual and relational effects of revealing the secret, but they also may consider how those effects are likely to evolve over time. The short-term effects of revealing a secret may differ from the long-term effects. That is, a positive effect in the short-term (e.g., more status or power for the person who reveals the secret) may become negative in the long term (e.g., fewer close friends). Conversely, a negative short-term outcome (e.g., the loss of trust) may evolve into a positive effect over time (e.g., safe guarding the physical or mental well-being of a person who was engaging in risky behavior). Individuals may decide to tell a secret because it is "the right thing to do" in the long-run even though it violates certain moral commitments (e.g., keeping a promise or being loyal) in the short-run.

In addition to evaluating possible changes in the effects of their disclosure, people who are considering whether to divulge a secret are likely to think about whether—and to what degree—the disclosure will influence their goals. Some outcomes may be consistent with their goals, whereas others may run in opposition to their goals. Further, as noted by Caughlin (2010) individuals hold multiple goals and some of those goals may conflict with others. Decisions about whether to reveal another person's secret sometimes force people to confront conflicting goals. For instance, individuals considering disclosure may have to weigh goals they have about being liked by others against goals about maintaining certain moral standards.

The evaluations that people make concerning their goals and the various outcomes associated with divulging a secret are evidenced in the criteria they employ to determine whether or not to reveal the secret to others. Those criteria, in turn, offer information about the moral reasoning involved in people's decisions about disclosing the secret as well as the extent to which they will use discretion in telling the secret to others.

## CRITERIA FOR REVEALING SECRETS

Criteria for revealing secrets are "the prerequisites or standards people use to judge whether they should divulge secret information" (Vangelisti, Caughlin, & Timmerman, 2001, p. 1). When people describe the conditions under which they would tell a secret, most will acknowledge that some of those conditions or prerequisites are more worthy, morally defensible, or important to uphold than others. In other words, they recognize that some criteria involve more positive effects on the well-being of individuals or their relationships than do others. For instance, criteria that involve others' physical welfare, prosocial outcomes, and long-term relational goals may be seen as better reasons for divulging a secret than those that focus on self-promotion or self-gratification. Decisions based on the former set of criteria, thus, are likely to be viewed as more moral or ethical than are those based on the latter set.

Although theoretical evidence that people evaluate criteria for revealing secrets is relatively clear, empirical evidence has not been as forthcoming. The conditions under which people reveal secret information, however, offer some insight into the criteria individuals use in making decisions about disclosing secrets. Vangelisti et al. (2001) argue that people disclose personal or secret information under several conditions. The first is when keeping the secret threatens individuals' well-being. Clinicians, researchers, and theorists have argued that the failure or inability to disclose secrets can have deleterious effects on people's psychological and physical health (Finkenauer & Rime, 1998; Imber-Black, 1993; Karpel, 1980). Studies have demonstrated, for example, that individuals who kept personal secrets from others were more anxious and depressed than those who did not (Larson & Chastain, 1990). Further, people who supressed their feelings and thoughts about traumatic events visited health centers more often and exhibited poorer immune function than did those who expressed their thoughts and feelings (Greenberg & Stone, 1992; Pennebaker & Beall, 1986; Pennebaker, Kiecolt-Glaser, & Glaser, 1988; Petrie, Booth, Pennebaker, Davison, & Thomas, 1995).

Although most researchers accept the notion that withholding information can be associated with negative outcomes, it is important to acknowledge that the portrayal of secrecy as uniformly negative has been deemed short-sighted (see Bochner, 1982; Parks, 1982). The way people express their thoughts and feelings can affect whether divulging secrets is linked to positive or negative outcomes. For example, Pennebaker, Mayne, and Francis (1997) found that the words individuals used in revealing personal information were associated with their well-being. People who used words related to insightful or causal thinking engaged in more adaptive behavior and had greater improvements in their health than those who did not. There also is evidence that continually thinking or talking about negative events can increase distress (Wegner & Wenzlaff, 1996). Richards and Sillars

(2014) found that people who frequently thought about interactions associated with their secrets had poorer health outcomes than did those who did not. It may be that divulging negative information is initially linked to positive psychological and physical outcomes, but that repeated disclosure encourages people to ruminate about the negative information and, as a result, is linked to relatively negative outcomes.

A second condition under which people reveal secrets is when they anticipate the response they will get from a confidant is positive. When individuals divulge their secrets to others, they place themselves in a vulnerable position (Kelvin, 1977). Others may evaluate the content of their disclosure or the act of disclosure as undesirable, inappropriate, or immoral. Because disclosing personal information is risky (Petronio, 2000), people tend to be selective about who they choose as confidants, evaluating whether potential confidants will respond to the disclosure in positive or negative ways (T. Afifi & Steuber, 2009; Brown-Smith, 1998; Fisher, 1986; Omarzu, 2000).

Kelly and McKillop (1996) suggest that individuals assess several qualities of a potential confidant to evaluate the response they are likely to receive when they disclose a secret. One is the degree to which the confidant is discreet. Kelley and McKillop argue that people should target individuals for disclosure who are unlikely to reveal the secret to others. The authors also suggest that possible confidants should be non-judgmental. Indeed, studies show that people are more likely to reveal personal information to others who are accepting (Pennebaker, 1990) and less likely to disclose when the image portrayed by the disclosure is viewed by others as undesirable (Rosenfeld, 1979). Finally, Kelly and McKillop note that confidants should provide people with support or offer them a new perspective on issues associated with the secret, suggesting that good confidants are those who offer some sort of reward in exchange for the disclosure. In line with these recommendations, W. A. Afifi and Caughlin (2006) found that when people revealed secret information and perceived the target's reaction as positive, they were less likely to ruminate about the secret.

Of course, a positive response from a confidant often is contingent upon the context in which a disclosure occurs. A third condition associated with the revelation of secret information is when the communication context creates an opportunity for disclosure. Researchers and theorists have long acknowledged that prior disclosures (or the lack thereof) create a context for current disclosures. More specifically, the "norm of reciprocity" (Gouldner, 1960) or the "dyadic effect" (Jourard, 1971) suggests that people often return another individual's disclosure by revealing personal information themselves (Dindia, Fitzpatrick, & Kenny, 1997). People also may divulge personal or secret information in response to inquiries. Studies suggest that general questions about an individual's well-being sometimes are viewed as opportunities for disclosure (Petronio, Reeder, Hecht, & Ros-Mendoza, 1996).

In addition to characteristics of the conversation, characteristics of the physical environment can create an opening for divulging secret information (Altman, 1975). Petronio and her colleagues (1996) found that children who were sexually abused chose particular circumstances to reveal information about their abuse to others. The researchers noted, for example, that the children sought out places that made them feel relatively comfortable and that minimized the fears they had. By selecting some physical contexts over others, the children were able to control some of the risks associated with their disclosure.

A fourth circumstance when people reveal secrets is when they perceive the impact of divulging the secret will be positive for others. Even though secrets often involve information that people see as negative (Karpel, 1980; Vangelisti, 1994), there are situations when revealing that negative information has positive outcomes. For instance, disclosing negative information can serve as a form of social support. Therapeutic support groups are based on this premise. When one person in the group reveals a negative experience or a poor choice, others in the group can benefit. Revealing the secret can allow group members to seek input and can alleviate some of their negative feelings about their own experiences (Derlega, Metts, Petronio, & Margulis, 1993). Another case when divulging a secret can have positive outcomes for others is when it draws individuals' attention to a problem that needs to be addressed. People often hide information about substance abuse, mental health challenges, and physical abuse from others (Imber-Black, 1993). Revealing a secret about a friend's alcoholism, a romantic partner's manic episodes, or a family member's abusive behavior often is risky, but it may be morally justified because it is the only means to encourage the friend, romantic partner, or family member to change his or her behavior.

While there are many cases when divulging a secret is risky, there are also instances when disclosure involves relatively little risk and substantial reward for the teller. A fifth circumstance under which people reveal personal or secret information is when the impact of the disclosure is rewarding. Because secret information often is deemed important, revealing that information can accord individuals a degree of power or status. Bok (1983) notes that people who show they have access to secrets have power because they are able to grant access to others. Individuals also can divulge secrets as a means of obtaining validation for their ideas or experiences (Derlega & Grzelak, 1979). Telling a secret about a hurtful incident or a difficult relationship to the right person can provide the teller with a confirming, empathetic response that would not be obtained otherwise.

Although the aforementioned circumstances for revealing secrets provide a picture of some of the criteria individuals use when making decisions about divulging secrets, they do not indicate how people evaluate those criteria. Research suggests not only that individuals evaluate criteria for telling secrets in terms of whether they are good or important, but also that good or important reasons sometimes take precedence over other reasons. Vangelisti, Caughlin, and Timmerman (2001) found that when people were asked to rate various criteria they might use in deciding to reveal a family secret, they rated having an "important reason" as significantly higher than any of the other criteria. Even those who reported they were unlikely to divulge a secret noted they would consider revealing it if there was a good or important reason to do so.[2] These findings indicate not only that individuals evaluate possible criteria for revealing secrets, but also that they assess some criteria as better, more important, or more worthy than others. The findings also raise questions about how people conceptualize good or important reasons for divulging secrets—some reasons may be seen as good because they are moral, whereas others may be viewed as good because they are efficient or rewarding.

## "GOOD REASONS" FOR REVEALING SECRETS: A STUDY

Given that relatively little is known about the way people evaluate criteria for revealing others' secrets, our understanding of the secrets people reveal and the reasons they reveal them is limited. When individuals make a decision to divulge a secret about someone else, they make a number of assessments about their own well-being, the response of possible confidants, the communication context, and possible outcomes for themselves and others. Each of these assessments may have moral implications. Still, the nature of secrets that people think they should disclose and the reasons they believe they should disclose those secrets are unclear. The current study was conducted to investigate the secrets that individuals say they disclose for *good reasons* and to explore what individuals perceive as good reasons for telling others' secrets. To examine the topics of secrets that people reveal for good reasons and as well as people's understanding of the reasons they divulged those secrets, the following two research questions were posited:

RQ1: What are the topics of secrets that people reveal for *good reasons*?
RQ2: What do people perceive are *good reasons* for revealing a secret?

### Method

Three hundred twenty-nine undergraduate students enrolled in communication courses served as respondents in the study. Of the total, 192 were women and 136 were men. One participant opted not to report his or her sex. The average age of participants was 20.11 years ($SD = 1.48$).

Participants were asked to recall and describe a secret about someone else that they told another person because they thought there was a good reason to reveal it. Then they were asked to explain the reason they decided to reveal the secret.[3]

The topics of the secrets described by participants were coded using the category scheme initially developed by Vangelisti (1994) to describe family secrets. A coder first read all of the responses generated by the first prompt and then categorized them into one of the 20 topic categories. To check the reliability of this procedure, a second coder independently read and coded approximately 25% of the data. Kappa was calculated at .93.

Participants' descriptions of the reasons they revealed the secrets were coded using inductive analysis (Bulmer, 1979). Two coders separately read approximately half of the data and each generated a category scheme. They met to discuss the categories they generated, refine them, and develop definitions for each category. Then, one of the coders categorized the data. To check the reliability of this procedure, the second coder categorized approximately 25% of the data (Kappa = .87).

## Results

**Secret topics.** Findings indicated that the secrets people reported revealing for good reasons revolved around a variety of topics. They included *extradyadic relationships, mental health, sexual relations, dating partners, substance abuse, illegal activities, physical health problems, physical/psychological abuse, breaking rules, drinking/partying, sexual preferences, premarital pregnancy, family problems, grades/academic achievement, abortion, personality conflicts, finances, religion, death,* and *cohabitation* (see Table 1).

Table 1. Descriptions and Frequencies of Secret Topics Revealed for "Good Reasons."

| Description | Frequency |
| --- | --- |
| *Extradyadic relationship*: romantic relations outside of an existing relationship that the focal person has had or is having | 71 (21.5%) |
| *Mental health*: issues or problems surrounding the mental state or capacity of the focal person | 42 (12.8%) |
| *Sexual relations*: sexual history, sexual relationships, or sexual activities of the focal person | 30 (9.1%) |
| *Dating partners*: information related to who the focal person is/was dating | 29 (8.8%) |
| *Substance abuse*: the abuse of or addiction to drugs or alcohol by the focal person | 21 (6.4%) |
| *Illegal activities*: activities carried out by the focal person that are illegal | 18 (5.5%) |
| *Physical health problems*: problems relating to the focal person's physical health | 16 (4.8%) |

Table 1. (Continued)

| Description | Frequency |
| --- | --- |
| *Physical/Psychological abuse*: physical, mental or sexual abuse; the focal person is/was abused or knows about someone else who is/was abused | 13 (3.9%) |
| *Breaking rules*: actions of the focal person that violate known rules or regulations | 12 (3.6%) |
| *Drinking/partying*: behaviors that involve the social consumption of alcohol/drugs by the focal person | 12 (3.6%) |
| *Sexual preferences*: sexual preferences of the focal person with regard to sex and/or specific practices | 10 (3.0%) |
| *Premarital pregnancy*: pregnancy prior to marriage that directly involves the focal person | 8 (2.4%) |
| *Family problems*: divorce or other family-related issues experienced or known by the focal person | 7 (2.1%) |
| *Grades/Academic Achievement*: the academic performance or activities of the focal person | 6 (1.8%) |
| *Abortion*: circumstances or issues concerning the intentional termination of a pregnancy by the focal person | 5 (1.5%) |
| *Personality conflict*: circumstances or qualities associated with long-term conflict between the focal person and someone else. | 2 (0.6%) |
| *Finances*: issues related to money, business, or other financial matters involving the focal person | 2 (0.6%) |
| *Religion*: issues related to religious or ideological beliefs or practices of the focal person | 1 (0.3%) |
| *Death*: issues or circumstances surrounding the death of someone in the focal person's life | 1 (0.3%) |
| *Cohabitation*: the premarital cohabitation of a focal person with a romantic partner | 1 (0.3%) |

*Note.* Uncodable responses are not included in the table (*n* = 22, 6.7%).

The most frequently noted secret topic focused on *extradyadic relationships*. One participant reported, for example, "One of my guy friends was cheating on his girlfriend who was a really good friend of mine." Another wrote, "My buddy has been cheating on his soon to be wife. It has always been rather easy for him to get girlfriends, so it just kind of happens." In the majority of cases, people revealed the information about the extradyadic relationship to the individual who was the victim of the affair. However, in some cases, they decided to divulge the secret to a third party. For instance, one participant noted, "I revealed a very personal secret to my best friend. I told him that his father was cheating on his mother." Participants clearly viewed these extradyadic relationships as wrong and felt a moral imperative to inform certain individuals about them.

Secrets involving *mental health* issues also were disclosed relatively frequently. Individuals revealed secrets about the psychological or emotional problems experienced by an acquaintance, friend, or family member. One participant wrote, "My friend had problems with hurting herself by cutting different parts of her body." Another reported that "One of my friends was thinking about committing suicide. She had mentioned it to a few of my [other] friends." A third noted, "My girlfriend had an eating disorder." Participants' descriptions of secrets about mental health typically involved issues that posed a threat to an individual's safety or well-being.

People also frequently disclosed secrets about *sexual relations*. These secrets involved sex, but were distinct from those focused on extradyadic relationships in that they did not include cheating on a partner. For instance, one individual noted, "My ex-best friend slept with this guy on the deck of another one of my best friend's lake house." In this case, the participant told the owner of the lake house (one of her best friends) about her former friend's sexual activities at the house. Another person wrote, "A classmate on an out of town trip was staying in the same hotel room as me. He and another guy had engaged in sexual relations while they thought I was asleep." This person was disturbed about the sex he witnessed and told a third party about it. One participant reported, "My best friend in high school would sneak out of her house to have sex with her ex-boyfriend." Like the participants in the other two examples, this person saw the sexual activities as wrong or inappropriate—and felt that others (her best friend's parents) also would see them as such.

Although several of the secret topics only were reported by one or two individuals, they were nonetheless described as salient. Indeed, the least frequently noted topics—*religion*, *death*, and *cohabitation*—involved information that participants noted affected individuals' relationships in substantial ways. For example, one person who described a secret about religion noted, "One of my guy friends talked to me a while ago and told me some interesting things about his girlfriend. He said that she wished she was a bigger Christian … he told me not to tell anybody. I didn't realize he was going to break up with her a week later." Another individual who divulged a secret about death reported, "My friend's dad died when she was really little … nobody talks about it." A third person who revealed information about cohabitation said, "I told my mom that my college best friend was no longer living at our apartment b/c she had essentially moved in with her boyfriend … I was worried because I hadn't heard from or seen my friend in several weeks." In all three of these cases, people noted the hidden information was cause for concern—either for themselves or for others who were unaware of the secret.

**"Good reasons" for revealing secrets.** As can been seen in Table 2, people offered a number of different explanations as good reasons for revealing the secrets they reported. These included *concern for welfare, right to know, storytelling/gossip, self-expression, relationship influence,* and *self-interest.*

Table 2. Descriptions and Frequencies of "Good Reasons" for Revealing Others' Secrets.

| Description | Frequency |
| --- | --- |
| *Concern for welfare*: to promote the well-being of the focal person | 86 (26.1%) |
| *Right to know*: to provide the recipient with information that he or she deserves to know | 83 (25.2%) |
| *Storytelling/Gossip*: to contribute to a conversation because the secret was interesting or humorous | 56 (17.0%) |
| *Self-expression*: to make one's own thoughts or feelings about the secret known | 47 (14.3%) |
| *Relationship influence*: to affect or maintain the state of a relationship | 29 (8.8%) |
| *Self-interest*: to defend or protect the self from negative circumstances and/or to benefit from the secret information | 15 (4.6%) |

*Note.* Uncodable responses are not included in the table ($N$ = 13, 4.0%)

The reasons participants noted most often were *concern for* (the focal person's) *welfare* and the recipient's *right to know*. Individuals who told a secret to a third party because they were concerned for the focal person's welfare gave explanations such as, "We decided to tell because we were concerned about her. We didn't want anything bad to happen." These individuals often were worried about the risk associated with the focal person's behavior. For instance, one participant explained, "I told my friend [about what his girlfriend was doing] because of the potential danger his girlfriend was putting herself in." Another person noted, "I was worried about his health and safety," whereas another simply stated, "B/c she needed help!"

In contrast to those who were concerned for the focal person, individuals who revealed the secret because someone had a right to know were concerned that someone was unaware of the concealed information. These people suggested that a particular individual deserved to know about the secret because it affected his or her well-being. For example, one participant wrote, "I didn't think it was right for the girl to keep that from her boyfriend. He deserved to know what she did so he didn't waste any more of his time with her." Another explained, "I felt that she needed to know because relationships should be based in truth. Plus if the same happened to me I would want to know so I could make the most informed decision."

The reasons mentioned least frequently by respondents were *self-interest* and *relationship influence*. People who divulged a secret because of self-interest explained that they told to protect themselves or to obtain something they desired. For instance, one person who told about a roommate's illegal activities noted, "I felt like if his enemies found out where he lived then I might get in trouble just by association." Another explained that, "She hadn't told her parents and she had back-stabbed me—[I told them to get] revenge." Another said, "I guess I told people because, in a way, it validated my own self-worth." For these individuals, telling the secret was a means to guard themselves, support their identity, or attain something they wanted or needed.

Those who disclosed a secret in order to influence a relationship noted that revealing the information would help them shape the quality of a particular relationship. In some cases, individuals' motives appeared to be prosocial. For instance, one person said that she told a secret to help a group of friends understand the behavior of another friend. She noted, "I just wanted them to be able to empathize with her and let her know we were there for her. I just didn't want our friends to be angry with her for acting different." By contrast, other people indicated that their motives were less than positive. One participant reported, for instance, that she told a secret "so my current best friend would hate my roommate." This individual divulged the secret information to negatively affect the association between her best friend and her roommate. Spoiling that particular relationship may have been an indirect way for the participant to maintain a closer relationship with her best friend.

## WHEN IS REVEALING SECRETS MORAL? FACTORS THAT MAY AFFECT "GOOD REASONS" FOR REVEALING SECRETS

Because secrets typically are kept to protect people's identity, their goals, their actions, and their possessions (Bok, 1983), revealing secret information about another person is a moral act. Decisions about whether to disclose a secret can affect the well-being of individuals and their relationships. The effects may be evident immediately or they may occur over time—they may be consistent with people's goals or they may interfere with their goals. As such, the moral issues involved in decisions people make about divulging others' secrets can be quite complex.

Although the conditions under which individuals reveal secret information provide an indication of the criteria they use in deciding whether to reveal a secret, research examining the way those criteria are evaluated has not been forthcoming. The exploratory study described in the current chapter was conducted to examine individuals' assessments of secrets they revealed for "good reasons." The topics of secrets people said they divulged for good reasons were investigated as were the reasons individuals revealed those secrets. The study's findings indicated that the most frequently reported topic people disclosed involved extradyadic relationships. Individuals also told secrets about mental health and sexual relations relatively frequently. The "good reasons" individuals described for revealing other's secrets ranged from being worried about the welfare of others to self-interest. People most frequently explained that they disclosed the secret information for reasons that are inherently moral in nature—because they were concerned for the other person's welfare or because they thought someone had a right to know the secret.

The findings of the current study, in conjunction with extant research and theory, suggest that people evaluate some reasons for revealing secrets as better, more important, or more moral than others. While the data presented in this chapter provide an indication of the secret topics people are likely to reveal and the explanations they see as good or important reasons for divulging a secret, those topics and reasons are likely to vary depending on a number of factors. For instance, individuals' evaluations probably depend, in part, on the quality of their relationship with the person who is the focus of the secret. People may be more discrete when the secret concerns someone they are close to and may, as a consequence, be relatively selective in the reasons they endorse for revealing the secret. They may only disclose secrets about a person they are close to when keeping the secret would be harmful. That is, close relational ties may prohibit individuals from telling most secrets, but morally obligate them to reveal a secret when a partner is in danger. By contrast, when they are not close to the person who is the focus of the secret—or when they are dissatisfied with their relationship with that person—they may be less cautious. They may, for example, believe that any benefit or advantage they would obtain from revealing the information is reason enough to reveal it.

In a similar vein, the reasons people endorse for revealing a secret may vary based on their relationship with the individual to whom they disclose the secret. In general, people are fairly selective about the individuals they choose as confidants (Tardy, Hosman, & Bradac, 1981). However, if the confidant is someone they feel close to and if they are relatively satisfied with their relationship with that person, they may be more liberal about the good reasons they are likely to endorse. In other words, the quality of their relationship with the potential recipient may reduce their need to exercise caution in evaluating reasons for divulging a secret. In fact, when people trust a potential confidant, they may not perceive that telling a secret is much of a violation because they may believe the secret will be safe. Conversely, if the person to whom they reveal a secret is someone they are not as close to or someone with whom they have a dissatisfying relationship, they may exercise a great deal of caution opting to reveal a secret only under relatively dire conditions.

There also is some evidence that women and men may evaluate secret topics and reasons for telling secrets differently. Women may be more likely to believe they have good reasons to reveal secrets focused on some topics whereas men may be more likely to believe they have good reasons for revealing other topics. If, as suggested by some researchers, women are regarded as being responsible for the well-being of their relationships (Chodorow, 1978), they may be more concerned about secrets emphasizing relationship issues. Indeed, Last and Aharoni-Etzioni (1995) found that girls were more likely than boys to keep secrets concerning family issues, while boys were more likely than girls to keep secrets about possessions and moral transgressions. Further, and in a similar vein, the reasons that women and men decide to divulge others' secrets may vary. Although sex differences in individuals' moral orientation are relatively small (Jaffe & Hyde, 2000), Gilligan (1982) has argued that women's moral reasoning is more focused on interpersonal responsiveness and empathy (an ethic of care) whereas men's moral reasoning is more centered on relatively objective standards (an ethic of justice). Inasmuch as this is the case, women, again, may be more wary of keeping secrets that involve relationship issues (dating partners, extradyadic relationships, sexual relations) than are men and men may be more concerned about issues associated with rules (e.g., rule breaking, illegal activities) than are women. Exploratory analyses of the current data set provide some support for these gendered moralities as women reported revealing more secrets than did men about *mental health*, *sexual relations*, and *physical or psychological abuse* and men reported disclosing more secrets than did women about *illegal activities*. Women also provided more reasons associated with *concern for the focal person's welfare* and *relationship influence* than did men.

Finally, the sophistication of individuals' moral reasoning may influence the way they evaluate the topics of secrets that they reveal as well as the reasons they might reveal others' secrets. Researchers have long argued that people vary with regard to their moral development. For instance, children's moral reasoning often is based on punishment and self-interest whereas adolescents' and adults' moral reasoning is more likely to include consideration of social roles and societal expectations (Kohlberg, 1973). The emerging adults who participated in the current study clearly reflected on roles and expectations in deciding whether to reveal the secret they described. Many of them evaluated expectations associated with their own role as a friend, son or daughter, or sibling (e.g., "She was my best friend, so I had to say something."), as well as expectations associated with the roles of others who were involved in the secret ("It was important to tell them ... they were her parents."). Also, consistent with the work of Arnett and his colleagues (Willoughby & Arnett, 2013), much of the moral reasoning described by participants revolved around behavior in dating and romantic relationships (e.g., "He was engaged to be married ... he shouldn't have cheated on her."). Because emerging adulthood is a time during the life course when individuals are learning to negotiate sexual and intimate behaviors, those behaviors may be a particularly salient part of the secrets that young adults choose to conceal or reveal. Further, while emerging adults may be more practiced than adolescents at deciding when and how to reveal secrets about sexual behavior and romantic relationships, they are likely less practiced—and less sophisticated—than they will be at later points in their life.

Although age is a key factor influencing the sophistication of moral reasoning, it is important to note that people can vary in moral development regardless of their age (Rest, Narvaez, Bebeau, & Thoma, 1999). Differences in moral development may be due to individual traits (i.e., empathy, hostility), relational history (i.e., how long a couple has been together, whether one partner has cheated on the other), or critical life events (i.e., the birth of a child, death, divorce). These variables may shape moral development in distinct ways and, in turn, may affect both the secrets that people opt to disclose and the reasons they decide to divulge those secrets.

Of course, individuals' moral development, their biological sex, and their relationships with others are only a few of the factors that influence the way they evaluate criteria for revealing others' secrets. The assessments people make in deciding to divulge a secret about another person are imbued with moral issues—each of which may affect, and be affected by any number of variables. "Good reasons" for revealing secrets, in short, are complex and multifaceted. A good reason for one person may not be a good reason for another person. And a reason that is seen as good at one point in time might not be viewed as good at another point in time. Identifying and explaining the factors that distinguish good reasons for revealing others' secrets—and for concealing them—is an important task for researchers to undertake.

## REFERENCES

Afifi, T., & Steuber, K. (2009). The revelation risk model (RRM): Factors that predict the revelation of secrets and strategies used to reveal them. *Communication Monographs, 76*, 144–176. doi:10.1080/03637750902828412

Afifi, W. A., & Caughlin, J. P. (2006). A close look at revealing secrets and some consequences that follow. *Communication Research, 33*, 467–488. doi:10.1177/0093650206293250

Altman, I. (1975). *Environment and social behavior: Privacy, personal space, territory, and crowding.* Monterey, CA: Brooks/Cole.

Bochner, A. P. (1982). On the efficacy of openness in close relationships. In M. Burgoon (Ed.), *Communication Yearbook 5* (pp. 109–124). New Brunswick, NJ: Transaction Books.

Bok, S. (1983). *Secrets: On the ethics of concealment and revelation.* New York: Vintage Books.

Brown-Smith, N. (1998). Family secrets. *Journal of Family Issues, 19*, 20–42. doi:10.1177/019251398019001003

Bulmer, M. (1979). Concepts in the analysis of qualitative data. *Sociological Review, 27*, 651–677. doi:10.1111/j.1467-954X.1979.tb00354.x

Caughlin, J. P. (2010). A multiple goals theory of personal relationships: Conceptual integration and program overview. *Journal of Social and Personal Relationships*, 27, 824–848. doi: 10.1177/0265407510373262

Caughlin, J. P., Scott, A. M., Miller, L. E., & Hefner, V. (2009). Putative secrets: When information is supposedly a secret. *Journal of Social and Personal Relationships*, 26, 713–723. doi:10.1177/0265407509347928

Caughlin, J. P., Vangelisti, A. L., & Mikucki-Enyart, S. L. (2013). Conflict in dating and marital relationships. In J. Oetzel & S. Ting-Toomey (Eds.), *The Sage handbook of conflict communication* (2nd ed., pp. 161–185). Thousand Oaks, CA: Sage.

Chodorow, N. J. (1978). *The reproduction of mothering: Psychoanalysis and the sociology of gender*. Berkeley, CA: University of California Press.

Derlega, V., & Grzelak, J. (1979). Appropriateness of self-disclosure. In G. Chelune (Ed.), *Self disclosure: Origins, patterns, and implications of openness in interpersonal relationships* (pp. 151–176). San Francisco, CA: Jossey-Bass.

Derlega, V. J., Metts, S., Petronio, S., & Margulis, S. T. (1993). *Self-disclosure*. Newbury Park, CA: Sage.

Dindia, K., Fitzpatrick, M. A., & Kenny, D. A. (1997). Self-disclosure in spouse and stranger interaction: A social relations analysis. *Human Communication Research*, 23, 388–412. doi:10.1111/j.1468-2958.1997.tb00402.x

Finkenauer, C., & Rime, B. (1998). Keeping emotional memories secret: Health and subjective well-being when emotions are not shared. *Journal of Health Psychology*, 3, 147–158. doi:10.1177/135910539800300104

Fisher, D. V. (1986). Decision-making and self-disclosure. *Journal of Social and Personal Relationships*, 3, 323–336. doi:10.1177/0265407586033005

Gilligan, C. (1982). *In a different voice: Psychological theory and women's development*. Cambridge, MA: Harvard University Press.

Gouldner, G. W. (1960). The norm of reciprocity: A preliminary statement. *American Sociological Review*, 25, 161–178. doi:10.2307/2092623

Greenberg, M. A., & Stone, A. A. (1992). Writing about disclosed versus undisclosed traumas: Immediate and long-term effects on mood and health. *Journal of Personality and Social Psychology*, 63, 75–84. doi:10.1037/0022-3514.63.1.75

Imber-Black, E. (1993). Secrets in families and family therapy: An overview. In E. Imber-Black (Ed.), *Secrets in families and family therapy* (pp. 3–28). New York, NY: W. W. Norton.

Jaffe, S., & Hyde, J. S. (2000). Gender differences in moral orientation: A metaanalysis. *Psychological Bulletin*, 126, 703–726. doi:10.1037/0033-2909.126.5.703

Jourard, S. (1971). *Self-disclosure: An experimental analysis of the transparent self*. New York, NY: Wiley.

Karpel, M. A. (1980). Family secrets: Implications for research and therapy. *Family Process*, 19, 295–306.

Kelly, A. E., & McKillop, K. J. (1996). Consequences of revealing personal secrets. *Psychological Bulletin*, 120, 450–465. doi: 10.1037/0033-2909.120.3.450

Kelvin, P. (1977). Predictability, power, and vulnerability in interpersonal attraction. In S. W. Duck (Ed.), *Theory and practice in interpersonal attraction* (pp. 355–378). New York, NY: Academic Press.

Kohlberg, L. (1973). The claim to moral adequacy of a highest stage of moral judgment. *Journal of Philosophy*, 70, 630–646. doi:10.2307/2025030

Larson, D. G., & Chastain, R. L. (1990). Self-concealment: Conceptualization, measurement, and health implications. *Journal of Social and Clinical Psychology*, 9, 439–455. doi:10.1521/jscp.1990.9.4.439

Last, U., & Aharoni-Etzioni, A., (1995). Secrets and reasons for secrecy among school-aged children: Developmental trends and gender differences. *Journal of Genetic Psychology: Research and Theory on Human Development, 156,* 191–203. doi:10.1080/00221325.1995.9914816

Omarzu, J. (2000). A disclosure decision model: Determining how and when individuals will self-disclose. *Personality and Social Psychology Review, 4,* 174–185. doi:10.1207/S15327957P-SPR0402_05

Parks, M. R. (1982). Ideology in interpersonal communication: Off the couch and into the world. In M. Burgoon (Ed.), *Communication Yearbook 5* (pp. 79–107). New Brunswick, NJ: Transaction Books.

Pennebaker, J. W. (1990). *Opening up: The healing powers of confiding in others.* New York, NY: Morrow.

Pennebaker, J. W., & Beall, S. K. (1986). Confronting a traumatic event: Toward an understanding of inhibition and disease. *Journal of Abnormal Psychology, 95,* 274–281. doi:10.1037//0021-843X.95.3.274

Pennebaker, J. W., Kiecolt-Glaser, J., & Glaser, R. (1988). Disclosure of traumas and immune function: Health implications for psychotherapy. *Journal of Consulting and Clinical Psychology, 56,* 239–245. doi:10.1037//0022-006X.56.2.239

Pennebaker, J. W., Mayne, T. J., & Francis, M. E. (1997). Linguistic predictors of adaptive bereavement. *Journal of Personality and Social Psychology, 72,* 863–871. doi:10.1037//0022-3514.72.4.863

Petrie, K. J., Booth, R. J., Pennebaker, J. W., Davison, K. P., & Thomas, M. G. (1995). Disclosure of trauma and immune response to a hepatitis B vaccination program. *Journal of Consulting and Clinical Psychology, 63,* 787–792. doi:10.1037//0022-006X.63.5.787

Petronio, S. (2000). The boundaries of privacy: Praxis of everyday life. In S. Petronio (Ed.), *Balancing the secrets of private disclosures* (pp. 3749). Mahwah, NJ: Erlbaum.

Petronio, S., Reeder, H. M., Hecht, M. L., & Ros-Mendoza, T. M. (1996). Disclosure of sexual abuse by children and adolescents. *Journal of Applied Communication Research, 24,* 181–199. doi:10.1080/00909889609365450

Rest, J., Narvaez, D., Bebeau, M., & Thoma, S. (1999). A neo-Kohlbergian approach: The DIT and schema theory. *Educational Psychology Review, 11,* 291–324. doi: 10.1023/A:1022053215271

Richards, A. S., & Sillars, A. L. (2014). Imagined interactions as predictors of secret revelation and health. *Communication Research, 41,* 236–256. doi:10.1177/0093650212438392

Rosenfeld, L. R. (1979). Self-disclosure avoidance: Why am I afraid to tell you who I am? *Communication Monographs, 46,* 63–74. doi:10.1080/03637757909375991

Tardy, C. H., Hosman, L. A., & Bradac, J. J. (1981). Disclosing self to friends and family: A reexamination of initial questions. *Communication Quarterly, 29,* 263–268. doi:10.1080/01463378109369414

Vangelisti, A. L. (1994). Family secrets: Forms, functions, and correlates. *Journal of Social and Personal Relationships, 11,* 113–135. doi:10.1177/0265407594111007

Vangelisti, A. L., Caughlin, J. P., & Timmerman, L. (2001). Criteria for revealing family secrets. *Communication Monographs, 68,* 1–17. doi:10.1080/03637750128052

Wegner, D. M., & Wenzlaff, R. M. (1996). Mental control. In E. T. Higgins & A. W. Kruglanski (Eds.), *Social psychology: Handbook of basic principles* (pp. 466–492). New York, NY: Guilford Press.

Willoughby, B. J., & Arnett, J. J. (2013). Communication during emerging adulthood. In A. L. Vangelisti (Ed.), *The Routledge handbook of family communication* (2nd ed., pp. 287–301). New York, NY: Routledge.

## NOTES

1. Of course, if the person who is the focus of the secret is not aware of the disclosure, he or she may not be affected. Alternatively, any effects he or she experiences are likely to be indirect.
2. The topic of the secrets described by participants were not related to any of the criteria reported. However, there were significant associations between people's perceptions of the secrets and several of the criteria. Specifically, people who closely identified with the secret and who saw the secret as negatively valenced or intimate were more likely to endorse a number of the criteria.
3. Other methodological details of the study are available from the first author.

# CHAPTER EIGHT

# Moral Standards, Emotions, AND Communication Associated WITH Relational Transgressions IN Dating Relationships

LAURA K. GUERRERO & MEGAN COLE

## MORAL DIMENSIONS, EMOTIONS, AND COMMUNICATION ASSOCIATED WITH RELATIONAL TRANSGRESSIONS IN CLOSE RELATIONSHIPS

*My boyfriend was on deployment with the US Navy. He had already been gone for five and a half months with only one and a half to go. He sent me an email saying that he wanted to be by himself when he got home. I was devastated. I've waited for him and sent him everything he's needed with much support and then he didn't want to spend time with me.*

*We hung out for two weeks during winter break and she called me her boyfriend. When school started back up we did a lot of texting and snapchatting but didn't hang out. She kept saying she was too busy but continued to flirt with me and act like she was interested in me when we texted. This went on for a couple of months. Then she stopped texting me back. When I confronted her she said that she never wanted anything serious, it was all just for fun. I really liked her and felt that she deceived me and led me on. What a waste of my time.*

*One night after hanging out he looked me straight in my face and out of nowhere said he wanted to be single. He said he loves me and wanted a future with me, but he just wanted to be single right now. What made it worse was we had sex like 5 minutes before that. I felt used. You just don't treat people you are supposed to care about that way.*

The three scenarios above are actual accounts of relational transgressions that occurred in dating relationships among college students. Transgressions occur when the rules of a relationship—whether explicit or implicit—are broken (Metts, 1994). According to Metts (1994), "If the behavior is considered sufficiently untoward by the offended partner, the misconduct will be considered a relational transgression" (p. 217). In other words, relational transgressions can be any number of acts, but are subjective in that only the people involved can decide if the act in fact breaks a relational rule. In some cases, partners agree that a rule has been broken. In other cases, only one partner thinks a transgression has occurred. Relational transgressions are especially common in close relationships because people expect their partners to treat them with fairness, respect, and consideration. When people violate this expectation by engaging in hurtful behavior, one or both partners may regard that behavior as a transgression.

This type of violation is evident in all of the above scenarios. In the first case, the writer expected that her boyfriend would want to be with her, but he wanted to be alone. In the second case, the writer believed that the young woman he liked had deceived him and led him on rather than being honest. Finally, in the third case, the writer felt that her ex-boyfriend treated her in an uncaring manner. The transgressors in these scenarios did more than violate relational rules; they also violated moral standards that underlie relational rules. These standards revolve around how people should be treated by others in relationships. Sometimes these moral standards are explicitly negotiated, agreed upon, and accepted by relational partners. Other times these standards are assumed based on cultural and social norms about how people treat one another in relationships.

This chapter explores how violations of moral standards are associated with transgressions as well as the emotions and communication associated with transgressions. The study reported herein uses both qualitative and quantitative data to suggest that transgressions often violate moral standards of fidelity, honesty, caring, and autonomy. Specifically, this exploratory study focuses on how these four moral standards are related to: (a) different types of transgressions, (b) the emotions that accompany transgressions, and (c) the communicative responses that follow transgressions within a college-age sample of students who have been transgressed against in a romantic relationship within the past year. The goal of this study is to provide initial insight into the role that violations of moral standards play in the process of responding to and coping with relational transgressions. Importantly, this study is limited to understanding the perspective of the person who was transgressed against rather than the perspective of the transgressor.

## RELATIONAL TRANSGRESSIONS IN DATING RELATIONSHIPS

Transgressions can occur in any type of relationship: romantic, friendship, family, or even work-related (Metts, 1994). The present research, however, focuses on transgressions within dating relationships since research suggests that most people experience at least some hurt within the context of their romantic relationships (Fehr & Harasymchuk, 2005). Although a variety of transgressions can occur, when people are asked to name a transgression that they have experienced in their romantic relationship, studies suggest that the most frequently mentioned transgressions are sexual infidelity, deception, and flirting with or dating another person (Guerrero & Bachman, 2008; Metts, 1994). In addition, Metts and Cupach (2007) identified inappropriate interaction, lack of sensitivity, extra-relational involvement, relational threat confounded with deception, disregard for relationship, abrupt termination, broken promises, secrets, and abuse as transgressions (Metts & Cupach, 2007). In a related line of research, Feeney (2004, 2005) listed five main types of hurtful events: active disassociation, which involves been rejected or abandoned; passive disassociation, which involves being ignored or excluded; criticism, which includes insults; sexual infidelity; and deception, which includes lying and breaking promises. Bachman and Guerrero (2006a) found that breakup was a common form of active disassociation, and that in addition to criticism, people reported that statements of relationship devaluation (e.g., "I never thought our relationship was that serious) or preference for others ("I'd rather be with my friends") were hurtful. Similar to earlier work by Metts (1994) on transgressions, flirting or showing interest in others was also a commonly reported transgression, as was sexual infidelity.

These studies demonstrate that although sexual involvement with another person is the prototypical example of a transgression, misconduct can range anywhere from unfair fighting while in an argument to jealousy to emotional involvement with an ex-partner to physical abuse (Metts, 1994). To provide a context for studying moral standards within the sample of college students participating in this study, the present study takes another look at what transgressions are common in dating relationships by asking:

RQ1: What relational transgressions are commonly reported in romantic relationships among college students?

## Moral Standards That Relational Transgressions Commonly Violate

Given that relational transgressions violate implicit or explicit rules about how people should conduct themselves in relationships, it follows that sometimes transgressions have a moral dimension. This is because many of the "rules" that guide relationships are grounded in moral standards. LaFollette (1996) suggested that several moral issues are relevant to how relationships function. These include trust, honesty, fairness, caring, patience, fidelity, and commitment. In a perfect world, people would always treat each other in line with these moral standards.

However, people are not perfect and they often fall short of these standards by engaging in behavior that is distrustful, dishonest, unfair, uncaring, impatient, unfaithful, disloyal, or shows a lack of commitment. These types of actions devalue the partner and the relationship, and feeling devalued is a key defining feature of transgressions and hurtful events (Leary, Springer, Negel, Ansell, & Evans, 1998). In line with this reasoning, LaFollette (1996) argued that "there is an intricate connection between morality and personal relationships" (p. 194). In healthy relationships, people generally engage in behavior that reflects the moral standards that have been negotiated or are expected given the level of commitment in the relationship whereas in distressed relationships people tend to engage in behavior that deviates from moral standards and elicits negative emotion. As of yet, however, there is little information on how moral standards are connected to relational transgressions even though work in the related area of interpersonal conflict suggests that when a partner's behavior elicits anger, the receiver often evaluates the sender's behavior as immoral and unjust (Baumeister, Stillwell, & Wotman, 1990). Therefore, a second research question is advanced:

RQ2: How are various relational transgressions associated with violations of moral standards of conduct?

## Transgression-Induced Emotion

Hurt feelings typically accompany relational transgressions, especially for the person who has been transgressed against. Indeed, some scholars contend that hurt is the key characteristic defining transgressions (e.g., Feeney, 2005). People typically experience hurt, which is an unpleasant and often intense emotion, when they have been psychologically injured by another person (Folkes, 1982; Vangelisti & Sprague, 1998). According to Leary et al. (1998), hurt can occur as a result of any number of events ranging from sexual infidelity to criticism, and these events can strain or end relationships. Furthermore, Leary et al. suggested that relational devaluation underlies most messages and events that lead to hurt feelings. They defined relational devaluation as "the perception that another individual does not regard his or her relationship with the person to be as important, close, or valuable as the person does" (p. 1225). Thus, since relational transgressions are grounded in breaking a relational rule, which in some cases may also involve not meeting a moral standard, a transgression can signal to one partner that the relationship is not important to the other partner. As a result, hurt feelings typically follow a transgression. Feeney (2005) extended this line of research by showing that while some transgressions lead people to feel devalued, other transgressions, and especially those that revolve around issues of distrust, lead people to feel injured and betrayed more than devalued. In either case, transgressions violate rules related to valuing and being able to trust others in relationships.

While hurt is the most prototypical and common emotion associated with transgressions for the person who has been betrayed, other emotions such as anger, frustration, disappointment, jealousy, embarrassment, and sadness can surface in the aftermath of transgressions. This is not surprising given Berscheid's (1983, 1991) emotion-in-relationships model, which suggests that negative emotions are a reaction to events that disrupt an individual's plans and goals. Most of the time, these events are unexpected. For example, if a man observes his girlfriend flirting with her ex-boyfriend, this would likely trigger jealousy because he expects her not to flirt with others. Such behavior also disrupts and threatens his goal of wanting a close, exclusive relationship with his girlfriend. Other transgressions, such as being deceived, cheated on, or criticized harshly are events that tend to be unexpected and to disrupt relational goals. In her study on hurt in romantic relationships, Feeney (2005) identified several "emotion terms" that accompanied hurt feelings, including: "hurt, angry, betrayed, upset, sad, confused, used, embarrassed, depressed, shocked, rejected, and pained" (p. 262). Barnes, Brown, and Osterman (2009) confirmed that anger was a common reaction to transgressions. Leary and his colleagues (1998) found that the more people experienced hurt feelings after being transgressed against, the more likely they were to experience anxiety, general distress, and negative self-feelings, and the less likely they were to experience positive affect.

Research has demonstrated that there are differences in emotional reactions based on the type of transgression. Specifically, Feeney (2004) asked participants about a hurtful event as well as their immediate emotional reactions to that event. Participants identified five event types: infidelity, deception, criticism, active disassociation, and passive disassociation. Of these, the first three were related to the highest levels of anger, while the latter two were related to the highest levels of fear. In a later study, Feeney (2005) replicated this result and also demonstrated that sadness occurred more often in response to active and passive disassociation than criticism, whereas fear was most likely to occur in response to active disassociation. Bachman and Guerrero (2006a) showed that sexual infidelity and disassociation through breakup elicited the most hurt among the transgressions they examined. Sexual infidelity can also cause intense feelings of jealousy, anger, fear, and sadness (Guerrero, Trost & Yoshimura, 2005).

Moral standards of good conduct may help further explain why different transgressions result in various emotional experiences. For example, breaches of fidelity tend to elicit anger and jealousy (Feeney, 2005). Being treated unfairly has also been identified as a primary elicitor of anger (Canary, Spitzberg, & Semic, 1998). These types of transgressions may be seen as conscious choices, and therefore as more purposeful and immoral, leading to more anger. On the other hand, breaches of caring and commitment tend to elicit sadness or disappointment (Feeney, 2005). Feeling rejected is also a primary elicitor of sadness (Shaver, Schwartz,

Kirson, & O'Connor, 1987). Being rejected or uncared for may violate a different type of moral standard than something like infidelity. People cannot help how they feel about others, but there is variability in how people can communicate rejection and criticism. Moral standards dictate that such messages should be communicated in ways that minimize rather than maximize hurt. Finally, McCornack and Levine (1990) reviewed research suggesting that people tend to experience emotions such as resentment, disappointment, and sadness upon discovery of a partner's deception. The emotions people experience upon discovering deception may vary according to the moral standards that were violated. For example, when deception is enacted for selfish reasons it is likely to elicit different emotions than when it is enacted to protect someone. These possibilities suggest that the following question is worth exploring:

RQ3: Which emotions are associated with each of the moral standard violations that underlie transgressions?

## Moral Standards and Communication

Research has also been conducted that identifies the ways in which partners communicate following a relational transgression (Bachman & Guerrero, 2006a; Guerrero & Bachman, 2008; Roloff, Soule, & Carey, 2001). Bachman and Guerrero (2006a) identified seven different communicative responses to hurtful events. These seven communicative responses were then divided into two categories: constructive and destructive responses. The researchers determined that there were three prosocial, constructive responses: relational repair, integrative communication, and loyalty. According to Bachman and Guerrero (2006a), *relational repair tactics* include strategies aimed at restoring the relationship after a transgression, such as trying to be more romantic and affectionate. *Integrative communication* focuses on disclosing to one's partner and solving relational problems through actions such as explaining feelings and talking about the relationship. *Loyalty* is a passive but prosocial response (Rusbult & Zembrodt, 1983) that involves staying in the relationship, being patient, and hoping things will get better.

Bachman and Guerrero (2006a) also identified four antisocial or destructive communicative responses to hurtful events that tend to further damage one's romantic relationship: de-escalation, distributive communication, revenge, and active distancing. *De-escalation* strategies focus on behaviors that facilitate breakup. According to Bachman and Guerrero (2006a), this response category was based on the neglect and exit strategies proposed by Rusbult and Zembrodt (1983), and includes actions such as dating other people and letting the relationship fall apart. *Distributive communication* includes actions that are negative and aggressive in nature, such as making hurtful or mean comments or acting rude. *Revenge* focuses on getting back at one's partner. Finally, *active distancing* is about creating distance between oneself and one's partner through behaviors such as ignoring and stopping communication.

The moral standards that are violated when people transgress may help explain why people utilize different communicative responses to hurtful events. When a transgression occurs, at least one relational rule has been broken. Depending on which rules have been broken, the victim may engage in different communicative responses. For example, when people are unfaithful or otherwise disloyal, their partners are likely to feel an acute sense of betrayal that could lead to destructive responses such as revenge and distributive communication. In addition, since infidelity and disloyalty are key predictors of breakup and divorce (Amato & Previti, 2003), fidelity violations should also be positively related to de-escalation and may have a stronger relationship to de-escalation than other types of violations. When people have their trust violated, they may be especially likely to distance themselves from their partner and keep information private. When one partner violates moral standards related to being caring and respectful, the other partner may react by engaging in reciprocal behavior that shows a similar lack of regard. To test these types of possibilities, a final research question is asked:

RQ4:    Which communicative responses to hurtful events are associated with each of the moral standards that underlie transgressions?

## METHOD

Data were collected from undergraduate students enrolled in communication courses at a large university in the Southwestern region of the United States. To participate, students had to have experienced a transgression or hurtful event within a dating relationship sometime during the past year. If they had experienced more than one transgression, they were told to report on the most current one. Students who wished to participate in exchange for extra credit were given directions via their instructor's Blackboard page. In these instructions, a transgression was defined as "anything a partner says or does that breaks a spoken or unspoken rule in your relationship and causes hurt feelings. Examples of these kinds of events include cheating, insults, and lies, but these are only three of many such events. The key is that you feel that what your partner said or did violated a rule and hurt you. The partner who hurt you should be someone who you dated at least once or had some kind of romantic relationship with at the time the event occurred." This definition of transgressions is consistent with work reviewed earlier in this chapter, which showed that rule violations and hurt feelings are central to the concept of transgressions. Students who met these criteria were asked to download a questionnaire marked "hurtful events." Students who did not meet these criteria were directed to a different link. Participants were directed to complete the questionnaire independently in a private place and return it to their instructor by a certain date. Students placed their questionnaires in a box in the classroom and then signed a separate sheet to receive extra credit. In this way, all responses remained anonymous. Respondents were informed that participation was voluntary and asked not to put their names anywhere on the questionnaire.

These procedures resulted in a total of 708 returned questionnaires. Of these, 83 were eliminated from analysis because the participant did not provide a sufficient description of the hurtful event or left a page or more of the questionnaire unanswered. This left 625 usable questionnaires, which were completed by 331 women and 294 men, who averaged 20.2 years old (SD = 2.12, range = 18 to 31 years old). Most of the participants ($n$ = 384) reported being in serious dating relationships, followed by casual dating relationships ($n$ = 163), friends with benefits relationships ($n$ = 42), and engaged relationships ($n$ = 36). The average time since the transgression was 7.40 months prior to data collection (range = 1 month to 12 months; SD = 3.89 months). Nearly 80% of respondents classified themselves as European American/White, with the rest of the sample divided nearly equally among those who identified as Mexican American/Hispanic/Latino/a, Asian American, African American, and other.

## The Transgression

At the beginning of the questionnaire, respondents were reminded that the goal of the study was to better understand how people respond to transgressions in romantic relationships. The definition of transgressions that was given to them in the initial instructions was repeated, and participants were asked to provide a detailed description of the hurtful event, including what happened and why it was hurtful. Half of this page was blank so participants had ample space to write their descriptions.

## Moral Standards of Conduct

Next, the instructions noted that "As mentioned above, transgressions occur when a spoken or unspoken rule is broken in a relationship. These rules commonly involve things like being caring and loyal to each other. To what extent do you believe that your partner's actions broke each of the following rules of conduct for how people should behave in relationships?" The "rules" were prefaced by the stem: "My partner's actions showed that s/he was ..." followed by a list of these adjectives: dishonest, unfair, uncaring, impatient, critical, untrustworthy, unsupportive, disloyal, uncommitted, selfish, possessive, inconsiderate, judgmental, unfaithful, controlling, deceptive, manipulative, and clingy. These adjectives were chosen by looking at descriptions of hurtful events given by participants in a previous study (e.g., Bachman & Guerrero, 2006a). The participants in that study used these terms, or similar terms, when describing their partner's untoward behavior. Endpoints were 1 = not at all and 7 = to a great extent.

An exploratory factor analysis using the maximum likelihood method and direct oblimin rotation was conducted to determine how the adjectives that reference moral standards group together. The scree plot and the eigenvalues over 1.0 suggested that four underlying factors were present. The items that loaded on each factor all had primary loadings over .50 and secondary loadings that were below .30, so a clean factor structure emerged. The first factor included the items dishonest, untrustworthy, and deceptive. These three items formed a reliable scale for measuring *honesty violations* ($\alpha$ = .96; M = 4.89, SD = 1.72). The second factor, labeled *fidelity violations*, included the items disloyal, unfaithful, and uncommitted ($\alpha$ = .90; M = 3.77, SD = 1.80). The third factor, labeled *care violations*, included the items uncaring, unsupportive, selfish, and inconsiderate ($\alpha$ = .88; M = 5.41, SD = 1.38). The fourth factor, labeled *autonomy violations*, included possessive, controlling, manipulative, and clingy ($\alpha$ = .75; M = 3.12, SD = 1.61). The remaining items (unfair, impatient, critical, and judgmental) did not load strongly on any of the factors or had split factor loadings. The correlations among these four factors ranged from −.11 to .38, with the largest correlation between fidelity and honesty violations.

## Emotions

To assess the emotions experienced after the transgression, participants were given the following prompt: "Please indicate the extent to which you felt each of the following emotions as a result of the hurtful event that you described at the beginning of this questionnaire." The stem then read, "I felt ..." Endpoints were 1 = not at all and 7 = to a great extent. Participants were then given a set of emotions that are likely relevant to transgressions based on several typologies (e.g., De Smet, Loeys, & Buysse, 2012; Feeney, 2005; Guerrero et al., 2005): angry, anxious, bitter, betrayed, depressed, disappointed, disgusted, distress, embarrassed, empty, fearful, frustrated, grief, hate, heartbroken, humiliated, hurt, jealous, lonely, mad, panic, rage, resentful, sad, shame, shock, sorrow, surprise, taken advantage of, and used.

The emotion items were factor analyzed in accordance with the procedures described above for the factor analysis of the moral standard items. Five factors emerged. The first factor, labeled *angry emotions*, included angry, betrayed, bitter, frustrated, hate, mad, and resentful ($\alpha$ = .86; M = 5.11, SD = 1.51). The emotions in this factor are similar to what other scholars have labeled hard emotions (e.g., Sanford, 2007) or hostile emotion (Guerrero & Andersen, 2000). The second factor, labeled *vulnerable emotions*, included disappointed, empty, heartbroken, sad, taken advantage of, and used ($\alpha$ = .84; M = 5.01, SD = 1.83). The emotions in this factor are similar to those labeled as soft emotions by Sanford (2007, 2010). Soft emotions reflect vulnerability and stem from experiencing loss, rejection, or psychological injury. In Sanford's work, hurt and sadness are the key emotions underlying soft emotions. In the present study, feeling disappointed, empty, heartbroken, taken advantage of, and used also fall under this factor, which suggests an emphasis on feeling vulnerable. The third factor, labeled *distress*, included anxious, distressed, and fearful ($\alpha$ = .81; M = 3.82, SD = 1.61). The fourth factor, labeled *embarrassment*, included embarrassed, humiliated, and shame ($\alpha$ = .81; M = 3.97, SD = 1.44). The final factor, labeled *shock*, included shock and surprise ($\alpha$ = .76; M = 4.78, SD = 1.68). The correlations among these factors ranged from .18 to .33.

## Communicative Responses to Hurt

Participants were asked to think about how they communicated with their partner after the transgression occurred. The items used to measure communicative responses to hurt on a 1 (strongly disagree) to 7 (strongly agree) scale were the same items used by Bachman and Guerrero (2006a). Items measuring *relational repair* ($\alpha$ = .87; M = 3.11, SD = 1.37) included being extra affectionate and romantic. Items measuring *integrative communication* ($\alpha$ = .88; M = 5.09, SD = 1.41) focused on disclosure and problem solving. Items measuring *loyalty* ($\alpha$ = .83; M = 4.01, SD = 1.52) were taken from Rusbult and Zembrodt (1983) loyalty measure, and included being patient and waiting for things to get better. Items measuring *de-escalation* ($\alpha$ = .84; M = 3.13, SD = 1.71) focused on behaviors designed to decrease closeness or end the relationship. Items measuring *distributive communication* ($\alpha$ = .91; M = 4.03, SD = 1.58) included aggressive responses such as yelling and calling the partner names. Items measuring *revenge* ($\alpha$ = .90; M = 2.91, SD = 1.80) focused on getting "back at" or "even with" the partner. Finally, items measuring *active distancing* ($\alpha$ = .76; M = 4.84, SD = 1.55) included strategically trying to make the partner feel badly by limiting contact, communication, and affection.

## RESULTS

### Transgression Types

To answer the first research question, the descriptive data on the hurtful events were analyzed. Initially, an undergraduate research assistant was given descriptions of the various types of transgressions identified in past research (Feeney, 2004, 2005; Metts, 1994), including sexual infidelity, third party involvement (i.e., dating or flirting with a third party), deception, passive association, break up, criticism/insults, physical abuse, and betrayed confidences. The undergraduate student then read each of the descriptions and identified which of the transgressions were implicated in the description. The assistant was told that she could identify more than one transgression per description. Indeed, in nearly 1/3 of the descriptions, participants mentioned more than one transgression. For example, the description below was coded as containing three transgressions: passive disassociation, third party involvement, and break up.

> *My girlfriend and I been on and off with our relationship for two years but then our relationship got really serious. We started spending a lot of time together and talking about a future together. Then towards the end of the summer, she started to ignore my texts/phone calls, did not want to hang out anymore. I told her I could not handle our relationship anymore if it was going to be like that. She did not seem to care. Next day, I found out she's with another guy in a new relationship and wants to end our relationship for good.*

The research assistant was also told to identify any additional transgressions that were not in the original list. She came up with several additional categories, including misrepresented relational intent (e.g., leading someone on, acting like the relationship was more serious than it was), inconsiderate behavior (e.g., engaging in behavior that was insensitive or inconsiderate, such as forgetting a birthday or not listening to a problem), unfounded jealousy (e.g., partner is suspicious or worried about a third party when s/he shouldn't be), manipulation (e.g., tricking the partner into doing or feeling something), dangerous behavior (e.g., continuing to drink, smoke weed, or drink and drive against the partner's objections), social network disapproval (e.g., not getting along with a partner's family and friends), stealing (e.g., partner took something and didn't return it), and talking behind the partner's back (e.g., partner said negative things about the other partner to her/his friends). The research assistant created definitions for each of these new transgressions. Definitions for the original transgressions were also developed based on how they were described in the literature.

The primary investigator then read the definitions, went through the descriptions, and identified the transgressions that were present. After the initial coding, there was a high level of agreement between the research assistant and the primary investigator (over 91% across all categories). The research assistant and primary investigator met to resolve any inconsistencies in their ratings. This process resulted in nine transgressions being identified as present in 5 percent or more of the descriptions, as shown in Table 1. The other transgressions listed above were identified in less than 5 percent of the descriptions, and therefore were not analyzed when answering the remaining research questions.

## Violations of Moral Standards

The second research question asked how moral standards were associated with various relational transgressions. Although this question was primarily tested via quantitative methods, there was also qualitative evidence that moral standards are indeed part of the fabric of transgressions since many of the descriptions that participants gave included references to violations of fidelity, honesty, care, and autonomy standards. For example, the following description shows a violation of the fidelity standard:

Table 1. The Most Commonly Identified Transgressions with Examples.

*Third Party Involvement*—19.9% (the transgressor dated, flirted with, or otherwise showed interest in a third party)

My boyfriend flirted with and then kissed another girl at a party.

*Sexual Infidelity*—18.1% (the transgressor had sex with a third party)

My girlfriend cheated on me with some other guy.

*Criticism/Insults*—11.2% (the transgressor was critical, insulting, or engaged in name-calling)

He said I was lazy and need to lose weight because I don't look as good as I used to.

*Break Up*—10.8% (the transgressor ended the relationship)

We were together for almost a year then one night after a great date (with gifts etc.) he told me he was leaving me to go back with his ex-wife because of the kids!

*Passive Disassociation*—8.4% (the transgressor distanced her/himself from the partner and/or relationship)

Did not return phone calls or text messages for three days

*Deception*—8.0% (the transgressor lied or broke a promise).

She lied to me about something really important that happened in her past.

*Misrepresented Relational Intent*—7.3% (the transgressor led the partner on or acted like the relationship was more serious than it was)

He acted like he was really into me, even told me he loved me a couple of times, but then said that he didn't see us as a "long term thing."

*Inconsiderate Behavior*—6.1% (the transgressor engaged in insensitive or inconsiderate behavior that ignores the needs of the partner)

My boyfriend insisted that we see the movie that he wanted to see even though it was my turn to decide.

*Unfounded Jealousy*—5.9% (the transgressor acted overly suspicious or possessive when s/he had nothing to worry about)

She basically got mad when I gave another girl my phone number. The girl was someone who I knew in high school. She didn't answer my calls after that so I was basically done with her. I have too much pride for a girl to try to play games with me and not trust me.

*I had been in the relationship for about 8 months and I caught him talking about me in a negative way through an online journal with another girl. They had wrote to each other about our whole relationship and it was all negative towards me. I expected him to be loyal to me and not badmouth me in front of some girl.*

A lot of descriptions also explicitly mentioned characteristics that were in violation of the care standard, such as the partner being selfish, unsupportive, or purposefully hurtful. Here are two descriptions that exemplify violation of this standard:

*We went to the San Diego zoo on the day of my birthday—only because he wanted to go. He was acting selfish and short with me on "my" special day. I was really hurt by his selfishness …*

*He said I was "just like every other bitch out there." … The worse insult was when he said I was just like his ex (if you knew her you'd know why). It was obvious that he was trying to push my buttons and hurt me.*

Violations of the honesty standard were mentioned quite often. In many cases, honesty standards were violated in connection with fidelity standards, as shown in the following description.

*I was seeing this guy for almost a year. Little did I know he had a girlfriend for over two years at the same time he was seeing me. He led me on and lied to me the entire time when all he really wanted was a friends with benefits thing since his girlfriend goes to a different school. I felt incredibly used and deceived.*

Finally, violations of the autonomy standard were less common but were nonetheless found in some of the descriptions. Many of these descriptions focused on unfounded jealousy and a lack of trust, as illustrated in the following account.

*She refused to believe me with regard to a sexual encounter she accused me of having between one of our break ups. It didn't happen but she kept insisting it did and after that she was always checking up on me, looking through my phone, asking me about girls and stuff, until I felt like I couldn't even talk to another girl without her getting mad. We got into a huge stupid fight about it even though I didn't do anything wrong.*

To quantitatively test the second research question, which asked how transgressions were associated with the moral standards, four regression analyses were conducted. For each analysis, the transgressions were dummy coded and entered as independent variables. Participants were given a 1 if a particular transgression was mentioned in their description and a 0 if it was not. Since many of the descriptions referenced multiple transgressions, a participant could have more than one transgression dummy coded with a 1. All nine transgressions served as independent variables. The dependent variables were the four types of moral standard violations: fidelity, honesty, care, and autonomy.

All four models were significant. In first regression model, $F(9,595)$ = 122.83, $p < .001$, $R = .81$, adjusted $R^2 = .59$, third party involvement, sexual infidelity, misrepresented relational intention, break up, and passive disassociation were all positively associated with violating the fidelity standard. In the second model, $F(9,595) = 107.76$, $p < .001$, $R = .70$, adjusted $R^2 = .49$, deception, sexual infidelity, and misrepresented relational intention, were positively associated with violating the honesty standard, whereas criticism was negatively associated. In the third model, $F(9,595) = 99.15$, $p < .001$, $R = .65$, adjusted $R^2 = .41$, break up, passive disassociation, inconsiderate behavior, misrepresented relational intention, and criticism were all positively associated with the care standard. Finally, in the fourth model, $F(9,595) = 68.91$, $p < .001$, $R = .58$, adjusted $R^2 = .31$, unfounded jealousy, misrepresented relational intention, and deception were all positively associated with the autonomy standard. Beta weights and $t$-values for the independent variables in each of these models can be found in Table 2.

Table 2. Significant Associations in the Regression Analyses looking at the Associations among Relational Transgressions and Violations of Moral Standards.

| Dependent Variable | Predictor Variables | $\beta$ | $t$-Value |
|---|---|---|---|
| Fidelity Violation | Sexual Infidelity | .61 | 20.99*** |
| | Third Party Involvement | .54 | 19.56** |
| | Misrepresented Relational Intention | .13 | 4.86*** |
| | Criticism | .12 | 4.32*** |
| | Passive Disassociation | .10 | 3.61** |
| Honesty Violation | Deception | .46 | 13.98*** |
| | Misrepresented Relational Intention | .45 | 13.83*** |
| | Sexual Infidelity | .18 | 2.18* |
| | Criticism | -.24 | -5.18 |
| Care Violation | Break Up | .52 | 20.82*** |
| | Passive Disassociation | .46 | 18.53*** |
| | Inconsiderate Behavior | .26 | 12.59*** |
| | Misrepresented Relational Intention | .16 | 7.86*** |
| | Criticism | .13 | 6.25*** |
| Autonomy Violation | Unfounded Jealousy | .54 | 22.38*** |
| | Misrepresented Relational Intention | .20 | 9.16*** |
| | Deception | .18 | 7.89*** |

*Note.* ** $p < .01$, *** $p < .001$, two-tailed.

## Emotions

The third research question examined how various emotions are related to each of the moral standards that underlie transgressions. To test this question, four regression analyses were conducted. The five emotion measures—angry emotions, vulnerable emotions, distress, embarrassment, and shock—served as the predictor variables. The analysis was set up this way to tap into how the various emotions studied herein associate with each moral standard. Since the data were collected at one point in time, the causal nature of these findings cannot be ascertained. Thus, moral standards may be predictive of emotions, or emotions may color the extent to which people recall that their partner violated certain moral standards. The four moral standards—fidelity, honesty, care, and autonomy—were dependent measures in separate analyses. In the first regression model, $F(5,599) = 71.71$, $p < .001$, $R = .61$, adjusted $R^2 = .37$, angry emotion, vulnerable emotion, embarrassment, and shock were all positively associated with violations of fidelity. In the second model, $F(5,599) = 17.08$, $p < .001$, $R = .35$, adjusted $R^2 = .12$, vulnerable emotion and shock were positively associated with honesty violations and distress was negatively associated with honesty violations. In the third model, $F(5,599) = 34.63$, $p < .001$, $R = .47$, adjusted $R^2 = .22$, vulnerable emotion, distress, and angry emotions were positively associated with care violations. Finally, in the fourth model, $F(5,599) = 20.93$, $p < .001$, $R = .38$, adjusted $R^2 = .14$, vulnerable emotion and distress were positively associated with autonomy violations (see Table 3).

Table 3. Significant Associations in the Regression Analyses Looking at the Associations among Emotions and Violations of Moral Standards.

| Dependent Variable | Predictor Variables | $\beta$ | $t$-Value |
|---|---|---|---|
| Fidelity Violation | Angry Emotion | .56 | 17.05*** |
| | Vulnerable Emotion | .19 | 5.87*** |
| | Embarrassment | .13 | 3.81*** |
| | Shock | .11 | 3.31*** |
| Honesty Violation | Vulnerable Emotion | .27 | 5.84*** |
| | Shock | .12 | 2.91** |
| | Distress | -.11 | -2.74** |
| Care Violation | Vulnerable Emotion | .31 | 8.38*** |
| | Distress | .30 | 8.16*** |
| | Angry Emotion | .13 | 3.59*** |
| Autonomy Violation | Vulnerable Emotion | .31 | 10.22*** |
| | Distress | .22 | 5.92*** |

Note. ** $p < .01$, *** $p < .001$, two-tailed.

Communicative Responses to Hurt

The fourth research question examined how various communicative responses to hurt are associated with each of the moral standards that underlie transgressions. To test this question, four regression analyses were conducted. The seven communicative responses—relational repair, integrative communication, loyalty, de-escalation, distributive communication, revenge, and active distancing—served as the predictor variables. The four moral standards—fidelity, honesty, care, and autonomy—were dependent measures in separate analyses. Similar to the earlier analyses, the models were set up this way to explore how the various communicative responses associate with each moral standard, without implying causality in either direction. The first regression analysis, $F(7,597) = 52.68, p < .001, R = .62$, adjusted $R^2 = .38$, showed that distributive communication, revenge, and de-escalation were positively associated with fidelity violations, whereas relational repair, integrative communication, and loyalty were negatively associated with fidelity violations. In the second analysis, $F(7,597) = 17.18, p < .001, R = .41$, adjusted $R^2 = .16$, distributive communication, de-escalation and active distancing were positively associated with honesty violations, whereas repair and integrative communication were negatively associated with honesty violations. The third regression, $F(7,597) = 12.38, p < .001, R = .36$, adjusted $R^2 = .12$, produced a model showing that distributive communication and active distancing were positively associated with care violations, whereas relational repair and integrative communication were negatively associated with care violations. Finally, the fourth regression analysis $F(7,597) = 20.03, p < .001, R = .45$, adjusted $R^2 = .20$, demonstrated that distributive communication, active distancing, relational repair, and integrative communication were all positively associated with autonomy violations (see Table 4).

## DISCUSSION

The goal of this exploratory study was to provide an initial glimpse into the role that moral standards play in the process of responding to and coping with relational transgressions. A basic assumption guiding this study was that because transgressions constitute violations of relational rules, they also usually involve the violation of moral standards of conduct. To that end, four moral standards associated with transgressions were identified: fidelity, honesty, care, and autonomy. Before exploring how the violations of these moral standards are associated with emotions and communicative responses, links between these moral standards and various transgressions were established.

Table 4. Significant Associations in the Regression Analyses Looking at the Associations among Communicative Responses to Hurt and Violations of Moral Standards.

| Dependent Variable | Predictor Variables | $\beta$ | $t$-Value |
|---|---|---|---|
| Fidelity Violation | Distributive Communication | .48 | 12.64*** |
| | Revenge | .27 | 6.57*** |
| | De-escalation | .11 | 3.33** |
| | Relational Repair | -.16 | -4.33*** |
| | Integrative Communication | -.15 | -3.63*** |
| | Loyalty | -.09 | -2.67** |
| Honesty Violation | Distributive Communication | .35 | 71.30*** |
| | De-escalation | .19 | 4.12*** |
| | Active Distancing | .12 | 3.06** |
| | Relational Repair | -.19 | -4.09*** |
| | Integrative Communication | -.10 | -2.41* |
| Care Violation | Distributive Communication | .33 | 7.08*** |
| | Active Distancing | .13 | 3.06** |
| | Relational Repair | -.16 | -3.93** |
| | Integrative Communication | -.11 | -2.84** |
| Autonomy Violation | Distributive Communication | .29 | 7.19*** |
| | Active Distancing | .28 | 7.10*** |
| | Relational Repair | .18 | 4.16*** |
| | Integrative Communication | .17 | 4.01*** |

*Note.* $*p < .05$, $** p < .01$, $*** p < .001$, two-tailed.

## Transgressions in Dating Relationships

The present study was consistent with past research showing that third party involvement (i.e., dating, flirting, or otherwise showing interest in others), sexual infidelity, and deception are three of the most commonly identified transgressions in college-age romantic relationships. Similar to Bachman and Guerrero (2006a), break ups were also identified as a common transgression in the present study. This study also replicated Feeney's (2004, 2005) work by showing that passive disassociation and criticism/insults were common transgressions. A separate category called inconsiderate behavior also emerged in the present study. This category was distinct from criticism/insults because it focused on behavior that was selfish or did not meet the needs of one partner. Two additional transgressions that have not surfaced much in past literature were also identified in the present study—misrepresented relational intent and unfounded jealousy. Misrepresented relational intent is a special form of deception that involves misrepresenting one's feelings and intentions about a partner and a relationship. Participants in the present study sometimes reported that their partners led them to believe that they liked them more than they did or that they wanted a more serious relationship than they actually wanted. Unfounded jealousy occurred when people felt that their partner was acting jealously or possessively when they should have instead trust them.

## Violations of Moral Standards of Conduct

The present study also confirmed that violations of fidelity, honesty, care, and autonomy underlie many relational transgressions. These four violations were also found by Feeney (2005) who looked at the types of rules that are commonly violated during hurtful events. She found that people reported feeling hurt when their partners violated rules related to loyalty/fidelity, openness (which is related to honesty), supportiveness (which was conceptualized similar to how care is defined in the present study), and autonomy. Feeney, however, identified additional rule violations, including similarity display, shared time, equity, and romance. In her study, people were hurt if their partners did not show enough similarity, spend enough time with them, treat them equitably, or engage in enough romantic behavior. Future work on violations of moral standards related to transgressions should determine if any of these issues are relevant. It may be, however, that some of these behaviors (especially similarity and romantic behavior) are not moral standards as much as they are negotiated rules within a relationship. The standards examined in the present study—fidelity, honesty, care, and autonomy—may be somewhat more universal, as might standards related to equity. Next, each of the moral standards identified in the present study is discussed in more detail.

## Violations of the Fidelity Standard

Not surprisingly, many transgressions were associated with violating the fidelity standard. It is also unsurprising that third party involvement and sexual infidelity are at the top of this list. These two transgressions are the prototypical examples of being unfaithful or disloyal—instead of being monogamous and devoted to one's partner, the transgressor has sex with or shows interest in a third party. These are clear acts of betrayal and disloyalty. Misrepresenting relational intentions was also associated with violating the fidelity standard. Partners discovered to be insincere in their expressed intentions were perceived to be disloyal. Break ups can also violate the fidelity standard. Indeed, breaking up with someone, especially if it is unexpected, may be the ultimate act of disloyalty and unfaithfulness since one has chosen to leave the relationship. Furthermore, when describing transgressions, just over 18% of participants in the present study reported both break up and sexual infidelity, whereas around 13% of participants reported both break up and third party involvement. In these cases, issues related to involvement with a third party may have precipitated the break up, such that the break up was also a consequence of violating the fidelity standard. Finally, passive disassociation may sometimes be seen as a violation of the fidelity standard because ignoring the partner and spending time apart may communicate a lack of commitment and loyalty. Thus, all of these transgressions appear to reflect some level of betrayal and disloyalty.

Violations of the fidelity standard were also associated with a variety of emotional and communicative responses. Past research has shown that compared to other types of transgressions, infidelity, third party involvement, and break up are associated with relatively high levels of anger and hurt as well as a lack of forgiveness (Bachman & Guerrero, 2006a, 2006b; Feeney, 2005). Since these transgressions were verified to be associated with violations of the fidelity standard, it is logical to expect that the fidelity standard would also be related to angry emotions and vulnerable emotions. Feeling betrayed by someone who has been disloyal and has shown a lack of commitment likely elicits vulnerable emotions such as sadness because a relationship has been lost or diminished. As Fehr and Harasymchuk (2005) noted, "the dissolution or loss of an intimate relationship is widely regarded as one of life's most heart-wrenching experiences" (p. 181). The angry feelings that stem from violations of the fidelity standard may reflect that an implicit or explicit promise has been broken—namely the promise to be faithful and loyal to one's partner.

Two other emotions were associated with violating the fidelity standard— embarrassment and shock. Although these associations were smaller than those for angry emotions, they are still a significant part of the emotional experience that reportedly accompanies violations of the fidelity standard. As Afifi, Falato, and Weiner (2001) demonstrated, the discovery of infidelity can be embarrassing because it can cause a loss of face, especially if others outside of the relationship know about it. When a transgressor engages in acts that violate the fidelity standard, the victim may lose face because others may think he or she cannot hold onto a relational partner. Whether the fidelity violation involves flirting with a third party, having sex with a rival, breaking up, backing away from the relationship (after misrepresenting it), or disassociating with the partner, all of these transgressions suggest that the person is somehow not wanted, respected, or good enough, which can lead to emotions such as embarrassment and shame. Finally, violations of the fidelity standard may sometimes be associated with shock and surprise, as would be the case if infidelity was discovered unexpectedly or a break up occurred with little warning.

The finding that violations of fidelity standards are associated with strong, angry emotions is paralleled by the finding that these violations are positively associated with three out of the four destructive communicative responses to hurt—distributive communication, revenge, and de-escalation—and negatively associated with all three constructive responses to hurt. These three destructive communicative responses were all positively associated with angry emotion as well ($r = .48$ for distributive communication, $r = .37$ for revenge, and $r = .31$ for active distancing, $p < .001$ for all). Taken together, these findings suggest that violations of the fidelity standard, angry emotions, and destructive communication may function as a cluster of related experiences and expressions. Interestingly, violations of the fidelity standard were the only type of violations that correlated with revenge in the present study. Thus, violations of the fidelity standard are somewhat unique in that they may lead people to want to get back at their partner. Given these findings, it is not surprising that violating the fidelity standard was negatively associated with the constructive responses of relational repair, integrative communication, and loyalty. As McCullough, Worthington, and Rachal (1997) suggested, people are unlikely to engage in conciliatory behavior toward their partner following a relational transgression unless they have forgiven their partner, and violations of infidelity appear to be perceived by many to be one of the most unforgivable and hurtful acts that occur in relationships (Bachman & Guerrero, 2006a, 2006b).

## Violations of the Honesty Standard

A somewhat different set of transgressions, emotions, and communicative responses were associated with violations of the honesty standard. Understandably, the transgression that was most associated with violating the honesty standard was deception. But this was not the only transgression that was considered to be a violation of the honesty standard. Sexual infidelity and misrepresented relational intention were also positively associated with this type of violation. Given that the qualitative data showed that sexual infidelity and deception often went hand-in-hand (e.g., people were caught lying about being unfaithful), the association between sexual infidelity and violating the honesty standard could be a side effect of the strong correlation between violation of the honesty standard and deception. Indeed, around 18% of the participants in the present study described joint acts of infidelity and deception in their descriptions of the transgression that they had experienced. However, acts of infidelity may also be regarded as a type of deception in some cases, especially if the partner has promised to be faithful. Misrepresenting relational intentions is a more clear-cut violation of the honesty standard because such misrepresentations imply that the transgressor knowingly misled the partner. Finally, perhaps surprisingly, criticism was negatively associated with violating the honesty standard. This may be because some forms of criticism may contain a kernel of truth or even be completely true. Vangelisti (1994) found that some of the most hurtful statements are informative—the sender says something true such as "I hate the way you do that" or "Your constant nagging is getting on my nerves."

Interestingly, angry emotion was not associated with violations of the honesty standard, despite the association between infidelity and dishonesty. Instead, vulnerable emotions and shock were associated with violations of the honesty standard. Recall that vulnerable emotions are composed of feeling disappointed, empty, heartbroken, sad, taken advantage of, and used. Deception may stir these emotions when people are disappointed and heartbroken that their partner was not open and honest with them, while also feeling that they were used and taken advantage of if the deception benefitted the transgressor in some way while hurting them. Shock and surprise may occur when the behavior that violates the honesty standard is inconsistent with information that the partner formerly believed. For example, one participant in the study wrote: "*I was shocked to find out that she still had feelings for him. She had told me that they were completely over and that she hated him so to find out that she still loved him and that I was just a rebound guy was a total shock.*" Notice that this example also shows how misrepresented relational intentions can violate the honesty standard.

In terms of communication, violating the honesty standard was positively associated with distributive communication, de-escalation, and active distancing. This makes sense. All of these responses involve aggression or avoidance, which McCullough et al. (1997) argued are common reactions to transgressions. Revenge was not associated with violating the honesty standard, perhaps because engaging in more deception would be seen as counterproductive or hypocritical. People were also unlikely to report using relational repair or integrative communication in response to violations of honesty. Since the transgressor was the person who engaged in the violation, the partner may feel that she or he is not the one responsible for fixing the situation. Positive forms of communication may also be less likely because trust is a cornerstone of close relationships, and violations of the honesty standard destroy trust.

## Violations of the Care Standard

People expect their partners to be caring, supportive, unselfish, and considerate. When they are not, a violation of the care standard has occurred. This standard seems to be a basic tenet in relationships and a reason why people form close relationships in the first place; people want someone who will care for and support them. It is not surprising, then, that several transgressions are associated with violating the care standard. Breaking up represents the likely end of support and care from someone who was once important in one's life, and passive disassociation often entails the temporary removal of support and care. Inconsiderate behavior and criticism are almost by definition violations of the care standard since the behaviors that constitute these transgressions are the opposite of caring. Finally, misrepresenting relational intentions shows a disregard for one's feelings. When transgressors are misleading about what they want from a relationship, they set their partners up for eventual disappointment—and finding out that one's partner wants less from the relationship than one thought can also make a person feel uncared for and used.

Violations of the care standard are associated with emotions as well. In particular, violations of this type were associated with vulnerable emotions, distress, and angry emotions. When a valued relational partner acts in an uncaring manner, it follows that the receiver will feel sad and hurt. Such behavior shows a disregard for the receiver's feelings. When the uncaring behavior is also aggressive or insulting, it is likely to elicit angry emotions. As Canary et al. (1998) noted, when people feel they have been unfairly criticized, insulted, or blamed for something, anger is a typical reaction. Distress, which was comprised of distress, fear, and anxiety, may accompany some care violations, especially if people are worried that the transgressor will continue to act in an uncaring, unsupportive, and possibly even aggressive manner.

The communicative responses associated with care violations were similar to what was found for fidelity and honesty violations. People reported engaging in relatively high levels of distributive communication and active distancing, and relatively low levels of relational repair and integrative communication to the extent that they believed their partner violated the care standard. In many ways this finding represents a reciprocity effect. Violations of the care standard often take the form of specific behaviors, such as ignoring one's partner (passive disassociation), showing up late for a date (inconsiderate behavior), leading someone on (misrepresented relational intention), or insulting one's partner (criticism). Distributive communication represents a reciprocal response to many of these behaviors, as does passive aggressive behavior such as active distancing. Break ups are also likely to elicit aggressive and avoidant responses unless the partner is trying to get back together. Relational repair and integrative communication would be compensatory responses that would be designed to get the relationship back on track. Apparently, however, the stronger the violations of care are, the less likely people are to engage in these types of compensatory responses. Thus, these types of responses were unlikely when people reported that their partners had violated standards of care.

## Violations of the Autonomy Standard

The final moral standard, autonomy, may not be as obvious as the other three. However, people have a right to freedom and personal space. Communication researchers taking a dialectic perspective (e.g., Baxter, 1990; Baxter & Montgomery, 1996) have long held the position that autonomy is just as important as closeness and connection. According to this viewpoint, humans require both autonomy and connection; even though these forces seem to be contradictory, they are actually complementary. Thus, just as people expect their partners to give them love, support, care, and connection, they also expect their partners to give them freedom and personal space, to value their individuality, and to trust them when they are on their own. Work on face needs (Brown & Levinson, 1987; Metts & Grohskopf, 2003) also highlights the importance of respecting a partner's need for autonomy. This work suggests that in addition to wanting to be liked by others (positive face), people want to be free from restraint so that they are able to control their time, resources, and activities (negative face). When people act in controlling, possessive, and mistrustful ways, they are threatening their partner's negative face and also impinging upon their autonomy. In this way, violations of the autonomy standard may represent a moral imperative related to freedom, trust, and respect.

Three transgressions were related to violating the autonomy standard: unfounded jealousy, misrepresented relational intention, and deception. Of these, unfounded jealousy seems the most obvious. If transgressors become jealous when they have no real reason to be, the partner is likely to feel that the transgressor should trust them more. In addition, the qualitative data suggests that people who display unfounded jealousy sometimes express that jealousy by being possessive and controlling. In fact, these types of communication may be part of what determines whether unfounded jealousy crosses over to become a relational transgression. If jealous individuals talk to their partners and re-evaluate the situation so that trust in their partner is restored, a transgression would be unlikely to be reported. In this study's data, reports of unfounded jealousy as a transgression usually (about 62% of the time) included mention of possessive behavior or lack trust. For example:

> At a restaurant when with friends, she noticed the waitress was interested in me. Every time she came to our table to check on us she kept calling me her boyfriend and giving her dirty looks. Then she called me a flirt and a male slut in front of our friends. It was super annoying and embarrassing. She needs to chill and trust me more.

Misrepresented relational intention can also impinge upon one's autonomy. In the qualitative data, some individuals referred to partners who led them on as a "waste of my time" (see the second scenario in the introduction) or as controlling (e.g., one participant said, "he controlled me by making me think he liked me when the whole time he was just playing games"). Deception can also be related to violations of autonomy, especially if the deception is aimed at controlling or manipulating the partner.

Two emotions were associated with violating the autonomy standard: vulnerable emotions and distress. Vulnerable emotion is the only emotion category that was related to all four violations of moral standards. This suggests that hurt is the key emotion that defines relational transgressions, as Feeney (2005) argued. When people believe that their partner does not trust them or is controlling and manipulative, feelings of disappointment, hurt, and sadness may follow. Because violations of autonomy may reflect insecurity on the part of the transgressor, people may respond to these types of transgressions with sadness rather than angry emotions. Distress could surface when people believe that the transgressor is so controlling that they become threatening, or that their autonomy is being encroached upon.

The pattern of associations between violations of the autonomy standard and communicative responses to hurt was unique. For all of the other violations, the destructive responses were positively associated to violations of moral standards, whereas the constructive responses were negatively associated. However, for violations of the autonomy standard, all of the associations were positive. The more people reported that a transgression violated the autonomy standard, the more they tended to report engaging in distributive communication, active distancing, relational repair, and integrative communication. Perhaps people try to reassure their partners by becoming more affectionate and trying to solve the problem. This seems likely given some of the qualitative descriptions, where people described that things would be better if their partner trusted them or knew how much they really loved them. However, partners may also respond with antisocial behavior, such as arguing (distributive communication) or giving the partner the silent treatment (active distancing) because of the negative emotion that autonomy-restricting behavior elicits.

## Limitations and Conclusions

This study represents an initial step in understanding how violations of moral standards function in relation to transgressions. The significant associations that emerged suggest that this is a fruitful avenue of research. However, there are several limitations in the present research that should be remedied in future work, the most important of which are discussed next. First, the present study focused on college students' romantic relationships. People experience transgressions in various types of relationships (e.g., family, friend, and romantic) at different times in their life. Certain transgressions are likely to be more common in some relationships and particular life stages than others. For example, relational misrepresentation is less likely to occur in committed relationships than new relationships. Thus, this study provides a limited view of transgressions in one type of relationship during one phase of life. Second, and similarly, all of the participants in the present study were college students; individuals with different levels of education and life experience may not react the same way to transgressions. Education and life experiences may make people more or less tolerant of certain types of moral violations. Third, the present study was exploratory in nature and cannot determine causality. Some of the reasoning in the literature suggests that transgressions lead to emotions, which then lead to communication, but these causal links are not supported by the questionnaire data in the present study, so aside from the qualitative data, this study only tells us how the variables of interest are associated with one another. Fourth, other moral standards may be violated when people transgress. This study included a limited number of terms related to moral standards and some of the rule violations that Feeney (2005) identified may also be associated with moral standards. Some of the items included in this study, such as impatient and unfair, did not load on a factor but may still represent violations of important moral standards. Indeed, these were among the moral standards in relationships that LaFollette (1996) discussed. Finally, the present study focuses on the victim's perspective. Transgressors may feel differing amounts of guilt, as well as other emotions, and engage in different types of remedial strategies depending on the extent to which they believe they violated moral standards related to fidelity, honesty, caring, and autonomy. Thus, future research should examine both the victim's and the transgressor's perceptions.

Despite these limitations, this exploratory study provides a springboard for future research on moral standards that are violated by transgressors. The study shows a clear link between transgressions and violations of moral standards, such that moral standards regarding infidelity, honesty, care, and autonomy are associated with different sets of transgressions. The study also shows that violations of all four of these moral standards are associated with vulnerable emotions, which reinforces the idea that hurt is at the heart of what constitutes a relational transgression. The other emotions—angry emotion, distress, embarrassment, and shock—associated with some types of violations but not others. Finally, most of the communicative responses followed a similar pattern; the more people believed the transgressor violated the moral standards of fidelity, honesty, or care, the more they reported engaging in destructive communication and the less they reported engaging in constructive communication. The exception to this rule was for violations of the autonomy standard. The more this standard was violated, the more people were likely to engage in distributive communication, active distancing, relational repair, and integrative communication—which represent a mix of constructive and destructive responses. The constructive responses may help people alleviate fears that cause autonomy-restricting behaviors, whereas the destructive responses may represent a way to push back against those same behaviors. This finding, along with the rest of the data reported herein, suggests that the type of moral violation that occurs matters in terms of the emotion people experience and the way people communicate those emotions. Hopefully more researchers will pay attention to the moral component that underlies relational transgressions as research in this area advances.

# REFERENCES

Afifi, W. A., Falato, W. L., & Weiner, J. L. (2001). Identity concerns following a severe relational transgression: The role of discovery method for the relational outcomes of infidelity. *Journal of Social and Personal Relationships, 18*, 291–308.

Amato, P. R., & Previti, D. (2003). People's reasons for divorcing: Gender, social class, the life course, and adjustment. *Journal of Family Issues, 24*, 602–626.

Bachman, G.F., & Guerrero, L. K. (2006a). Relational quality and communicative responses following hurtful events in dating relationships: An expectancy violations analysis. *Journal of Social and Personal Relationships, 23*, 943–963.

Bachman, G.G., & Guerrero, L. K. (2006b). Forgiveness, apology, and communicative responses to hurtful events. *Communication Reports, 19*, 45–56.

Barnes, C. D., Brown, R. P., & Osterman, L. L. (2009). Protection, payback, or both? Emotional and motivational mechanisms underlying avoidance by victims of transgressions. *Motivation and Emotion, 33*, 400–411.

Baumeister, R. F., Stillwell, A., & Wotman, S. R. (1990). Victim and perpetrator accounts of interpersonal conflict: Autobiographical narratives about anger. *Journal of Personality and Social Psychology, 59*, 994–1005.

Baxter, L. A. (1990). Dialectical contradictions in relationship development. *Journal of Social and Personal Relationships, 7*, 69–88.

Baxter, L. A., & Montgomery, B. M. (1996). *Relating: Dialogues and dialectics.* New York: Guilford Press.

Berscheid, E. (1983). Emotion. In H. H. Kelley, E. Berscheid, A. Christensen, J. H. Harvey, T. L. Huston, G. Levinger, E. McClintock, L. A. Peplau, & D. R. Peterson (Eds.), *Close relationships* (pp. 110–168). New York: Freeman.

Berscheid, E. (1991). The emotion-in-relationships model: Reflections and update. In W. Kessen & A. Ortony (Eds.), *Memories, thoughts, and emotions: Essays in honor of George Mandler* (pp. 323–335). Hillsdale, NJ: Erlbaum.

Brown, P., & Levinson, S. (1987). *Politeness: Some universals in language usage.* Cambridge, UK: Cambridge University Press.

Canary, D. J., Spitzberg, B. H., & Semic, B. A. (1998). The experience and expression of anger in interpersonal settings. In P. A. Andersen & L. K. Guerrero (Eds.), *Handbook of communication and emotion: Research, theory, applications, and contexts* (pp. 189–213). San Diego, CA: Academic Press.

De Smet, O., Loeys, T., & Buysse, A. (2012). Post-breakup unwanted pursuit: A refined analysis of the role of romantic relationship characteristics. *Journal of Family Violence, 27*, 437–452.

Feeney, J. A. (2004). Hurt feelings in couple relationships: Towards integrative models of the negative effects of hurtful events. *Journal of Social and Personal Relationships, 21*, 487–508.

Feeney, J. A. (2005). Hurt feelings in couple relationships: Exploring the role of attachment and perceptions of personal injury. *Personal Relationships, 12*, 253–271.

Fehr, B., & Harasymchuk, C. (2005). The experience of emotion in close relationships: Toward an integration of the emotion-in-relationships and interpersonal script models. *Personal Relationships, 12*, 181–196.

Folkes, V. S. (1982). Communicating the causes of social rejection. *Journal of Experimental Social Psychology, 18*, 235–252.

Guerrero, L. K., & Andersen, P. A. (2000). Emotion in close relationships. In C. Hendrick & S. S. Hendrick (Eds.), *Close relationships: A sourcebook* (pp. 171–186). Thousand Oaks, CA: Sage Publications.

Guerrero, L. K., & Bachman, G. F. (2008). Communication following relational transgressions in dating relationships: An investment-model explanation. *Southern Journal of Communication, 73,* 4–23.

Guerrero, L. K., Trost, M. R., & Yoshimura, S. M. (2005). Romantic jealousy: Emotions and communicative responses. *Personal Relationships, 12,* 233–252.

LaFollette, H. (1996). *Personal Relationship: Love, Identity, and Morality.* Cambridge, MA: Blackwell Publishers.

Leary, M. R., Springer, C., Negel, L., Ansell, E., & Evans, K. (1998). The causes, phenomenology, and consequences of hurt feelings. *Journal of Personality and Social Psychology, 74,* 1225–1237.

McCornack, S. A., & Levine, T. R. (1990). When lies are uncovered: Emotional and relational outcomes of discovered deception. *Communications Monographs, 57,* 119–138.

McCullough, M. E., Worthington, E. L., & Rachal, C. (1997). Interpersonal forgiving in close relationships. *Journal of Personality and Social Psychology, 73,* 321–336.

Metts, S. (1994). Relational transgressions. In B. H. Spitzberg & W. R. Cupach (Eds.), *The dark side of interpersonal communication* (pp. 217–239). Mahwah, NJ: Lawrence Erlbaum Associates.

Metts, S., & Cupach, W. R. (2007). Responses to relational transgressions: Hurt, anger, and sometimes forgiveness. In B. H. Spitzberg & W. R. Cupach (Eds.), *The dark side of interpersonal communication* (pp. 243–274). Mahwah, NJ: Lawrence Erlbaum Associates.

Metts, S., & Grohskopf, E. (2003). Impression management: Goals, strategies, and skills. In J. O. Greene & B. R. Burleson (Eds.), *Handbook of communication and social interaction skills* (pp. 357–402). Mahwah, NJ: Lawrence Erlbaum.

Roloff, M. E., Soule, K. P., & Carey, C. M. (2001). Reasons for remaining in a relationship and responses to relational transgressions. *Journal of Social and Personal Relationships, 18,* 362–385.

Rusbult, C. E., & Zembrodt, I. M. (1983). Responses to dissatisfaction in romantic involvements: A multidimensional scaling analysis. *Journal of Experimental Social Psychology, 19,* 274–293.

Sanford, K. (2007). Hard and soft emotion during conflict: Investigating married couples and other relationships. *Personal Relationships, 14,* 65–90.

Sanford, K. (2010). Perceived threat and perceived neglect: Couples' underlying concerns during conflict. *Psychological Assessment, 22,* 288–297.

Shaver, P., Schwartz, J., Kirson, D., & O'Connor, C. (1987). Emotion knowledge: Further exploration of a prototype approach. *Journal of Personality and Social Psychology, 52,* 1061–1086.

Vangelisti, A. L. (1994). Messages that hurt. In B. H. Spitzberg & W. R. Cupach (Ed.), *The dark side of interpersonal communication* (pp. 53–82). Hillsdale, NJ: Lawrence Erlbaum.

Vangelisti, A. L., & Sprague, R. J. (1998). Guilt and hurt: Similarities, distinctions, and conversational strategies. In P. A. Andersen & L. K. Guerrero (Eds.), *Handbook of communication and emotion: Research, theory, applications, and contexts* (pp. 123–154). San Diego, CA: Academic Press.

# CHAPTER NINE

# Mindfulness AS Morality

## Awareness, Nonjudgment, and Nonreactivity in Couples' Communication

VALERIE MANUSOV

Most of us want what we would consider to be a good primary love relationship. That is, we want a space where we can, for example, be ourselves and connect deeply to another. The criteria we may have for such a relationship can vary across the people who hold those judgments (that is, I may want one thing out of a close relationship; my neighbor may have a very different idea about an ideal or good bond). But the subject of what is and how to create relationships that reflect our best sense of *what matters to us* (i.e., our morality) has produced an abundance of scholarship.

Whereas there is still much to be learned about how intimate pairs communicate with one another—for good *or for ill*—one thing we know is that couple members respond to each other through interpretive lenses they develop over time. That is, when our partner acts a certain way (for example, he talks a lot about his past, or she brings home an unexpected gift), we make sense of the action through a set of existing beliefs, experiences, and emotions we have about that partner, our relationship, and ourselves.

The set of constructs through which we understand our partner's behavior—or any behavior, for that matter, including our own—has been referred to variously as our *filter, lens, knowledge structure, schemata,* or *interpretive frame,* among other

The author thanks the Department of Communication at the University of Washington for an internal grant to support, and Jacquelyn Harvey-Knowles and John Crowley for their help with, the project from which the data in this chapter are drawn.

terms. Such lenses or frames represent a confluence of cultural learning, family background, mood, dispositions, and experiences with our partner and with relationships more generally. They also reflect our views of relational morality: our hopes and expectations of what we want from our relationship and our partner and our sense of whether or not we are receiving what we wish to receive. Moreover, our lenses tend to influence how we relate to others, often in ways that reinforce our existing filter. This process of filtered interpretation/action can be harmful, particularly when our frames place us or our partner in an unwarranted negative light.

Researchers who study intimate—or "romantic"—relationships, particularly heterosexual married couples, and who are interested in the ways in which people think about or make sense of their partner's behaviors, often do so under the rubric of Attribution Theories (Spitzberg & Manusov, in press). Attribution Theories state explicitly that people work actively, at least to some degree, to understand social behavior. Heider (1958) called us "naïve scientists," in that we engage without formal theories or methods but nonetheless scan our environments to try to make sense of what occurs within them. We do this with our own behavior ("Why do I always choose partners who seem afraid of intimacy?") and for others' behavior ("Why is she so affectionate with her friends?"). When we provide answers to those "why" questions, we are making *attributions* for our own and others' actions. Importantly, these attributions are colored by the larger frames we have for ourselves and for others and, in so doing, reflect our sense of good and bad, our view of morality.

Early theorizing about attributions provided models for how people should make "good" (i.e., logical, accurate) attributions (see, e.g., Kelley, 1971), another way to think about the morality of sense-making. Looking across the ways people actually make sense of behavior, however, has shown that people more typically make such attributions in "biased" rather than "logical" ways (Crittenden & Wiley, 1985; Ross, 1977), which we tend to think of as problematic, inherently. Often these "biases" reflect short cuts to a full assessment of all the things that could have caused an action. So, for instance, we tend toward what has been called the "fundamental attribution error," in that we are likely to make personal or dispositional attributions (what Heider, 1958, called "internal" attributions) rather than attributions that cite the cause outside of the other, perhaps because there are fewer internal explanations than there are external ones or because our focus is already on the person when we are trying to understand his or her action. Although such biases are "natural," in that we are programmed cognitively toward meaning-making short cuts, they can also be seen as less "good" than more careful and "logical" assessments.

Attribution-making, in whatever form it takes, is something we do across time, people, and places. But much of it is likely to occur within the minds and discourse of couples as they navigate their way through their days with one another. In "romantic" pairs, particular types of biases have been discovered; these will be discussed in more detail as this chapter unfolds, but suffice it to say that we can make sense of our partner's actions in more or less benign, relationally- and personally-supportive ways. In this paper, I argue that these attributions for our partners' behaviors—even very positive attributions that make the other "look good" in our minds and may make us or our partners feel happy—need to be understood as *obscured by our own conceptual filters* and as such may be problematic for us and our relationships. At minimum, they tend to be relatively quick judgments of why our partner acted as he or she did, very likely minimalizing the complexity of a situation that may close down discussion about the behavior and what underlies it.

This chapter reviews the research on couples' attributions for one another's communication, with additional focus on the appearance of attribution-making in childhood. It also, however, goes a step further than reviews of this nature by suggesting that even the most positive sense-making is still biased, still *a way of seeing* that privileges our judgment over other possibilities; moreover, we are often unaware of the role our own perspective has on how we make sense of and engage with others. As such, they may be problematic inherently for a relationship. For these, and other, reasons, investigating and possibly working to lessen the degree to which we understand our partner through our own lenses may be an approach to relating with greater morality. That is, rather than making sense of our partners' actions on our terms, *we can act with more integrity—with greater goodness—if we move toward fewer assumptions and less judgment.*

With this in mind, I offer a different possibility, a means for stepping back from judgment and, instead, entering intimate interactions with greater awareness and openness. This other way of being, referred to as *mindfulness*, stems from Buddhist philosophy and suggests a different frame for morality in our relationships, one based on observing—of paying attention—but without the judgment, background, and set of expectations we usually bring to our relationships and to ourselves. I provide some data showing what a mindful approach to a partner's behavior may look like and compare it with more "filtered" sense-making. I also review some research that shows the benefits of mindfulness learning in adolescence and suggest that encouraging mindfulness in young people may enhance their ability to go into adult relationships in a more mindful—and more moral—way. In making this move toward mindfulness rather than adherence to existing ways of thinking, I suggest a divergent conception of moral thought and behavior than may be taken elsewhere.

## ATTRIBUTIONS

There are many ways scholars approach the study of meaning for our communication behaviors. The focus of this chapter centers on the work done regarding the general process of *making attributions*. As noted, attributions are the ideas we have about why a person acted as he or she did. So, when our partner behaves a particular way that catches our attention—for example, acting more formally in a conversation than usual—we typically search for why he or she may have done so. I have argued elsewhere (e.g., Manusov, 1990, 2002; Manusov & Spitzberg, 2008) that the choice of an answer to the "why" question leads us down a path toward one set of meanings for the behavior; if we chose a different attribution, we would have other interpretations open to us.

The attribution we provide for the behavior ("I think he's acting formally because he is mad at me"; "He is feeling grumpy"; "Something must've happened at work"; "He is such a jerk"; "I pissed him off") is important in its own right for how we make sense of things, and because it may lead us to respond in a particular way that follows from our attribution (Manusov, 2002). This is consequential for many reasons including the finding that, in people who are interdependent, particularly intimate couples, one person's behavior can lead to a similar behavior from a partner, creating cycles of behavior, both negative (Gottman, Markman, & Notarius, 1977) and positive (Manusov, 1995). Given that negative cues tend to be noticed and acted on more often than are positive cues (Pszyszynski & Greenberg, 1981), the effects of attributions become even more pronounced.

As well, *we often communicate our attributions to others in our everyday talk* with our partners or with others (Burleson, 1986; Hilton, 1990). The focus on how our attributions (thoughts) play out in behavior—and the ways in which the attributions may be communicated to others—has compelled communication scholars to look at these processes, though the study of attributions was originally and is still largely the domain of social psychologists. In this section, I provide a brief overview of the commonplace and consequential nature of attributions from this large body of work, beginning with work on children's attribution-making.

## Starting Early

Abundant research exists that shows we start making attributions early in life. These sense-making attributions range from judgments of the intentionality of characters in a story (Ronfard & Harris, 2014; Rybash, Roodin, & Hallion, 1979) to attributions about family arguments (Weston, Boxer, & Heatherington, 1998) and one's own hostile intent (Halligan Cooper, Healy, & Murray, 2007). Children develop this attribution-making ability quickly: At age four, accurate attributions can be made for simple judgments, but by age six, the ability to make more interconnected attributions increases significantly (Sodian, 1988). Children's attributions show sophisticated thinking: Even children as young as five years old make somewhat complex attributions for why others act as they do. Moreover, biases show up early: Weston et al. (1998) note that the attributions children provide show differential ways children think of their mother's and father's behavior and diversity in how those attributions play out in children's "adjustment" to their parents' actions.

Other researchers have also found early evidence of attributional biases. Finlay et al. (2014), for example, reported patterning in attribution-making for fathers' behavior. Girls, for instance, made more stable attributions (the definition of which will be discussed in the next section) for their fathers' positive behaviors than did boys. In addition, European American youth and those from "intact" families were more likely than Mexican American youth or adopted children to make stable attributions. That is, the former group tended to see the father's character or something unchanging in the environment as the cause for the favorable ways the fathers acted.

Not surprisingly, children's attributions are affected by the quality of the communication around them. Fincham, Beach, Arias, and Brody (1998) studied girls and boys between 10 and 12 years old interacting with their parents and noted that the children's attributions for their parents' behaviors were correlated with how positive their relationships were with their parents (see, also, Brody, Arias, & Fincham, 1996). Likewise, L. E. Miller, Howell, and Graham-Bermann (2014) found that children from 4–6 years old already showed problematic attributions, including self-blame, for the violence that occurred in their homes. Such attributions actually increased over time, particularly girls' attributions of self-blame. The authors concluded that "without intervention, young children may be at risk of developing relatively stable maladaptive cognitive patterns, thereby heightening their risk of subsequent psychopathology" (p. 1535). Whether the attributions were positively or negatively-valenced, however, there is a direct link between the larger familial world in which they grew up and how the children made their attributions; this occurred when the children lived with their families and also colored attributions years later (Gardner, Busby, Burr, & Lyon, 2011).

Other researchers have likewise found that what happens to us as children shows up in the ways we think about the world and others in it, but such biased sense-making can be changed. Chodkiewicz and Boyle (2014), for instance, ... found that children can learn to change negative attributions they make regarding their own behavior, a process the authors refer to as "retraining." As will be discussed later, the ability to change one's learned and habitual ways of thinking—particularly when they are negatively toned—provides the basis for suggesting mindfulness training as a useful avenue toward self- and other-acceptance.

## Attributional Variation

In some of the earliest work seeking to describe and understand attributions, scholars argued that attributions—whether offered by children or adults—take many different forms, and these can be delineated from one another based on a number of dimensions. Weiner (1985) is perhaps most well-known for discussing these attributional dimensions. He noted that, in addition to the causal locus (i.e., making an attribution to something internal—such as a disposition—or external—such as an environmental feature—to person whose behavior is being observed), attributions vary from one another based on, for example, how stable or unstable they are, how specific or global they appear, and the like. So, a wife may see her husband's affectionate behavior as due to his kind nature (an internal, stable, global attribution) or to the fact that it's their anniversary (an external, specific, but yet stable cause).

Some studies on attribution-making focus on just one of the many attributional dimensions or types that exist; others center on several at once. Responsibility attributions are often looked at as the sole sense-making dimension, and it often makes sense to do so. When people make judgments of who or what was responsible for a certain event or behavior, they are often also making the most obviously "moralistic" judgment among all attribution types. For instance, researchers have looked at how people judge who or what was responsible for why someone contracted HIV; when people judge *the person* as "responsible" (i.e., engaging in risky behavior rather than receiving a blood transfusion with the virus), that are also likely to receive less sympathy from others (Badahdah & Alkhder, 2006). Greater responsibility attributions for negative behaviors have also been found to lead to more negative reciprocity and greater displays of anger (Bradbury & Fincham, 1992). The moral implications of such sense-making are clear.

Myriad studies using multiple attributions also exist. Silvester, Arnon, Stratton, and Hanks (1995), for instance, emphasized attributions of control and causal locus (in their study, "locus" was defined as located in the parent or the child); based on spoken attributions, the authors looked at parents' talk about children's behavior to see how they talked about who was more or less in control of the parent's physical abuse of the child. The authors were able to find that families they categorized as "good" (meaning that they were likely to be rehabilitated) included parents who were more likely to see themselves rather than the child as the source of the abuse and to understand that they had more control over their own behavior than did their child.

Other scholars have offered an array of other underlying structures for attributions that arise in interactions. For example, researchers have identified *relational* attributions, where an aspect of the relationship is identified as the cause of a behavior (Berscheid, Lopes, Ammazzalorso, & Langenfeld, 2001; Vangelisti, Corbin, Lucchetti, & Sprague, 1999), *interpersonal* attributions (Fletcher, Fincham, Cramer, & Heron, 1987; Newman, 1981; Vangelisti et al., 1999) where "interaction between partners is the focus" of the attribution (Manusov & Koenig, 2001, p. 142), and *communication* attributions, where explanations for behavior are tied directly to what was being communicated (Manusov & Koenig, 2001).

Additional attribution dimensions include assessments of *intentionality* (e.g., Manusov, 1996) and, as noted earlier, *responsibility* (e.g., Bugental, Shennum, Frank, & Ekman, 2001; Weiner, 1995). As can be seen, attributions are not only ubiquitous in our everyday lives; they also take myriad forms.

## Attribution-Making in Relationships

As asserted earlier in this paper, these common, multi-faceted forms of sense-making occur often in—and may be particularly consequential for—our romantic, partner relationships. One of the most consistent findings about attributions in intimate relationships is the recognition of how attribution-types differentiate satisfied from dissatisfied couples (Manusov, Floyd, & Kerssen-Griep, 1997). Most notably, Holtzworth-Munroe and Jacobson (1988) argued that certain combinations of attribution dimensions work together to characterize what they called "distress-maintaining" (i.e., multi-dimensional attributions for negative events that accentuate their impact and that minimize positive behavior) and "relationship enhancing" attributions (i.e., attributions that minimize the impact of negative events and maximize it for positive behavior). Negative biases in particular are "a dysfunctional way to view marital events and a stress generation process" (Peterson, Smith, & Windle, 2009, p. 478), though positive biases have also been described as "attributional charity" (Cropley & Reid, 2008).

Sense-making for a negative behavior that places blame on a spouse, views the cause as stable, and that represents something larger or global about that spouse are considered "distress-maintaining," because they assume the worst in explaining a partner's behavior. On the other hand, more external, unstable, and specific attributions for a negative behavior are thought to be "relationship enhancing"; such attributions reduce the negative valence of the attribution and place less blame on one's spouse for the action and its consequences. The opposite pattern occurs for distress-maintaining and relationship-enhancing attributions for positive behaviors (i.e., a happy spouse sees her partner's "good" behaviors as caused by something stable and global about the spouse ["He is just such a great guy"]). Focusing one's attributions on the relationship when the behavior is negative is also seen as distress-maintaining (Manusov & Koenig, 2001).

Importantly, *both satisfied and dissatisfied couples make both forms of attributions at times* (Manusov & Koenig, 2001); more often, however, they occur in the ways Holtzworth-Munroe and Jacobson (1988) predicted. What is more, Bradbury and Fincham (1990) argued that relational biases "underlie the patterns of behavior exchange that differentiate distressed and nondistressed couples" (p. 4); that is, attributions often result in *how we act toward the person about whose behavior we have made the attribution,* an argument that has received widespread support (e.g., Davey, Fincham, Beach, & Brody, 2001; Johnson, Karney, Rogge, & Bradbury,

2001; Miller & Bradbury, 1995; Manusov, 2002; G. E.). Importantly, when couples change their attributions, particularly negative ones, their behavior toward one another also changes (Sanford, 2006).

There are additional ways in which partners make "distress-maintaining" attributions. Watching the tape of an interaction in which they just engaged, Sillars, Leonard, Roberts, and Dunn (2002) asked couple members to report on what they were thinking (and what they believed their partner was thinking) during the taped conflict episode. Sillars and his colleagues found that spouses categorized as "aggressive" tended to attribute less *constructive engagement* and more *avoidance* to their partner than they attributed to themselves, reflecting what has been referred to elsewhere as a type of "actor-observer bias." The authors also noted that the tendency for husbands in aggressive relationships to pay heightened attention to communication, and the likelihood that their attributions for their wives' communication will be distress-maintaining, "presents a combustible situation" (Sillars et al., 2002, p. 101) in these relationships.

## Mindfulness

It is clear from this review that there are patterned—and potentially biased— ways of making attributions for our own and others' actions. An argument can be made that, when looking at the relationship between relational satisfaction and attribution-making, it may be that couple members are just right. That is, happy wives may correctly attribute better intent to their spouses because their spouses do have better intent than do those in unhappy relationships. But researchers (e.g., Baucom, 1987; Durtschi, Fincham, Cui, Lorenz, & Conger, 2011; Johnson et al., 2001; Lavner, Bradbury, & Karney, 2012) suggest that it is often the way we make sense of things *coming into a relationship* that matters most. That is, those who tend to be highly critical and/or make maladaptive attributions (based in childhood trauma or an array of other causes) tend to also become dissatisfied in their relationships. Changing the ways one makes attributions can also bring about greater satisfaction and decrease negative behavior, even in abusive relationships (Durtschi et al., 2011; Hrapczynski, Epstein, Werlinich, & LaTaillade, 2012).

As noted, there are ways in which people can be "retrained" to alter their global cognition or frame as well as their patterned ways of making attributions. On the face of it, doing so seems to promote a more positive morality in those relationships. Indeed, it is easy to want to encourage only relationship-enhancing attributions, as they are linked to greater satisfaction and lead to more positive behaviors at times. But doing so, I argue, may keep us from seeing our partner fully "where she is," in all of her complexity and changeability. This view is consistent with Cropley and Reid's (2008) contention that seeing partners' behavior in a too positive light is "attributional charity" and not necessarily consistent with reality. As such, in interpreting behavior through our own lenses—no matter how positive those are—we are not "being with what is" either with ourselves or in our relationships. A different perspective on being a good, moral, partner and person is to become more *mindful* in how we think about ourselves and others.

## Defining Mindfulness

Following the work of Kabat-Zinn (1990, 1994), mindfulness is defined generally as the ability to be aware of, and accept without judgment, experiences as they exist in the present moment (Brown & Ryan, 2003). More specifically, it "involves a receptive state of mind, wherein attention is kept to a bare registering of the facts observed ... the basic capacities for awareness and attention permit the individual to be present to reality ... rather than react to it or habitually process it" (Brown, Ryan, & Creswell, 2007, p. 212). Greco, Baer, and Smith (2011) note likewise that the "elements of mindfulness [include] ... observation of present-moment experience, behaving with awareness of one's current actions (rather than automatically or absentmindedly), and taking a nonjudgmental and nonreactive stance toward internal experiences such as cognitions, emotions, and bodily sensations" (p. 607). As can be seen, mindfulness differs significantly from our tendency to make attributions (i.e., judge) based on our existing perceptive lenses that tie us to past ways of understanding the world.

Mindfulness occurs in degrees, and higher levels of mindfulness have been linked with an array of positive benefits for psychological and physiological well-being (e.g., Brown et al., 2007; Dowd & McCleery, 2007), including lower levels of post-traumatic stress disorder (PTSD) symptoms, depression and anxiety, addictive behavior, and chronic distress or pain (Evans, Ferrando, Carr, & Haglin, 2010; Kabat-Zinn & Chapman-Waldrop, 1988; Kerr, Josyula, & Littenberg, 2011). These benefits are said to arise because, when mindful, personal biases or reflections on past encounters do not influence evaluations of the present moment (Brown & Ryan, 2003; Teasdale, 1999). Importantly, this large body of research conceptualizes mindfulness in two ways: as a characteristic that can be measured (i.e., a disposition or state), or a set of practices—including mindfulness meditation—that can be taught (for a review, see Manusov & Harvey-Knowles, in press).

## Mindfulness in Relationships

Clearly, there is a sizable body of research looking at the relationship between trait mindfulness and other variables important to healthy functioning. Based on its consistent relationships with and effects on increased wellness, Manusov and Harvey-Knowles (in press) argue that mindfulness is a form of resilience that allows people to better navigate through life's (and love's) vagaries. In so doing, the authors point to the emerging literature on mindfulness in personal relationships. According to Gambrel and Keeling (2010) "[t]he mindfulness process of awareness, acceptance and choice has powerful implications for personal relationships" (p. 416).

In particular, research has, similar to that on attributions, documented that mindfulness relates to *relationship satisfaction*. Wachs and Cordova (2007), for example, reported that couple members higher in dispositional mindfulness were more satisfied in their relationships; they were also likely to have higher scores on perspective taking, empathic concern, and lack of distress. Barnes, Brown, Krusemark, Campbell, and Rogge (2007) likewise found that greater trait mindfulness relates positively with relational satisfaction, and it also correlates with increased capacity to respond constructively to relational stress and to lower levels of concern about an upcoming conflict discussion. Additionally, those with higher *state* mindfulness had higher communication quality (i.e., lower verbal aggression and higher verbal support) during a conflict discussion. Jones, Welton, Oliver, and Thoburn (2011) also found a relationship between mindfulness and satisfaction, one that was mediated by attachment type.

## Seeing Mindfulness in Written Discourse

My colleagues and I conducted an initial exploratory study to look further at how dispositional mindfulness may play out in close relationships. We asked 91 participants in committed relationships (70.8% male; 27% female; 41% in same-sex relationships, and 59% in opposite-sex relationships; 57% of participants were married, 78% lived with their partner; mean length of relationship 119 months [9.9 years]; ages ranging from 22 to 66) to complete the Kentucky Inventory of Mindfulness Skills (KIMS) (Baer, Smith, & Allen, 2004) to assess their dispositional mindfulness. This instrument is one that has been used a lot in research on trait or dispositional mindfulness and assesses four mindfulness elements: observing, describing, acting with awareness, and accepting without judgment. *Observing* is the ability to attend to internal and external stimuli. *Describing* involves the capacity for labeling and defining present-moment stimuli and experiences. *Acting with awareness* refers to the capacity to focus attention on only one thing in the present-moment. *Withholding of judgment* involves the process refraining from evaluating our own and others behaviors.

We report on the quantitative data in three papers: Harvey-Knowles, Manusov, and Crowley (2013) refer to the ways in which dispositional mindfulness relates to self-reports of conflict engagement; Crowley, Manusov, and Harvey-Knowles (2014) reports on the data that tie mindfulness to forgiveness practices; and

Manusov, Harvey-Knowles, and Crowley (2014) investigate how mindfulness re-lates to emotional sensitivity to one's partner's behaviors and interpretations of a hypothetical nonverbal event. In this chapter, I provide some of the qualitative data derived from Manusov et al.'s part of the project.

To get written attributions, we gave the following prompt to our participants:

Imagine that you and your partner are watching television together at home. At some point, s/he moves farther away from you on the couch, sighs, and looks away from the show you are watching.

We then asked participants this open-ended request: Tell us what specifically you imagine would have gone through your head if you noticed the behaviors. Even though we encouraged them to write only if they would have thought about the cues, 89 of the 91 participants provided responses.

Most of the open-ended answers to what they would be thinking resulted in fairly detailed and specific answers, *suggesting a strong tendency to make attributions that reflected a set of beliefs about their partner and/or about themselves.* That is, the responses did not reflect a high degree of mindfulness, as we define it here. Rather, they showed pretty quick and clear attribution-making or, at least, explorations of a range of circumstances that may have led to the behaviors. The following reflect many of the responses we received:

I would assume my partner was upset and annoyed and believe it was something I had done (then or earlier in the day). I would be uncomfortable and want to know what he was feeling but may also be annoyed that he didn't speak up sooner perhaps. I would also be aware that it could be something unrelated to me and would want to help him process his feelings and support him.

What's wrong? Did the movie upset him? Is something bothering him? Is he ill? Must investigate and resolve to address my anxiety.

He's unhappy with his life—career, friends, how he spends his time. Same ole, same ole.

That I had done something, the show was boring or they were wishing they were some-where else.

Oh Jesus, what is it now?

My partner sometimes suffers from anxiety and obsessive thinking, so I would probably wonder what he was thinking about. I would probably wonder if it was something to do with me, but I wouldn't immediately jump to the conclusion that he was upset with me because he can often become distant just because he's worried about things at work and he can't stop thinking about it.

As can be seen, most of these answers offer one or more attributions for why the partner likely acted as s/he did. Most are more negative in tone (though not all) and either have an answer or suggest that they (the respondents) would try to figure out from several options what would have been the cause. Whereas we tend to think that trying to determine the meaning of our partner's behaviors suggests that our partners are important to us, *doing so also reflects a tendency to define/judge those actions in ways consistent with our existing views and not necessarily in more "accurate" ways.* As well, our meanings often reflect judgments of how well our partner met our expectations or acted as we wanted him/her to act.

The last of the entries provided above, however, suggests a somewhat different approach, though it still reflects a lens through which the attributor views his/her partner (i.e., knowledge of past anxiety and obsessive thinking). That is, the entry mentions "not jumping immediately to a conclusion," a response that can be labeled more mindful (at least in terms of non-judgment) than can the previous entries. Other respondents offered what seemed even more mindful internal discourse. Many of these responses emphasized curiosity/open wondering: "I would wonder and inquire about what caused her to move away from me. But I wouldn't give it meaning" and "I would wonder what was going on, but I wouldn't assume it was negative." Others suggested some meaning-making but more openness and a desire to ask the other rather than assume: "I would have thought she was slightly upset that what we were watching was taking time away from being with each other, and I would ask what the problem was and if she would like me to turn off the TV and spend one-on-one time with her."

For me, the data reflect how rapidly and, it seems, with some attributional confidence most partners make sense of one another's behaviors. Or they can think of a range of possibilities and ruminate over which one was likely. Whereas the attributions provided may well reflect a long history with their partner, they also suggest that we may pigeon hole our partner and his/her actions when there may be many other viable explanations for our partner's behavior. Moreover, having answers about rather than questions for why a partner acted a certain way can shut off dialogue that may be useful in getting to know our partner and helping make him or her feel seen by us. It is for these reasons I argue that a more mindful approach is also a more moral one than making attributions on our own. I return to this idea in the discussion.

## Mindfulness and Adolescents

This paper focuses on mindfulness in adult romantic relationships. Given its potential consequences, however, it is useful to look at mindfulness in earlier stages of life, particularly to see if it can be enhanced prior to entering into long-term relationships and at the same time as attributions are likely to be forming. Research has found that mindfulness in children and adolescents is similar overall, but developmentally different from, adult mindfulness. It is also a relatively new field of inquiry. Mindfulness in young adults can be both measured and increased, however. For instance, Greco et al. (2011) created and tested the Child and

Mindfulness Measure (CAMM). Relying on four studies and over 1400 participants, the authors also found that CAMM scores correlated positively and as expected with quality of life, academic competence, and social skills and was related negatively to "somatic complaints, internalizing symptoms, and externalizing behavior problems" (p. 606). Using a scale created for adults, Ciesla, Reilly, Dickson, Emanuel, and Updegraff (2012) also found dispositional mindfulness in young adults was related to mood and susceptibility to stress.

To fine tune how greater mindfulness can be taught at a young age, Ames et al. (2014) adapted the Mindfulness-based Cognitive Therapy program (one of the many mindfulness trainings) for adolescents with moderate depression. After the 8-week training, the authors interviewed the young people in their groups and saw reduced depression and rumination and increased mindfulness skills and overall life quality. Moreover, they learned through interviews that the adolescents thought that the training was something that was "acceptable" to them, meaning that it was a viable set of practices to undertake for people in their age group. Sibinga et al. (2013) studied young urban men and discerned that mindfulness training in schools reduced the adolescents' stress and rumination. Others (e.g., Jennings & Jennings, 2014) have found that using a modified, shorter training with peers worked well for adolescents to increase their mindfulness and decrease problematic thoughts.

This latter finding is important for the case made in this chapter. Even though most of the research focusing on both dispositional mindfulness and mindfulness training with adolescents has focused on young people who are dealing with issues such as aggression or depression and not on how mindfulness may impact sense-making in relationships, the existing evidence suggests that increased mindfulness may well help adolescents in much the same way that it supports adults. That is, findings such as those reported by Jennings and Jennings suggest that mindfulness may alter the way adolescents think about things. This could include how they think about the behaviors of those in their families and peer networks. As such, more mindfulness during adolescence could predict more mindful ways of engaging as adults. Thus, encouraging more or training in mindfulness done at a younger age may allow adolescents to engage less in (especially negative) attribution-making in both their present and future relationships. Given that the mode of attributions people tend to make and bring with them into their relationships is a strong predictor of relational satisfaction over time, encouraging mindfulness during adolescence—and perhaps even childhood—may result in better adult relating.

## DISCUSSION

In this chapter, I argue that one way to bring more morality to our intimate, romantic relationships is to bring less meaning-making. Whereas that goes against much of our teaching, it has a certain resonance when compared with understanding our partners—and ourselves—through our existing interpretive lenses. The idea is that, if we become more mindful (in the sense that we encourage awareness, being present, and not judging), we can be more fully with another person and ourselves *just as we are.* Nonjudgment does not mean that we do not discern when a way of being may be more or less harmful to us or to our partner. Indeed, being aware and present may allow us more opportunity to attend to what in ourselves, our partners, or our environment are inconsistent with what is truly good for us and others. Kabat-Zinn (1990) concurs, stating,

> [t]he path to developing our capacity to express love more fully is to bring awareness to our actual feelings, to observe them mindfully, to work at being non-judgmental and more patient and accepting. If we ignore our own feelings ... sooner or later our connections ... may become strained or badly frayed, even broken. This is especially so if we are unable to see and accept them for who they actually are. (p. 224)

Acting with mindfulness, being curious rather than confident about the meaning for behavior, allows, as was seen in the data reported here, for new information to arise, for learning to happen, for unexpected opportunities to emerge. Sometimes this leads to greater closeness; *it may also lead us to make choices that separate us from another.* But in either case, our choices are based on what is occurring rather than what we think is occurring or how we assess it in patterned, potentially biased ways.

One choice could be to engage in dialogue about the behaviors. Mindfulness does not lead directly to dialogue, nor would its practitioners say that it is always the best course. That is, noticing our own thoughts about our partner can lead to our own investigation. "Why did that upset me so?"; How come it feels so good when she says things like that?" Such self-inquiry can lead to significant life changes that can affect our relationship. Other times, however, mindfulness, particularly when we are genuinely "curious" about another's action, can start an open dialogue that allows us to learn more about the other or ourselves. In both cases, if handled with sensitivity and a real desire to learn, the results of greater mindfulness can be seen as particularly good—as moral—outcomes.

As noted, we can become more mindful. Indeed, it may be that this happens naturally over the course of our lives. The data my colleagues and I collected showed a positive relationship between age and mindfulness. But at any time—from childhood, particularly during adolescence, and as adults—we can learn to be more mindful, and this can be enhanced with training. The most well-known method of mindfulness training is Kabat-Zinn's (1990) Mindfulness Based Stress Reduction (MBSR) program, an 8-week course that teaches such activities as mindful eating and, most centrally, mindful meditation. This form of meditation encourages those who practice it to sit (or walk) in stillness. As thoughts come up—and they always do—the training encourages us to notice them and then focus again on stillness.

Among other things, mindfulness meditation and other practices allows us to notice our own thought patterns, all without judgment. For me, I noticed over time how often my own observations of others are accompanied by "should" and "should nots." So, for example, I noticed a woman crossing the street, walking very slowly while talking on her phone. My thought was "She should know she is holding people up, and she should therefore walk faster." Attending to this—and the myriad other similar messages—helped me see how often I project rules onto others and myself. Because of the mindfulness practice, I was able to be curious about this pattern and explore it, all without judgment (okay, with some judgment, as I am still learning mindfulness in my everyday life).

The MBSR is an incredible course, though it is only a beginning to a lifetime endeavor. It has also been adapted to work with more specific populations. Carson, Carson, Gill, and Baucom (2004), for instance, revised the MBSR to use with couples, creating a program known as Mindfulness-based Relationship Enhancement, and many of the activities (such as partner yoga) are done in tandem rather than individually. The authors provide evidence of its effectiveness in enhancing couples' relationships. Both courses are, however, big undertakings. Books and audio courses (e.g., Williams & Penman, 2011) also exist that teach many of the same practices. Some researchers are also exploring whether mindfulness can be increased with much shorter trainings. This would be promising, as it means that formal teaching would be able to reach a wider audience.

This chapter has been an intriguing one for me to write. Most of my academic career, I have been interested in how people make sense of and talk about the meanings for behavior. I have been particularly interested in the attributions couples make for one another's nonverbal cues, as such behavior can be "given" a range of meanings. I have asked for and analyzed people's attributions—even those provided by the media for public nonverbal events—but never asked myself if our tendency to be "naïve scientists" comes at a cost. As I have learned about mindfulness, I have come to believe that it does.

## REFERENCES

Ames, C. S., Richardson, J., Payne, S., & Leigh, E. (2014). Mindfulness-based cognitive therapy for depression in adolescents. *Child and Adolescent Mental Health, 19,* 74–78.

Badahdah, A. M., & Alkhder, O. H. (2006). Helping a friend with AIDS: A test of Weiner's attributional theory in Kuwait. *Illness, Crisis, & Loss, 14,* 43–54.

Baer, R. A., Smith, G. T., Allen, K. B. (2004). Assessment of mindfulness by self-report: The Kentucky Inventory of Mindfulness Skills. *Assessment, 11,* 191–206.

Barnes, S., Brown, K. W., Krusemark, E., Campbell, W. K., & Rogge, R. D. (2007). The role of mindfulness in romantic relationship satisfaction and responses to relationship stress. *Journal of Marital and Family Therapy, 33*(4), 482–500.

Baucom, D. H. (1987). Attributions in distressed relations: How can we explain them? In D. Perlman & S. Duck (Eds.), *Intimate relationships: Development, dynamics, and deterioration* (pp. 177–206). Newbury Park, CA: Sage.

Berscheid, E., Lopes, J., Ammazzalorso, H., & Langenfeld, N. (2001). Causal attributions of relationship quality. In V. Manusov & J. H. Harvey (Eds.), *Attribution, communication behavior, and close relationships* (pp. 115–133). Cambridge, England: Cambridge University Press.

Bradbury, T. N., & Fincham, F. D. (1990). Attributions in marriage: Review and critique. *Psychological Bulletin, 107*, 3–33.

Bradbury, T. N., & Fincham, F. D. (1992). Attributions and behavior in marital interaction. *Journal of Personality and Social Psychology, 63*, 613–628.

Brody, G., Arias, I., & Fincham, F. D. (1996). Linking marital and child attributions to family processes and parent-child relationships. *Journal of Family Psychology, 10*, 408–421.

Brown, K. W., & Ryan, R. M. (2003). The benefits of being present: Mindfulness and its role in psychological well-being. *Journal of Personality and Social Psychology, 84*, 822–848.

Brown, K. W., Ryan, R. M., & Creswell, J. D. (2007). Mindfulness: Theoretical foundations and evidence for its salutary effects. *Psychological Inquiry, 18*, 211–237.

Bugental, D. B., Shennum, W., Frank, M., & Ekman, P. (2001). "True lies": Children's abuse history and power attributions as influences on deception detection. In V. Manusov & J. H. Harvey (Eds.), *Attribution, communication behavior, and close relationships* (pp. 248–265). Cambridge, England: Cambridge University Press.

Burleson, B. R. (1986). Attribution schemes and causal inference in natural conversations. In D. G. Ellis & W. A. Donohue (Eds.), *Contemporary issues in language and discourse processes* (pp. 63–85). Mahwah, NJ: Erlbaum.

Carson, J. W., Carson, K. M., Gil, K. M., & Baucom, D. H. (2004). Mindfulness-based relationship enhancement. *Behavior Therapy, 35*, 471–494.

Chodkiewicz, A., & Boyle, C. (2014). Exploring the contribution of attribution retraining to student perceptions and the learning process. *Educational Psychology in Practice, 30*, 78–87.

Ciesla, J. A., Reilly, L. C., Dickson, K. S. Emanuel, A. S., & Updegraff, J. A. (2012). Dispositional mindfulness moderates the effects of stress among adolescents: Rumination as a mediator. *Journal of Clinical Child and Adolescent Psychology, 41*, 760–770.

Crittenden, K. S., & Wiley, M. G. (1985). When egotism is normative: Self-presentational norms guiding attributions. *Social Psychology Quarterly, 48*, 360–365.

Cropley, C. J., & Reid, S. A. (2008). A latent variable analysis of couple closeness, attributions, and relational satisfaction. *Family Journal, 16*, 364–374.

Crowley, J. P., Manusov, V., & Harvey-Knowles, J. A. (2014, May). *How we forgive: The mediating role of mindfulness in the forgiveness process.* Paper presented to the International Communication Association, Seattle.

Davey, A., Fincham, F. D., Beach, S. R. H., & Brody, G. H. (2001). Attributions in marriage: Examining the entailment model in dyadic context. *Journal of Family Psychology, 15*(4), 721–734.

Dowd, T., & McCleery, A. (2007). Elements of Buddhist philosophy in cognitive psychotherapy: The role of cultural specifics and universals. *Journal of Cognitive and Behavioral Psychotherapies, 7*, 67–79.

Durtschi, J. A., Fincham, F. D., Cui, M., Lorenz, F. O., & Conger, R. D. (2011). Dyadic processes in early marriage: Attributions, behavior, and marital quality. *Family Relations, 60*, 421–434.

Evans, S., Ferrando, S., Carr, C., & Haglin, D. (2010). Mindfulness Based Stress Reduction (MBSR) and distress in a community-based sample. *Clinical Psychology and Psychotherapy.* Published online in Wiley Online Library (wileyonlinelibrary.com). doi: 10.1002/cpp.727

Fincham, Beach, Arias, and Brody (1998). Children's attributions in the family: The Children's Relationship Attribution Measure. *Journal of Family Psychology, 12*, 481–493.

Finlay, A. K., Cookston, J. T., Saenz, D. S., Baham, M. E., Parke, R. D., Fabricius, W., & Braver, S. (2014). Attributions of fathering behaviors among adolescents: The role of gender, ethnicity, family structure, and depressive symptoms. *Journal of Family Issues, 35*, 501–525.

Gambrel, L. E., & Keeling, M. L. (2010). Relational aspects of mindfulness: Implications for the practice of marriage and family therapy. *Contemporary Family Therapy, 32*, 412–426.

Gardner, B. C., Busby, D. M., Burr, B. K., & Lyon, S. E. (2011). Getting to the root of relationship attributions: Family-of-origin perspectives on self and partner views. *Contemporary Family Therapy, 33*, 253–272.

Gottman, J. M., Markman, H. J., & Notarius, C. I. (1977). The topography of marital conflict: A sequential analysis of verbal and nonverbal behaviors. *Journal of Marriage and the Family, 39*, 461–477.

Greco, L. A., Baer, R. A., & Smith, G. T. (2011). Assessing mindfulness in children and adolescents: Development and validation of the Child and Adolescent Mindfulness Measure (CAMM). *Psychological Assessment, 23*, 606–614.

Halligan, S. L. Cooper, P. J., Healy, S. J., & Murray, L. (2007). The attribution of hostile intent in mothers, fathers and their children. *Journal of Abnormal Child Psychology, 35*, 594–604.

Harvey-Knowles, J. A, Manusov, V., & Crowley, J. P. (2013, November). *Minding your matters: Predicting relational satisfaction, commitment, and conflict styles from trait-mindfulness.* Paper presented to the National Communication Association, Washington D. C.

Heider, F. (1958). *The psychology of interpersonal relations.* New York: Wiley.

Hilton, D. J. (1990). Conversational process and causal explanation. *Psychological Bulletin, 107*, 65–81.

Holtzworth-Munroe, A., & Jacobson, N. S. (1988). Toward a methodology for coding spontaneous causal attributions: Preliminary results with married couples. *Journal of Social and Clinical Psychology, 7*, 101–112.

Hrapczynski, K. M., Epstein, N. B., Werlinich, C. A., LaTaillade, J. J. (2012). Changes in negative attributions during couple therapy for abusive behavior. *Journal of Marital and Family Therapy, 38*, 117–132.

Jennings, S. J., & Jennings, J. L. (2014). Peer-directed, brief mindfulness training with adolescents: A pilot study. *International Journal of Behavioral Consultation and Therapy, 8*, 23–24.

Johnson, M. D., Karney, B. R., Rogge, R., & Bradbury, T. N. (2001). The role of marital behavior in the longitudinal associations between attributions and marital quality. In V. Manusov & J. H. Harvey (Eds.), *Attribution, communication behavior, and close relationships* (pp. 173–192). Cambridge, England: Cambridge University Press.

Jones, K. C., Welton, S. R., Oliver, T. C., & Thoburn, J. W. (2011). Mindfulness, spousal attachment, and marital satisfaction: A mediated model. *The Family Journal, 19*, 357-361.

Kabat-Zinn, J. (1990). *Full catastrophe living: Using the wisdom of your body and mind to face stress, pain, and illness.* New York: Random House.

Kabat-Zinn, J. (1994). *Wherever you go there you are: Mindfulness meditation in everyday life.* New York: Hyperion.

Kabat-Zinn, J., & Chapman-Waldrop, A. (1988). Compliance with an outpatient stress reduction program: Rates and predictors of program completion. *Journal of Behavioral Medicine, 11*, 333–352.

Kelley, H. H. (1971). *Attribution in social interaction.* New York: General Learning Press.

Kerr, C. E., Josyula, K., & Littenberg, R. (2011). Developing an observing attitude: An analysis of patient diaries in a MBSR clinical trial. *Clinical Psychology and Psychotherapy, 8*, 80–93.

Lavner, J. A., Bradbury, T. N., & Karney, B. R. (2012). Incremental change or initial differences? Testing two models of marital deterioration. *Journal of Family Psychology, 26,* 606–616.

Manusov, V. (1990). An application of attribution principles to nonverbal messages in romantic dyads. *Communication Monographs, 57,* 104–118.

Manusov, V. (1995). Reacting to changes in nonverbal behavior: Relational satisfaction and adaptation patterns in romantic dyads. *Human Communication Research, 21,* 456–477.

Manusov, V. (1996). Intentionality attributions for naturally-occurring nonverbal behaviors in intimate relationships. In J. E. Aitken & L. J. Shedletsky (Eds.), *Intrapersonal communication processes* (pp. 343–353). Plymouth, MI: Midnight Oil Multimedia.

Manusov, V. (2002). Thought and action: Connecting attributions to behaviors in married couples' interactions. In P. Noller & J. A. Feeney (Eds.), *Understanding marriage: Developments in the study of couple interaction* (pp. 14–31). Cambridge, UK: Cambridge University Press.

Manusov, V., Floyd, K., & Kerssen-Griep, J. (1997). Yours, mine, and ours: Mutual attributions for nonverbal behaviors in couples' interactions. *Communication Research, 24,* 234–260.

Manusov, V., & Harvey-Knowles, J. A. (in press). On being (and becoming) mindful: One pathway to greater resilience. In G. Beck & T. Socha (Eds.). *Communicating hope and resilience across the lifespan.* New York: Peter Lang.

Manusov, V., Harvey-Knowles, J. A., & Crowley, J. P. (2014, November). *The role of mindfulness in sensitivity to and interpretation of nonverbal cues by couple members.* Paper presented to the National Communication Association, Chicago.

Manusov, V., & Koenig, J. (2001). The content of attributions in couples' communication. In V. Manusov & J. H. Harvey (Eds.), *Attribution, communication behavior, and close relationships* (pp. 134–152). Cambridge, England: Cambridge University Press.

Manusov, V., & Spitzberg, B. H. (2008). Attributes of attribution theory: Finding good cause in the search for theory. In D. O. Braithwaite & L. A. Baxter (Eds.), *Engaging theories in interpersonal communication* (pp. 37–49). Thousand Oaks, CA: Sage Publications.

Miller, G. E., & Bradbury, T. N. (1995). Refining the association between attributions and behavior in marital interaction. *Journal of Family Psychology, 9,* 196–208.

Miller, L. E., Howell, K. H, & Graham-Bermann, S. A. (2014). Developmental changes in threat and self-blame for preschoolers exposed to IPV. *Journal of Interpersonal Violence, 29*(9), 1535–1553.

Newman, H. (1981). Communication within ongoing intimate relationships: An attributional perspective. *Personality and Social Psychology Bulletin, 7,* 59–70.

Peterson, K. M., Smith, D. A., & Windle, C. R. (2009). Explication of interspousal criticality bias. *Behaviour Research and Therapy, 47,* 478–486.

Pszyszynski, T. A., & Greenberg, J. (1981). Role of disconfirmed expectancies in the instigation of attributional processing. *Journal of Personality and Social Psychology, 40,* 31–38.

Ronfard, S., & Harris, P. L. (2014). When will Little Red Riding Hood become scared? Children's attribution of mental state to a story character. *Developmental Psychology, 50,* 283–292.

Ross, L. (1977). The intuitive psychologist and his shortcomings. Distortions in the attribution process. In L. Berkowitz (Ed.), *Advances in experimental social psychology* (vol. 10, pp. 174–177). New York: Academic Press.

Rybash, J. M., Roodin, P. A., Hallion, K. (1979). The role of affect in children's attributions of intentionality and dispensation of punishment. *Child Development, 50,* 1227–1231.

Sanford, K. (2006). Communication during marital conflict: When couples alter their appraisal, they change their behavior. *Journal of Family Psychology, 20,* 256–265.

Sibinga, E. M. S., Perry-Parrish, C., Chung, S., Johnson, S. B., Smith, M., & Ellen, J. M. (2013). School-based mindfulness instruction for urban male youth: A small randomized controlled trial. *Preventative Medicine, 57,* 799–801.

Sillars, A. L., Leonard, K. E., Roberts, L. J., & Dunn, T. (2002). Cognition and communication during marital conflict: How alcohol affects subjective coding of interaction in aggressive and nonaggressive couples. In P. Noller & J. A. Feeney (Eds.), *Understanding marriage: Developments in the study of couple interaction* (pp. 85–112). Cambridge, England: Cambridge University Press.

Silvester, J., Arnon, B., Stratton, P., & Hanks, H. (1995). Using spoken attributions to classify abusive families. *Child Abuse & Neglect, 19,* 1221–1232.

Sodian, B. (1988). Children's attributions of knowledge to the listener in a referential communication task. *Child Development, 59,* 378–385.

Spitzberg, B. H., & Manusov, V. (in press). Attributes of attribution theory: Finding good cause in the search for theory. In D. O. Braithwaite & P. Schrodt (Eds.), *Engaging theories in interpersonal communication* (2nd ed.). Thousand Oaks, CA: Sage Publications.

Teasdale, J. D. (1999). Metacognition, mindfulness, and the modification of mood disorders. *Clinical Psychology & Psychotherapy, 6,* 146–155.

Vangelisti, A. L., Corbin, S. D., Lucchetti, A. E., & Sprague, R. J. (1999). Couples' concurrent cognition: The influence of relational satisfaction in the thoughts couples have as they converse. *Human Communication Research, 25,* 370–398.

Wachs, K., & Cordova, J. V. (2007). Mindful relating: Exploring mindfulness and emotion repertoires in intimate relationships. *Journal of Marital & Family Therapy, 33*(4), 464–481.

Weiner, B. (1985). An attributional theory of achievement motivation and emotion. *Psychological Bulletin, 92,* 548–573.

Weiner, B. (1995). *Judgments of responsibility: A foundation for a theory of social conduct.* New York: Guilford.

Weston, H. E., Boxer, P., & Heatherington, L. (1998). Children's attributions about family arguments: Implications for family therapy. *Family Process, 37,* 35–49.

Williams, M., & Penman, D. (2011). *Mindfulness: An eight-week plan for finding peace in a frantic world.* New York: Rodale.

# Epilogue

## Good Relationship Talk

DOUGLAS KELLEY & VINCENT WALDRON

This volume has focused on the discourse that makes relationships good. Each chapter author has examined how relationship partners negotiate moral aspects of their relationships. In light of these exploratory peeks into moral communication processes and various relationship phenomena, we offer three concluding questions regarding how we communicate about, and in, *good relationships*: What do relational partners understand as moral in their own relationships? How do relational partners engage in moral negotiation with one another? Is it useful to think of personal relationships in moral terms?

## WHAT IS A GOOD RELATIONSHIP?

By framing this section as, "What is good ..." or "What is moral ..." we hope *not* to do several things. First, we do not mean to discuss what people typically think is "moral" regarding specific issues (e.g., on average how many parents think premarital sex is wrong?). Second, we do not mean to prescribe moral stances for partners or parents. Finally, we sincerely hope not to cast this epilogue as the final moral word.

We do hope to carefully glean some of the significant moral elements of human interaction that have been represented by the chapter authors in this book, specifically by focusing on what relational partners consider to be overarching moral themes in their personal relationships. One of the most interesting aspects of editing this volume was engaging each author (and each other) as we all wrestled with the notion of morality in our research. Generally, the first drafts of each chapter focused on the more obvious dimensions of moral negotiation in personal relationships. However, the challenge was often to explore more subtle nuances of "moral" talk between relational partners and/or parents and children. In Doug's work, he and his research assistants had multiple conversations about what constituted justice talk in couples' relationships. This was a complicated task. For example, one of the terms that surfaced, *respect*, has numerous possible relational meanings. As it turns out, at times couples used *respect* to represent both distributive and processual justice. Respect was spoken of both as something partners held in equal amounts (distributive justice) and something couples enacted (respecting one another). Likewise, Vince and his co-authors grappled with decisions regarding memorable moral messages. One of the themes that ran through remembered-parent messages was *confidence building*. They had extensive discussions regarding this category. The idea of building confidence was often implied in participant remembrances ("It helps reassure me …", "I know I can overcome …", "made me realize I was not being the best version of myself …"), but these efforts to bolster moral identity are less familiar than, say, moral injunctions: "Don't cheat," "Always tell us the truth."

The chapters of this volume provide a rich and diverse overview of the themes characterizing moral communication. For example, Socha and Eller describe how parents develop character strengths and competency in both moral reasoning and ethical communication. Likewise, Waldron et al. report the content of memorable parental messages to include qualities of virtuous people and good personal relationships, including honesty and compassion. In addition, they found moral communication to include identity messages, such as the importance of self-development and self-respect, and some messages included references to outside moral authorities, such as God or Scriptures. Similarly, Soliz and Rittenour found memorable moral messages from grandparents to contain statements regarding "right" or "wrong" ways to live a fulfilling life, to develop and maintain relationships with grandparents and others, and pragmatic advice regarding such issues as finances and work.

Other researchers found moral themes to *emerge* as partners negotiate relational disruptions. Guerrero and Cole found various relational transgressions threaten standards of fidelity, honesty, care, and autonomy. Vangelisti and Nelson found that moral conversations often include revealing secrets. It turns out that we reveal secrets for what we consider are "good" reasons—concern for the welfare of others, right to know, storytelling/gossip, self-expression, relationship influence, and self-interest. Fisher and Wolf surfaced standards that guide the efforts of mothers and daughters to cope with breast cancer. Stay positive. Hide your doubts. Don't discuss death. Accept Mom's expressions of emotion.

Two of us focused on the enactment of one particular moral theme—justice. Baxter et al., examined the use of poetic justice in personal relationships. Interestingly, their work demonstrates that poetic justice is viewed as a moral response because it includes some of the following elements: symmetry between "wrong" behavior and the responses' form or consequences, benefitting others, lessons learned by the wrongdoer, and limited harm to the relationship. Doug found that couples' "just" communication involved words related to distribution and process, including relationship policies or rules, quality of interactions, and certain relationship characteristics. Together these studies demonstrate how individuals construe just behavior as fair, equitable, and that which benefits and teaches others to live well.

As we reflect on the data reported in this volume, we think a good representation of how individuals generally represent relational morality in their talk can be framed as follows: Is it good for you? Is it good for me? We do not think this is a shallow representation reflecting the narcissistic values of our current culture. Rather, it seems to us that even the most authority-based moral platitudes are often passed down because the giver believes that they are what is best for individuals, family, and culture. As is evident across the chapters in this volume, relationally-based moral messages are not generally intended to facilitate short-term positive feelings. Rather, they are intended to facilitate substantive, lasting good for each partner and their joint relationship. Fisher and Wolf's work represents this perspective as their data most often revealed morality as related to positive physical and psychological health outcomes. Likewise, Vince's work on memorable moral messages clearly emphasizes talk related to treating others well and treating one's self well often with the goal of developing particular character strengths. Doug's conceptualization of processual justice as including certain relationship characteristics emphasizes relational partners' desires to treat one another in just ways that reinforce the essence of their humanity (e.g., respect one another).

This common theme, that relational morality is behaving in ways that assimilates what is ultimately best for one's self and one's relational partner, is perhaps best represented in Manusov's essay. She suggests that mindfulness is a means, or a way of being, that allows one to live nonjudgmentally. More specifically, she states that through mindfulness, "we can be more fully with another person and ourselves *just as we are* ... Indeed, being aware and present may allow us more opportunity to attend to what in ourselves, our partners, or our environment are inconsistent with what is truly good for us and others."

## HOW DO RELATIONAL PARTNERS ENGAGE IN GOOD TALK?

If relational partners primarily view morality in their relationships as, What's good for you? What's good for me? the next question we are bound to ask is, How do relational partners engage in good talk? Or, How do relational partners negotiate what is good for them and their partners?

Most central to the question of "good talk" are the many and varied examples of how "moral" talk is negotiated in relationships presented in this volume. It is one thing to engage in moral reasoning and to even have "good" character, but it is another thing to be able to pass these elements on to one's children or to negotiate them with one's relational partner. As Socha and Eller state, "Sometimes individuals may know what the 'right' thing to do in a situation might be, but may also lack the abilities to reach their goals."

The essays presented here demonstrate that negotiating morality is a varied and, often, sophisticated process. Illustrative of this, Vince's work shows that more accepted parental messages are often those that convey moral content while simultaneously helping the recipient adapt the message to "real life" conditions. Baxter et al.'s analysis of poetic justice reveals it to be a subtle kind of revenge, one that must be used judiciously, a calibrated response to violations of community norms; Guerrero and cole determined that moral communication was adapted to the type of moral violation; Vangelisti and Nelson showed us that revealing secrets is a moral act often conducted for a complex set of "good" reasons; and, Doug's work reveals that, at times, partners use words that invoke justice plainly (e.g., discussions about things being fair in the relationship) and at other times, use more nuanced terms such as "balance."

What is essential here is that moral talk, even authoritatively-based moral talk, is rarely simple, either in its presentation or its effect. Embedded in each piece of discourse is a reminder that we negotiate morality with reference to the qualities of our relationship (e.g., a parent teaching a child or a relational partner dealing with a moral violation), our partner, and ourselves. It is evident that individuals need the foundational elements of good moral reasoning and good character. However, good thinking and good character will not guarantee good outcomes. The complexity of our relationships calls for a rich repertoire of moral communication strategies.

A focus on communication is a focus on process. In the spirit of Marshall McLuhan's (1964) well worn line, "The medium is the message," we suggest that moral meaning arises in part from the processes used to communicate about morality in our relationships. Is our partner really listening to our moral concerns? Are our decision-making processes fair? Are we being transparent about our motives?

Are we making a good faith effort to be present, empathetic, just? Even if we disagree on a given moral question ("Is it ever ok to spank our kid?") affirmative answers to these "process questions" may lead us to the conclusion that our relationship is good in the moral sense of that word.

This idea was made clear this past weekend when Doug conducted a relationship seminar for about 250 college students. He gave a brief introduction and then audience members texted their questions to a moderator who quickly posed them to Doug. These were real questions from students—curious, hurting, lost, looking for love and intimacy, and trying to safeguard their hearts. The preponderance of these texts were expressions of moral concern. The students were asking the same questions in a variety of ways: Am I in a good relationship? What is the right thing to do in my relationship? What does a good relationship really look like? Almost always, Doug's responses addressed the communication process. While he addressed the content of their concerns, Doug found himself focusing always on whether there was potential to talk out significant relationship differences? When one young woman asked, "How can I tell my boyfriend I want to stop having sex," Doug's response didn't address the morality of premarital sex, or the "how-tos" of sexual talk, but rather went something like this, "What a great opportunity to see how he responds to your request. You can find out if he is the kind of person who wants to understand you and talk through the nature of your relationship. Perhaps more important than whether you are having sex, or not, is determining whether you can work through issues like this, together." This response takes the moral weight off of sex and places it on how the couple is, to use Manusov's language, mindfully present together. Likewise, another of our students who was living with her boyfriend decided she wanted to move out, but still see him. However, she was afraid to tell him directly, until she had a new lease and was ready to move her things. When she asked for advice, the response was, "Is this the kind of relationship you want, one where you can't be honest and are afraid of his potential response. This is a good opportunity to find out if he is the kind of person (has the kind of moral character) you want to give yourself to, one who wants to understand you and work together to shape the relationship."

These examples demonstrate the importance of how we talk about morality in our relationships. They emphasize the need for relationship partners to communicate clearly regarding significant moral concerns. Yet, they highlight the fact that the process of communication itself is possibly more central to the moral question being posed. Manusov makes this point when she encourages us to consider focusing less on attributions and more on how we are present with our relational partner. This brings us to our final question, Is moral talk good for us?

## GOOD RELATIONSHIPS: IS MORAL TALK GOOD FOR YOU? GOOD FOR ME? GOOD FOR US?

In Arizona we are about to vote for our next governor and attorney general. Watching what one can stomach of local political ads rather painfully demonstrates that casting issues in moral terms is sometimes unhelpful and even annoying. The long list of moral and ethical infractions by candidates, and concomitant use of "should," "ought," "good," and "bad" makes one want to turn off the television until mid-November. While moral talk is certainly warranted and necessary in certain public and private contexts (take for instance the recent issues involving American football players and domestic abuse), we must be cognizant of the inherent risks of viewing our relationship problems exclusively through a moral lens.

Moralizing is quite different from moral dialogue. Moralizing polarizes positions and demonizes partners. Moralizing has the potential to turn complex challenges, into simplistic, black-and-white decisions. Try asking a struggling married couple if it is helpful or hurtful to frame their conflict in moral terms: "He 'should' better understand me," "She 'ought' to be able to balance a checkbook," "People just don't …," "I would never stay with someone who …," "Anyone who does … is a…." Moralizing undermines the flexibility needed to respond creatively to real world moral challenges. As Fisher and Wolf put it, "While at times moral discourse can inform healthy coping behavior, it can also complicate it. Families may have cultivated their own norms of behavior … but may also find it difficult to enact *flexible* coping behaviors when they are not reinforced by broader moral discourses at the societal level." (*emphasis in original*)

In contrast, moral dialogue represents honest, respectful conversation about those things that are most central to our relationships, the commitments we share and those we do not. A basic tenet of our negotiated morality theory, consistent with many of the essays presented here, is that human beings are moral creatures who negotiate their moral identities. The words we choose and the practices we endorse clearly show that we are, by nature, deeply concerned with morality. Inherent to our development as *human* beings is our growth as *moral* beings. As these chapters have illustrated so well, this lifelong process is enriched by complicated, fascinating, frustrating, and sometimes exhilarating conversations with our friends, family members, and lovers.

Yet, moral talk is not simply discussing the dos and don'ts of life in order to assess who is wrong and who is right. Manusov, in a wonderful moment of transparency, again helps us here:

> I have asked for and analyzed people's attributions—even those provided by the media for public nonverbal events—but never asked myself if our tendency to be "naïve scientists" comes at a cost. As I have learned about mindfulness, I have come to believe that it does.

Manusov reminds us that morality is a matter of perspective taking or "seeing," and that when this seeing is mostly oriented toward cause-and-effect judgments, there is a great relational price to be paid. Mindfulness moves us away from judgment, toward learning to "be" with one another and, ultimately, ourselves. We see this point reinforced in Fisher and Wolf's observations regarding an ethic of care, wherein solace behavior is primarily conceptualized as "being there." Perhaps simply being there for others is the most fundamental act of moral communication.

We finish our moral musings about what constitutes *good communication* in *good relationships* by returning to the idea of whether moral talk is good for us, and by reflecting on a recent development in our long study of forgiveness. This fall semester has been particularly busy as we have taken our research to the streets in the form of a forgiveness education program called *The Forgiveness Tree Ceremony*. During numerous local community-based *Forgiveness Tree* workshops a key theme has emerged over and over again—people are looking for a way to get unstuck from their moral pain. Feeling bitter, and angry, and shameful simply is not a sufficient response to deep moral hurt. It seems that dwelling on the moral aspects of our, or others', mistakes can keep us stuck and potentially diminish our humanness.

More optimistically, however, dwelling on the moral promise of our joint futures repeatedly shows itself to be a fruitful, life-giving endeavor that ensures our humanness. Philosopher Hannah Arendt (1958; Petersen, 2001) stated that, as humans, we are able to remember the irreversible past, but powerless to change it; and we are able to imagine the possible future, but powerless to control it. To paraphrase Arendt, forgiveness is the only suitable response to the past, and promise is all we can bring to the future. As we have often stated in our classrooms and community workshops—there is no perfect justice for past wrongs; however, we can seek wholeness by healing our damaged pasts and actively engaging *what's good for you* and *what's good for me* as we jointly construct a moral future. In this sense, moral talk, as it heals the past and constructs a positive future, truly is good.

## REFERENCES

Arendt, H. (1958). *The human condition.* Chicago: The University of Chicago Press.

McLuhan, M. (1964). *Understanding media: The extensions of man.* New York: McGraw-Hill.

Petersen, R. L. (2001). A theology of forgiveness. In R. G. Helmick, S. J., & R. L. Petersen (Eds.), *Forgiveness and reconciliation* (pp. 3–25). Philadephia: Templeton Foundation Press.

# Contributors

**Leslie A. Baxter** is Collegiate Fellow, College of Liberal Arts & Sciences, and Professor of Communication Studies at the University of Iowa, where she was also named F. Wendell Miller Distinguished Professor. She has published 160 scholarly articles, chapters, and books, and she is honored to have received several awards from various professional associations for her scholarship. She is interested in the discursive struggles of meaning making, especially in post-nuclear families.

**Dawn O. Braithwaite** is a Willa Cather Professor and Chair of Communication at the University of Nebraska-Lincoln. She studies how people in personal and family relationships interact and negotiate family change and challenges, focusing on communication in understudied and changing families, communication rituals, and dialectics of relating in stepfamilies and among voluntary kin. Dr. Braithwaite has authored over 100 articles and is co-editor or co-author of five books. She received the National Communication Association's Brommel Award for Outstanding Contributions in Family Communication, the division's Book Award, the University of Nebraska-Lincoln College of Arts & Sciences Award for Outstanding Research in Social Science. Dr. Braithwaite was named the Western States Communication Association Distinguished Scholar in 2014 and is currently a Senior Fellow with the Council on Contemporary Families. She is a Past President of the Western States Communication Association, received the Distinguished Service Award, and was President of the National Communication Association.

**Megan Cole** is a Ph.D. candidate at Arizona State University where she studies communication in mediated and face-to-face personal relationships and is active in the Conflict Transformation Project.

**Joshua Danaher** is an Assistant Professor of Communication Studies at Grand Canyon University. His teaching and research interests revolve around religious and philosophical discourse, persuasion, communication ethics, and interpersonal communication. He is coauthor of a book chapter in *Communicating Emotion at Work* (Polity, 2012) and has coauthored an article appearing in the *Journal of Family Communication*.

**Angela Eller** is a graduate student in Lifespan & Digital Communication at Old Dominion University in Norfolk, Virginia. She is a graduate from Bluefield College (Bluefield, Virginia) and has extensive experience in early-childhood education as a pre-school teacher. She is working on an MA thesis that is testing the efficacy of using a videogame that she designed and built as a platform for positive character education (i.e., teaching about kindness) in early-elementary education. She aspires to one day design positive-communication videogames in Silicon Valley.

**Carla L. Fisher,** Ph.D. is an Assistant Professor at George Mason University's Department of Communication and Center for Health & Risk Communication. She is a former Pre-doctoral Fellow with the National Institute on Aging with post-doctoral training in health behavior theory from the National Cancer Institute. Using a lifespan, developmental lens she examines how families cope with aging and health transitions and the therapeutic or long-term health implications of their interaction. She has received federal, private, and local funding and published in journals like *Health Communication* and *Journal of Genetic Counseling*. Her primary research program on mother-daughter communication, breast cancer coping, and prevention has been honored with national awards and involves collaborations with leading institutions like Mayo Clinic and Memorial Sloan-Kettering Cancer Center (research web site: www.motherdaughterbreastcancer.com). Her book, *Coping Together, Side by Side: Enriching Mother-Daughter Communication Across the Breast Cancer Journey,* was published in Hampton Press' health communication series.

**Carmen Goman** (M.A. Arizona State University West) is a Ph.D. student at Georgia State University. She studies forgiveness at the intersections of health, ethics, and interpersonal/international relationships.

**Laura K. Guerrero** studies communication in close relationships, with a special emphasis on emotional and nonverbal communication. Her research focuses on how communication affects relationships in positive and negative ways. She has studied how people communicate intimacy and forgiveness as ways to keep relationships healthy. She has also looked at how people communicate in situations where they are jealous, hurt, or angry. In these situations, certain forms of communication can enhance understanding and improve relationships, whereas other forms of communication can make problems worse. Dr. Guerrero has published over 100 articles and chapters on these topics and has received several research awards. She has created questionnaires that measure communicative responses to jealousy, conflict styles, and attachment styles. She has also developed an observational technique for coding behaviors showing nonverbal intimacy from videotapes.

**Douglas Kelley** (Ph.D. 1988, University of Arizona) studies interpersonal communication processes. His recent work includes the book *Marital Communication* (2012). In addition, his co-authored book with Vince Waldron, *Communicating Forgiveness* (2008), has received both the Distinguished Book in Family Communication Award and the Sue DeWine Distinguished Award for a Scholarly Book. Professor Kelley's work has also appeared in such outlets as the *Journal of Social and Personal Relationships, Journal of Applied Gerontology, Communication Quarterly*, and the *Journal of Communication and Religion*. Dr. Kelley, a recipient of the Centennial Professor Award, teaches relationship-based courses and conducts workshops in the community on forgiveness and reconciliation, marital and family communication, conflict processes, and relational communication (including intimacy and love). Of particular note is his service-learning course, Inner City Families. Doug lives in Phoenix, Arizona, and thinks about writing and teaching while hiking and kayaking.

**Dayna Kloeber** is a faculty associate at Arizona State University where she teaches courses such as conflict and negotiation, storytelling, public speaking and community forgiveness education. Most of Dayna's research centers on the topic of cultivating sustainable personal and professional relationships through communication. This book topic intersects nicely with a prevalent theme among Kloeber's research—authentic relationships occasionally require multivocal negotiations about forgiveness and morality. As such, Kloeber's primary research topic has been conditional forgiveness. Dayna is also passionate about taking forgiveness education to communities beyond the university. She is the founder of The Forgiveness Tree Ceremony and leads The Forgiveness Tree Project along with Vince Waldron and Doug Kelley.

Their group has conducted forgiveness education and tree ceremonies in an inner-city neighborhood center, art gallery, community college, residence hall, and an adult detention center.

**Valerie Manusov** (Ph.D. 1989, University of Southern California) is a Professor at the University of Washington. Her overall interests are in interpersonal and social interaction, with a particular concern for the ways in which people (in relationships and in the media) interpret nonverbal cues. She has used attribution theories to understand these processes and has also looked at the ways in which stereotypes and relational satisfaction plays out behaviorally in interactions. More recently, Dr. Manusov has turned to the study of mindfulness as an alternative way for understanding and promoting certain interpretive processes and to understand conflict and forgiveness practices. Her current work also looks at the reported effects of retreat, solitude, and silence as a means toward well-being and to make the case that time alone can foster better communication and relationships.

**Erin C. Nelson** (San Diego State University) is a Ph.D. candidate at The University of Texas at Austin. She studies interpersonal communication with an emphasis on health. Specifically she studies information and uncertainty management in personal relationships. Her research focuses on how individuals decide to disclose or avoid disclosure of personal health information to family members.

**Kristen M. Norwood** (Ph.D., University of Iowa, 2010) is an Assistant Professor and Director of Communication in the Department of English and Communication at Fontbonne University. Her research interests include connections between relational communication and cultural discourse surrounding issues of gender, identity, and family. Her work has been published in journals such as *Communication Monographs, Journal of Family Communication*, and *Management Communication Quarterly*.

**Sarah Nebel Pederson** received her Ph.D. from the University of Iowa, in interpersonal and family communication at the end-of-life. Her research interests focus on cultural understandings of death and dying and identity constructions in illness narratives. Sarah currently serves as a manager of a nonmedical home health company, where she works with older adults and trains families and caregivers in Alzheimer's and other dementias as well as hospice care. Sarah has previously served as a chaplain at an assisted living facility and has volunteered at three different hospices across the United States.

**Nicole Piemonte** is a Ph.D. candidate at The University of Texas Medical Branch in Galveston. After receiving a master's degree in Communication Studies at Arizona State University, she began her doctoral work at the

Institute for the Medical Humanities, where her research interests expanded to include patient-physician communication, medical ethics, social theory, and continental philosophy. Her experiences teaching medical students and learning alongside clinicians have led to her current dissertation research, which examines contemporary medical epistemology and pedagogy and the ways in which medical education might begin to better address the phenomenological and existential experience of illness and suffering. She intends to pursue a career in medical education where she can use the humanities to advocate for broader understandings of care and healing in medicine.

**Christine E. Rittenour** (Ph.D., University of Nebraska-Lincoln) is an Assistant Professor of Communication Studies at West Virginia University. She researches communication that occurs between *and* about people belonging to different social, role-based, and value-based identities. Within the family, she has looked at the communication of in-laws, mothers and daughters, and interracial family members. As in non-family contexts, these family members' unity coincides with the inclusive or exclusive nature of their communication with each other. Her research shows these trends seeping beyond family boundaries to non-family relationships. Ultimately—recognizing family as the first socializer of "difference"—she works to uncover those family communication trends that result in members' prosocial action toward non-family members, particularly those belonging to diverse outgroups. Dr. Rittenour's research has appeared in journals such as *Sex Roles, Journal of Family Communication, Communication Quarterly, Western Journal of Communication, Southern Communication Journal, Journal of Marriage and Family* and edited volumes.

**Thomas J. Socha,** Ph.D. is ODU University Professor, Professor of Communication, and Director of the Graduate Program in Lifespan and Digital Communication at Old Dominion University in Norfolk, Virginia. He has published six co-authored/co-edited books, over 35 chapters and articles, and sixty conference papers that focus on family communication, children's communication, and most recently positive communication. He was the founding editor of the *Journal of Family Communication* and a Past President of the Southern States Communication Association. He is the Series Editor of the *Lifespan Communication: Children, Families and Aging* book series (Peter Lang International).

**Jordan Soliz** (Ph.D., University of Kansas) is an Associate Professor of Communication Studies at the University of Nebraska-Lincoln. His research investigates communication and intergroup processes primarily in personal and family relationships, with a current emphasis on grandparent-grandchild relationships, multiethnic-racial families, and interfaith families. In addition to various edited volumes, his work has been published in *Communication Monographs, Communication Quarterly, Journal of Family Communication, Journal of Marriage and Family,* and the *Journal of Language and Social Psychology.* He is the current editor of the *Journal of Family Communication.*

**Anita L. Vangelisti** is the Jesse H. Jones Centennial Professor of Communication at the University of Texas at Austin. Her work focuses on communication and emotion in the context of close, personal relationships. She has published numerous articles and chapters and has edited or authored several books including *The Routledge Handbook of Family Communication, The Cambridge Handbook of Personal Relationships,* and *Hurt Feelings in Close Relationships.* Vangelisti was editor of the Cambridge University Press book series on Advances in Personal Relationships and has served on the editorial boards of over a dozen scholarly journals. She is recognized as a Distinguished Scholar by the National Communication Association and served as President of the International Association for Relationship Research. Vangelisti has received awards for her work from the National Communication Association, the International Society for the Study of Personal Relationships, and the International Association for Relationship Research.

**Vince Waldron** (Ph.D., Ohio State University) is Professor of Communication Studies at Arizona State University where he serves as faculty coordinator of the Family Communication Consortium: http://famcom.asu.edu/. His research interests include the communication of forgiveness in personal relationships, relationship resilience, and the communication of the "moral emotions" in work settings. In weaving together these strands of research, Vince focuses on the communication practices that make relationships good, in the moral sense of that word. Vince Waldron is author or coauthor of four books, including two with Douglas Kelley: *Communicating Forgiveness* (Sage, 2008) and *Marriage at Midlife: Analytical Tools and Counseling Strategies* (Springer, 2009). With Jeffrey Kassing he coauthored *Managing Risk in Communication Encounters: Strategies for the Workplace* (Sage, 2010). His most recent book is *Communicating Emotion at Work* (Polity, 2012). Vince's recent articles appear in *Journal of Social and Personal Relationships, Journal of Family Communication,* and *Aging Studies* among other outlets.

**Bianca Wolf** earned a Ph.D. in Communication Studies and an MPH, focusing on health communication, from the University of Iowa after working 12 years in health care as a practice management, software, and billing expert and later as a product and software expert in the insurance field. She is an Assistant

Professor of Communication Studies at the University of Puget Sound. Dr. Wolf has studied and taught health communication in a variety of contexts including: cancer communication among family members, patient-provider communication, and persuasion and influence in interpersonal and media health risk messages. Her research is focused on the reciprocal influences between family communication and health. She has presented her cancer communication research that focuses on individual and collaborative coping processes of family members dealing with breast cancer at interdisciplinary regional, national, and international conferences. Dr. Wolf also recently co-authored an empirically based communication skills textbook for dental professionals.

# Index

## LIFESPAN COMMUNICATION
### *Children, Families, and Aging*

Thomas J. Socha, *General Editor*

From first words to final conversations, communication plays an integral and significant role in all aspects of human development and everyday living. The Lifespan Communication: Children, Families, and Aging series seeks to publish authored and edited scholarly volumes that focus on relational and group communication as they develop over the lifespan (infancy through later life). The series will include volumes on the communication development of children and adolescents, family communication, peer-group communication (among age cohorts), intergenerational communication, and later-life communication, as well as longitudinal studies of lifespan communication development, communication during lifespan transitions, and lifespan communication research methods. The series includes college textbooks as well as books for use in upper-level undergraduate and graduate courses.

Thomas J. Socha, Series Editor | *tsocha@odu.edu*
Mary Savigar, Acquisitions Editor | *mary.savigar@plang.com*

To order other books in this series, please contact our Customer Service Department at:

(800) 770-LANG (within the U.S.)
(212) 647-7706 (outside the U.S.)
(212) 647-7707 FAX

Or browse online by series at www.peterlang.com